T0320983

Praise for *ROI in Marketing*

As a marketer, it's a constant struggle to demonstrate direct and irrefutable proof of the impact on marketing. *ROI of Marketing* makes clear the steps needed to measure marketing success through a straightforward, easy-to-understand approach. A great read for both seasoned executives and junior marketing professionals.

ERIK SAMDAHL, VP OF MARKETING, I4CP

Determining a return on investment (ROI) on marketing efforts has been an age-old problem in companies. Without a clear way of measuring ROI, managers typically underestimate or overestimate their marketing spend. This book helps managers and educators unlock ROI by sharing the measurements and a systematic process to address this important issue.

ELI JONES, PHD, DEAN AND PROFESSOR OF MARKETING, PEGGY MAYS
EMINENT SCHOLAR, MAYS BUSINESS SCHOOL, TEXAS A&M UNIVERSITY

Certain books belong at every professional's fingertips, to both study, guide, and refer back to over time. *ROI in Marketing* should be that book for all leading marketing professionals. The book provides a strategic and actionable methodology for marketers to help them design and deliver meaningful, measurable business results.

DAN NOVAK, FORMER CHIEF MARKETING AND
CHIEF COMMUNICATIONS OFFICER, QUALCOMM INC.

Illustrating the business impact and value that marketing delivers across an organization is extremely complicated but never more essential than in today's business environment. *ROI in Marketing* provides a structured methodology and comprehensive blueprint to enable marketing leaders and practitioners to showcase the broad *chain of impact* and value that their activities deliver.

NIKKI JASON, SVP, MARKETING & COMMUNICATIONS,
RESOURCE PRO, RETHINK OPERATIONS

As a former senior marketing executive at major consumers packaged goods companies, all I can say is: *finally*, someone has developed a disciplined approach to measuring the ROI on marketing investment! I'm very impressed with the author's step-by-step marketing value creation and ROI measurement models, which hold the CMO's hand through what had previously been a relatively undisciplined, imprecise process and an enormous source of frustration. And perhaps most importantly, they emphasize the importance of linking marketing objectives with the overall business objectives to ensure alignment with the CEO and CFO.

STEVEN BELLACH, PRINCIPAL, BOTTOMLINE MARKETING

ROI in Marketing gives the business world a fresh perspective on evaluating the value added by every marketing activity. ROI as a marketing concept has often languished as an afterthought in the back of pricing or CRM chapters. This evolutionary book shows how ROI is intertwined with the value chain. Marketing educators as well as practitioners now have a powerful new tool to assess how value flows throughout the entire marketing process.

DR. MICHAEL T. ELLIOTT, ASSOCIATE DEAN OF COLLEGE OF BUSINESS ADMINISTRATION, CO-CHAIR OF MARKETING DEPARTMENT, ASSOCIATE PROFESSOR OF MARKETING AT THE UNIVERSITY OF MISSOURI–ST. LOUIS

Provides a perspective, methodology, and principles for determining the impact, even the ROI, of marketing programs on business results. Design thinking principles, performance improvement standards, and a proven approach again demonstrate that it's possible to credibly answer questions about value delivered. Logically compelling and procedurally clear, with illustrative case studies.

JOHN LAZAR, LEADERSHIP/EXECUTIVE COACH, CEO, JOHN B. LAZAR & ASSOCIATES, INC.

Adding value is the most important factor in determining marketing success. Yet quantifying that value or convincing others of it has always been a challenge. The proliferation of technology and data should have made estimating the ROI of marketing easier, but it has actually done the opposite. *ROI in Marketing* is a brilliant guide to unlocking and more importantly articulating the value of your marketing. A must-read for C-suite executives and marketers of all channels, *ROI in Marketing* is a cogent call to rethink our traditional marketing paradigms and design our marketing programs for impact with purpose and clarity.

GUILLERMO MAZIER, FOUNDER COLLECTIVE INTELLIGENCE, VICE PRESIDENT, GLOBAL INNOVATION, CONWAY INC

ROI in Marketing delivers a masterclass in how to measure and improve the value of marketing for the long-term success of every business. Now more than ever, we need to make smart marketing choices. Every marketer and leader from every industry can learn from the practical and actionable wisdom offered in this book.

FAUZIA BURKE, AUTHOR OF *ONLINE MARKETING FOR BUSY AUTHORS*, FOUNDER OF FSB ASSOCIATES AND COFOUNDER OF PUB SITE

Every role in every company continues to morph. Marketing is no exception. Turning marketing from art to science is key, and this book is a tool in the arsenal you need to make that happen.

MITCHELL LEVY, GLOBAL CREDIBILITY EXPERT, THINKAHA

Calculating the profitability of marketing campaigns has never been more complex than it is today due to all the various channels, devices, and touchpoints occurring within the marketing funnel/journey. Trying to prove the value of a specific campaign, channel, or touchpoint to upper management can be difficult, to say the least. Data is coming from many different sources and systems today. This book breaks down the process into easy steps and helps any marketing professional at any level master the task. These authors understand the issue at hand and have written a great guide.

PERRY D. DRAKE, PHD, MARKETING DEPARTMENT CO-CHAIR AND ASSOCIATE TEACHING PROFESSOR OF MARKETING, UNIVERSITY OF MISSOURI–ST. LOUIS, COLLEGE OF BUSINESS

For executives, managers, and business students who want to a gain a more holistic perspective on how to measure, improve, and demonstrate the value of marketing programs, this book is not to be missed.

DOUGLAS E. HUGHES, PHD, FORMER EDITOR-IN-CHIEF OF THE *JOURNAL OF PERSONAL SELLING & SALES MANAGEMENT*; DIRECTOR, SCHOOL OF MARKETING & INNOVATION, PROFESSOR OF MARKETING, MUMA COLLEGE OF BUSINESS, UNIVERSITY OF SOUTH FLORIDA

ROI
IN
MARKETING

The Design Thinking Approach to Measure, Prove, and Improve the Value of Marketing

Jack J. Phillips, PhD
Frank Q. Fu, PhD, CPT
Patricia Pulliam Phillips, PhD, CPT
and Hong Yi, CPT

Mc
Graw
Hill

New York   Chicago   San Francisco   Athens   London
Madrid   Mexico City   Milan   New Delhi
Singapore   Sydney   Toronto

1 2 3 4 5 6 7 8 9   LCR   25 24 23 22 21 20

ISBN   978-1-260-46042-1
MHID   1-260-46042-8

e-ISBN   978-1-260-46043-8
e-MHID   1-260-46043-6

Library of Congress Cataloging-in-Publication Data

Names: Phillips, Jack J., 1945– author. | Phillips, Patricia Pulliam, author. | Fu, Frank Q., author. | Yi, Hong, author.
Title: ROI in marketing / Jack Phillips, Frank Q. Fu, Patricia Phillips, and Hong Yi.
Description: New York : McGraw-Hill, [2020] | Includes bibliographical references and index.
Identifiers: LCCN 2020020622 (print) | LCCN 2020020623 (ebook) | ISBN 9781260460421 (hardback) | ISBN 9781260460438 (ebook)
Subjects: LCSH: Marketing. | Rate of return.
Classification: LCC HF5415 .P4835 2020 (print) | LCC HF5415 (ebook) | DDC 658.8—dc23
LC record available at https://lccn.loc.gov/2020020622
LC ebook record available at https://lccn.loc.gov/2020020623

CONTENTS

Contents

ACKNOWLEDGMENTS

Although it sounds cliché, it is still so important to say: we could not write this book without the many clients we've worked with throughout the years. We have had many opportunities to evaluate marketing programs, from simple ads and promotions to corporate sponsorships and golf outings. We thank all the clients and customers who have invited us in to work with them and in some cases experiment with different possibilities. As we added value to our customers, we have learned from these experiences. We appreciate those individuals who have helped shape our work in the marketing field.

We would like to thank the ROI Institute staff for their continued support as a team. In particular, we would like to thank Hope Nicholas, director of publications, for her efforts with managing this process from the very beginning to delivering the final pages. Her contribution is amazing, and this book's success is due in large part to her great support.

Jack and Patti would like to thank their two coauthors, Frank Fu and Hong Yi. This has been a global team effort as we developed a book that will span many countries with diverse markets. Frank Fu and Hong Yi have been a delightful team to work with during the development and writing of this book. They are very knowledgeable and experienced and have added much to this publication.

Jack would like to thank Patti. Patti is not only my spouse and business partner but also my best friend. She is an outstanding consultant, skilled writer, engaging facilitator, meticulous researcher, and sought-after keynote presenter. She is a role model for all our partners around the world. Her important and timely contributions made this book practical and valuable.

Patti would like to thank Jack for putting ROI on the map in terms of its applicability to noncapital investments. Jack laid the foundation on which so many others have built their measurement, evaluation, and analytics practices. Over the years, he has given much more than he has received—and for that, we are all thankful!

Frank would like to thank Jack and Patti for the opportunity to work on this project. It is a privilege to apply their theoretically sound and empirically tested methodology to the field of marketing. He is grateful for the honor to work with Hong Yi, who not only created many of the tools and materials discussed and used in the book but also provided leadership, resources, and support to make this book a reality. Additionally, Frank is grateful for the many students and colleagues at the University of Missouri–St. Louis who have tested this methodology and the embedded tools, and have given encouragement and feedback as the materials evolved over the years.

Hong Yi would like to thank her three coauthors, Jack, Frank, and Patti, for the opportunity to contribute to the project and work on this global team. She thanks all the clients and customers in China who have invited her and her Sinotrac team to work on their marketing performance improvement projects over the years. Without their trust and support, it is impossible to develop many of the models, tools, and techniques discussed in the book. For that, she is deeply grateful. She also appreciates the Sinotrac staff for their dedicated commitment and continuous improvement efforts.

And finally, we thank the team at McGraw Hill. This is our seventh book with McGraw Hill. We would like to thank Cheryl Segura for her patience and perseverance in working with us to make this book a reality. Cheryl exemplifies the reputation of McGraw Hill as one of the most outstanding publishing companies in the world.

PREFACE

You've been there before, pitching a new marketing campaign to the executives. You were very proud of the campaign design and special features, and you knew it was going to make a difference. Halfway through the presentation, the executives asked, "Is there any way to forecast the ROI of this campaign?"

You instantly felt anxiety, and there was an unfortunate, dead silence. Your answer was probably, "We haven't done that, but we can."

You have to anticipate this request in today's economic climate. Perhaps the situation is even worse when asked that same question after you have completed the implementation of a marketing project.

This book shows you how to address the ROI issue. We will guide you step-by-step through the process of calculating the impact and even the financial ROI for any type of marketing program, initiative, campaign, or event. We will also show you how to forecast the impact and ROI of any marketing project in advance of the implementation. And we will show you how to evaluate marketing projects you may implement internally with the customer service teams or sales teams.

The ROI Methodology

The methodology presented in this book shows how to measure the success of any marketing initiative with five levels of outcomes:

Level 1: Reaction. How the customers reacted to the marketing campaign, project, program, or initiative.

Level 2: Learning. What the customers learned from the marketing initiative (the takeaways).

Level 3: Action. The actions customers take to move toward a purchase.

Level 4: Impact. The actual purchase.

Level 5: ROI. The financial ROI, which shows the monetary value add from the purchase, which will be the profit compared with the cost of the campaign. The ROI is calculated the same way that a chief financial officer would calculate the ROI for a capital expenditure, using the same formula at the end of the process.

Planning for evaluation, collecting data, analyzing data, and reporting results involve 12 logical steps that are the heart of this book.

Think about why this is necessary. The marketing function is growing, with many options and opportunities offered. Some of these opportunities add value, and some do not. You must be able to sort out the effective from the ineffective. The ultimate accountability compares the cost of the campaign with the value add from the campaign, expressed in monetary benefits.

Proven Method

This book follows more than 75 other books that have been written to support this methodology, along with case studies, and even tools, templates, and application guides. The books have been published in 38 different languages. We wrote this book because there was no book available like it for the marketing field. The process this book presents, the ROI Methodology, the most used evaluation system in the world. We have been using this process for years in the marketing field with marketing VPs, directors, managers, and specialists, showing them how to calculate the impact and ROI of their campaigns.

While there has been much discussion about ROI, marketing professionals often come up short when showing the ROI of their campaigns because they fear their campaign may actually deliver a negative ROI. It's not just about plugging numbers into an equation. The challenge is how do you obtain the numbers and what is the process that drives those numbers. Because of this fear of a negative ROI, the ROI Methodology actually designs for the success of the campaign. In essence, we use design thinking principles to make sure you design the marketing campaign to deliver success on all five levels of outcomes, with the desired outcome being impact and, yes, even ROI. This minimizes the likelihood of a negative ROI and removes some of the resistance to using this type of methodology.

The methodology presented in this book has been tested and proved, and it works. It is based on a classic logic flow of data as the success of a marketing campaign unfolds and as customers react to the message, understand the message, and take action, with a corresponding impact and, of course, ROI value. The ROI Methodology was originally developed in the 1970s, refined, and first published in a major book in the early 1980s. It was refined periodically with input from users. In 2017, the method was further refined and modified to its current version.

Designed for Three Audiences

The methodology satisfies three important audiences: The first audience is the *user*. The ROI Methodology is user friendly, using logically sequenced steps, and it operates like a drop-down menu as you proceed through each of the steps of the process. Also, it is void of complicated mathematics and financial concepts. They are not necessary. Its user-friendly design has resulted in it achieving the reputation of being the most used system in the world.

The second audience is the *chief financial officers and top executives*, who must have a credible process that they can believe in and support. The ROI Methodology process was developed with this audience in mind. The methodology is CFO friendly and will usually be supported by CFOs in an organization when they completely understand the process. This is essential in today's environment, where there is always a quest for credibility, accuracy, and a conservative approach.

Finally, the third audience is the *professors and business students*, who have to see an evaluation process as credible, reliable, and valid with conservative standards. Our success with this group is best illustrated by the fact that ROI Institute books on this methodology are now used in almost 100 universities for master's- and PhD-level coursework. This new book will be adopted by marketing professors and benefit the students in their classes.

To balance these three groups—users, CFOs and other executives, and professors and their students—is not an easy task. This process has been created to satisfy all three groups, which makes it extremely valuable, useful, and essential in today's environment.

Global Focus

This book truly presents a global focus with its many applications, case studies, and examples, offered throughout the book. This is an essential perspective for a major marketing book, because so many organizations have become global in their operations and distribution. Globalization has caused many large organizations to operate in many different countries. A marketing strategy that works in one country might also work in another country, but only the data can confirm this success. The ROI Methodology can be adapted to any culture, language, or custom. The scenarios in this book reflect not only the United States and China but Europe, the Americas, and Africa as well.

Authors' Experience

The author team is ideal for delivering this book. Patti and Jack Phillips founded ROI Institute more than 25 years ago to help organizations across the globe show the value of what they do. The ROI Methodology is now used in all types of organizations and has been adopted by over three-fourths of the Fortune 500 companies; 26 federal governments around the world; large nongovernmental organizations, such as the United Nations; and even universities, nonprofits, and charitable organizations. Patti and Jack have trained thousands of managers on how to use this process. Professionals in all functions have adapted and adopted the process in many different areas, with marketing being one important area. With this methodology, which is considered the gold standard of evaluation, Patti and Jack bring expertise in how to make it work in organizations. ROI Institute operates in 70 countries through ROI Institute global partners. Patti and Jack and the collective work of ROI Institute represent a great team for offering this book to the marketing community.

Frank Fu brings tremendous experience in the business world as well as in an academic setting. He is an associate professor of marketing at the University of Missouri–St. Louis and teaches his students this methodology at the university. He has worked as a researcher and consultant, with many organizations in China and the United States, to bring value to marketing organizations. Frank serves on the board of the International Society for Performance Improvement and has expertise in marketing management, sales management, and performance improvement process.

Hong Yi is the president of Sinotrac, a major performance improvement consulting company in China. Over the years, she and her team have worked on hundreds of marketing performance improvement projects. She and her team have also developed various tools and techniques to enable and empower marketers to see and show the value of their marketing solutions. It is through Hong Yi's efforts that this book will be simultaneously published in Mandarin for the Chinese market.

The Flow of the Book

The book flows in sequential chapters that match the model of the ROI Methodology:

Chapter 1 begins with an explanation of why this methodology is needed at this time.

Chapter 2 provides a summary of the complete model as a quick reference.

Chapter 3 presents the first step of the model, starting with *why*, suggesting that marketing projects should start with clear business measures.

Chapter 4 explains how to make it feasible, ensuring that you have the right solution to drive the business measures.

Chapter 5 details how to expect success, as objectives are set for all levels of outcomes, and the information is provided to all stakeholders to ensure success is achieved.

Chapter 6 describes how to make it matter to the customers and the others involved, by making sure the program is important to them, useful, timely, and engaging.

Chapter 7 covers how to make it stick, making sure that customers take the action, either systematically or when needed, to move toward the actual purchase. This ensures that the proper actions are taken because of the marketing initiative.

Chapter 8 shows how to make it credible by isolating the effects of the marketing project from other influences. There are so many influences on marketing outcomes that it is imperative to sort out the effects of your particular marketing initiative from other influences.

Chapter 9 explains how to make it credible by converting data to monetary values to make sure it's the value add. The monetary value will be either profit for sales-related measures or cost avoidance for measures like product returns or customer complaints. Data items that cannot be converted to money credibly with a reasonable amount of effort are left as intangibles measures.

Chapter 10 covers how to make it credible by including all the costs of the program, direct and indirect. Also, two very important and credible ROI calculations are presented, the benefit-cost ratio and the ROI, expressed as a percentage.

Chapter 11 shares how to tell the story, presenting the different ways in which the results of a marketing campaign (using numbers and narrative) can be reported to key stakeholders. These methods can range from executive briefings to short blogs and one-page infographics.

Chapter 12 shows how evaluation data are used to make improvements. One of the major reasons for evaluation is to make projects better, and the philosophy of this methodology is to continue to make improvements in a particular project so that, in effect, the ROI is optimized for the particular campaign. When this is accomplished with an ROI calculation, it is much easier to protect or increase the budget for marketing.

Chapter 13 explains in detail how to forecast the ROI of a project before the project is implemented. Forecasting prior to program approval is becoming very important. This chapter presents some of the most credible concepts for estimating the impact and ROI and using error adjustments. The key is the credibility of the analysis and the accuracy of the forecast.

Chapter 14 focuses on how to implement the ROI Methodology and make it a routine, systematic process. It shows how to sustain the use of the ROI Methodology with reasonable resources.

There you have it, the book in 14 chapters.

PART I

Why This Is Important

1

The Value of Marketing: A Critical Issue

Marketing is about values.

STEVE JOBS

Jessica was frustrated. For the first time since she was appointed as the chief marketing officer (CMO) of Midwest Brewing Company (MBC), she was feeling unsure about what she had been doing. Sipping from her coffee mug imprinted with the MBC logo, she could not help thinking about what had happened earlier this morning in the executive conference room. It was just last year that she had personally redesigned the company logo printed on the coffee mug; now she was wondering whether she should continue to work at MBC.

MBC was among the fast-growing brewing companies in the nation. The organization rode the wave of craft beer's wild growth in the past decade and emerged as one of the market leaders in this lucrative industry. For two and a half years, Jessica had been working as the chief marketer for the company and been busy with launching a variety of marketing programs. From advertising and public relations to social media campaigns, Jessica believed these programs had advanced the organization's marketing agenda. The feedback she received had been generally positive. She was convinced that everything was on the right track, until she met Andrew, the newly appointed CEO of MBC.

At the request of the new CEO, Jessica made a presentation to the executives this morning. She highlighted the variety of marketing activities her team had conducted in the past years. The marketing efforts included advertising campaigns on local TV and radio, in the newspaper, on billboards, and in direct mailing of coupons to the local communities. MBC marketing also utilized the company's taprooms and restaurants to attract and engage customers by offering live music, family-friendly shows, and other events. In addition, MBC provided guided tours of the brewery daily and free beer schools on Saturdays and Sundays. The free tours and class sessions included a brief history of craft beer in local communities, showed how MBC brewed beer, and educated people on how to taste and fully appreciate the different flavors MBC offers. The initiative Jessica was most proud of was the annual two-day event called "Taste of Community Festival," which attracted thousands of visitors last year.

Additionally, MBC sold half of its products through distribution channels. For this division, salespeople made calls to distributors, retailers, and bar owners to introduce new flavors and seasonal deals. Jessica understood the importance of professional selling, so as part of the internal marketing efforts, she hired brewery experts and invited beer aficionados to provide training courses to the sales team. Still, Jessica believed that more could be done. As most MBC target customers were savvy young professionals constantly on their phones, she understood the need for MBC to beef up its social media presence. Because of this, during this morning's presentation, she discussed an enhanced digital and social media marketing plan that she and her team had put together.

The presentation generated mixed reactions. Andrew commented, "Jessica, you and your team certainly have conducted many activities, and I find some of the marketing activities very interesting and creative. My concern is that the focus of your presentation was on the activities conducted, not the value created. We can all identify with the issues and challenges facing our team, but I am curious about what specific value these activities have contributed to the company's bottom line. Do you have a way of showing the success of these activities, the impact on the business, or even the ROI?"

Jessica replied, "We have improved sales, market share, and customer loyalty, and I'm sure these activities have made a difference. I have heard people talk about how much fun they had at the Taste of Community Festival. In addition, we have been collecting feedback from our customers every month. More than 80 percent of people surveyed said they are satisfied with our products."

Andrew added, "Do we have anything more specific? You know, the total budget of marketing this year has exceeded 20 percent of company revenue. Although our business has been growing steadily in the past two years, it is nothing spectacular."

Jessica quickly responded by saying, "I do know that the advertisements, guided tours, beer school, and sales force training cost money, but these efforts are critical to allow people inside and outside the community to know our brand, taste our beer, learn about our history, and get interested in our offerings. Our business could be worse if we had not engaged in these activities."

Andrew sensed the defensive tone in Jessica's voice and said, "I am not against these marketing activities, Jessica. I believe they have value. All I am asking is for you to calculate or estimate the value the marketing department generated and compare it with the expenses. The growth rate of our industry is beginning to slow down, and many companies are struggling. The Brewers Association reported this month that in the last year alone 97 craft breweries closed. If we are not generating enough growth and not careful with the budget, we may be the next organization to close. We have to understand the connection between our marketing projects and their impact on sales very clearly. We can no longer implement these campaigns and not know the results we achieve from them."

Andrew concluded with some encouragement, saying, "Please understand that I am not opposed to your marketing efforts, Jessica. But when we have a significant proportion of the budget dedicated to marketing, we need to make sure the expenditure is successful and adding value to the company's bottom line as expected by generating a positive ROI. We also need to make our marketing efforts more effective and efficient. I'll give you time to research how to do this, and you can let me know your thoughts on these issues in about two weeks."

Jessica was concerned about Andrew's inquiries, particularly since he made several positive comments about her marketing activities. Why was he questioning the value of marketing projects? Why was he concerned about the costs and ROI? Was there really a way to measure and improve the marketing programs? What was the best way to do it? These questions began to frustrate Jessica as she reflected over her tenure at MBC and all the marketing programs she and her team had implemented. Jessica always thought her marketing campaigns and events were useful to the company. She believed sales and profits had improved as a result of the efforts, although there was no way of knowing for sure just how much. With some types of marketing, you may never know if they've added value, right? Still, Jessica was facing a challenge in her career. How should she respond to this request from the new CEO?

Pressure on Marketers to Show Value

On March 23, 2017, the Coca-Cola Company announced several new C-level leadership appointments and shook up its marketing team.[1] One notable change was consolidating the marketing function into a new chief growth officer (CGO) role as its chief marketing officer stepped down. To many CMOs, this news was not surprising. Coca-Cola was simply following the examples of other Fortune 100 companies, such as Hershey and Kellogg's, that had appointed CGOs to revitalize their marketing functions in the past year. This trend continues into 2020 as more CMOs are under the pressure of "grow or go," a term coined by

CNBC to depict the situation that CMOs need to deliver growth or need to step aside.[2] There are multiple reasons leading to these changes. For many companies, growth is the number one priority for everyone in the marketing function. However, companies strive to grow not just to increase revenue and market share, but to translate that growth into positive customer experiences and solid financial returns.

As we will discuss in later chapters of this book, sales growth and return on investment are both indicators of value created by marketing. This news and the opening story of this chapter highlight the challenges faced by many marketing professionals: how to measure, demonstrate, and improve the value created by marketing programs. Similar conversations are frequently happening in the marketing departments of many large and small organizations across industries.[3] Many marketing leaders share the same frustrations and concerns experienced by Jessica. As a matter of fact, according to surveys conducted in recent years, two-thirds of CMOs have felt pressure from their boards to prove their marketing department's value.[4]

What's Causing the Pressure?

One possible reason for this pressure is the increasing costs of marketing initiatives. Corporate America spends nearly $300 billion every year on advertising.[5] The total amount on marketing could exceed $1,000 billion, if the expenditures on sales force management were included. As new product development and promotional campaigns become more and more expensive, marketing budgets have reached 11 percent of total company budgets on average, and some industries allocate nearly one-quarter of total budgets to marketing.[6] However, as one study shows, seven in ten enterprise CEOs believe that they are wasting money on marketing initiatives.[7]

> *Half the money I spend on advertising is wasted;*
> *the trouble is I don't know which half.*
> JOHN WANAMAKER

Failing to measure the success of marketing or show the value of marketing efforts causes serious consequences. Facing demanding customers and intense competition, CEOs and CFOs are increasingly concerned with sales growth and put marketers under pressure to demonstrate solid returns of their efforts.[8,9] If marketers fail to show the value of their initiatives, top management may not hesitate to slash the marketing budget, reduce funding, and shift support to other departments and teams that do show the value added. In fact, many companies have been doing just that. As shown in a CMO Spend Survey conducted by a research firm, marketing budgets slipped from 12.1 percent of company revenue in 2016 to 11.3 percent in 2017. Newly appointed CGOs in Fortune 100 companies such as Coca-Cola, Hershey, and Kellogg's have taken over the marketing functions as their CMOs step down.[10] Meanwhile, marketing giants like Procter & Gamble have been trimming advertising budgets and significantly reducing the number of marketing and media agencies they work with.[11]

Value Embedded in Marketing

Marketing is an exciting field. For many people, when they think of marketing, it brings to mind images of catchy advertisements, eloquent salespeople, and famous brands endorsed by celebrities. They may also think of the telemarketing phone calls during their dinnertime, deals and coupons sent to their mailbox, and pop-ups and web banners when they surf the internet. Although these are indeed marketing, the truth of the matter is that they are only part of the activities of marketing. Marketing is all of that and beyond.

For business professionals and entrepreneurial minds, marketing serves as a critical function that links an organization's vision and mission to its core focus, the customers. From small local firms to large multinational corporations, retail stores to nonprofit charities, marketing is an indispensable component of every organization. One thing that distinguishes marketing from other departments is that it is the one and only function that has frequent interactions with customers.

Although other departments such as finance, accounting, research and development, and production are also important, what determines the organization's future success and even survival is the extent to which an organization takes care of its target customers. Therefore, marketing performance, effectiveness, and efficiency are not only important to marketing professionals, but also relevant to stakeholders throughout the whole organization.

If you sincerely believe that "the customer is king," then the second most important person in this kingdom must be the one who has a direct interaction on a daily basis with the king.
MICHEL BON

Because value is embedded in marketing, it is a disappointment that so many marketers are struggling to show the value of their work.

Basic Definitions

The American Marketing Association (AMA), a professional association for marketing professionals and educators, defines marketing as "the activity, set of institutions, and processes for creating, communicating, delivering, and exchanging offerings that have *value* for customers, clients, partners, and society at large" (emphasis added).[12] Although marketing engages in activities and processes, all activities and processes serve the same purpose: understanding, creating, communicating, delivering, and exchanging values. It stresses the importance of discovering and delivering genuine value in the offerings of products, services, and concepts to customers with the goal to achieve customer satisfaction and meet organizational goals at the same time.

Similarly, marketing management is defined as "the art and science of choosing target markets and getting, keeping, and growing customers through creating, delivering, and communicating superior value."[13] Once again, the focus of this definition is on creation, delivery, and communication of value. In fact, the whole process of marketing management is built around value. Marketers conduct marketing research and use marketing analytics to understand customers' needs in order to determine value offerings. They segment the market, select target groups, and position the value offerings to fulfill customers' needs. Good understanding of the value needed in the marketplace leads to the development of products and service packages. Marketers then set prices reflecting value and choose appropriate distribution channels to deliver the value offerings. A critical task of marketing is to promote the value offerings. The purposes of the promotions include building awareness about the value offerings, convincing customers to purchase the value offerings, and reminding customers of the benefits of these value offerings. No wonder Professor Michael Porter of Harvard Business School treats marketing and sales as one of the five primary functions of his value chain analysis.[14]

In addition to academicians and marketing practitioners, entrepreneurs also emphasize values in their marketing endeavors. In 1997, Steve Jobs made the following presentation to Apple employees:

> To me, marketing is about values. This is a very complicated world; it's a very noisy world. And we're not going to get a chance to get people to remember much about us. No company is. And so, we have to be really clear on what we want them to know about us. Now, Apple fortunately is one of the half-a-dozen best brands in the whole world. Right up there with Nike, Disney, Coke, Sony, it is one of the greats of the greats. Not just in this country but all around the globe. And—but even a great brand needs investment and caring if it's going to retain its relevance and vitality.[15]

In this presentation, Steve stated that marketing is not about the fancy features of your products or about comparing yourself with your competitors; it is about identifying the core values of your offerings and then being able to communicate those value propositions clearly, convincingly, and consistently to your target audience. Value gets people's attention. Value enables you and your company to stand out in this complicated and noisy world. Value gives you the chance for people to learn and remember you. For employees at Apple, it was value that earned them the opportunity to succeed. At the end of the presentation, Steve introduced the now famous "Think different" TV commercial based on this value proposition and the core values of that proposition empowered Apple to come back, create an industry, and become the market leader.

Because the purpose of business is to create a customer, the business enterprise has two, and only two, basic functions: marketing and innovation. Marketing and innovation produce results; all the rest are costs. Marketing is the distinguishing, unique function of the business.

PETER DRUCKER

Three Types of Marketing

Depending on the different types of target customers, marketing practices fall into three categories: consumer marketing, business marketing, and internal marketing. Value creation is the key for all three types of marketing activities, but the way marketers create value may slightly differ.

Consumer Marketing

Consumer marketing is the marketing of goods and services to end users. These individuals make day-to-day household purchasing decisions for their families or themselves. The purchases could be convenience goods, such as toothpaste, magazines, and groceries, or shopping goods, such as cars, smartphones, and jewelry. A typical example of a consumer marketing activity is promotion through advertising. Imagine that a consumer packaging goods manufacturer develops a new product that can make consumers' lives more convenient and enjoyable. However, without knowing of the product's benefits or even of this new product's existence, consumers will not take any action to buy. Therefore, a new TV commercial designed to promote the new product will add value to this company's bottom line by increasing sales revenue and profits, because it induces purchases, enhances sales revenue, and ensures new product success.

Business Marketing

Business marketing is the marketing of goods and services to companies, nonprofit organizations, and government agencies for use in the creation of goods and services they provide to others.[16] Compared with their consumer marketing counterparts, business marketing professionals need to convince the purchasing managers and agents of manufacturers, retailers, charitable organizations, and government agencies to purchase their goods and services. The process tends to be complex, and multiple decision makers are typically involved. For example, the sales force of an industrial manufacturer sells a new service package to 100 distributors nationwide. As the salespeople successfully convince the purchasing agents of the distributors to take actions toward purchase, they add value to the manufacturer's business outcomes.

Internal Marketing

Both consumer marketing and business marketing focus on external customers, which include individuals and organizations that are outside of the company. Internal marketing, on the other hand, is inward focused and treats company employees as internal customers. It refers to the process for promoting the company and its mission, values, brands, and objectives to the employees.[17] Research shows that the attitudes of employees (for example, salespeople) toward a house brand are highly correlated with the attitudes of customers toward the brand. Indeed, when customers see the enthusiasm and loyalty of a company salesperson toward the brand, they are more likely to be convinced and place orders. An example of an internal marketing program could be an internal branding campaign. For instance, after merging with another firm, the executives of a company notice conflicts in the two organizational cultures and decide to run an internal branding campaign in order to enhance employee morale. The effort leads to reduced turnover rates, more satisfied customers, and superior financial outcomes—all indicators of the values created by the internal marketing campaign.

Different Ways to Measure Value

But what exactly is value? Before we can properly measure value, we need to clearly define it. The definition of value should use terms that most marketers can relate to and agree upon. Unfortunately, "value" is an ambiguous word, as it has various meanings to different people. Dictionary.com defines value as "the worth of something in terms of the amount of other things for which it can be exchanged or in terms of some medium of exchange."[18] For most people, value means the importance, worth, benefit, and usefulness of something. A more relevant question is what value means to you, the marketers. Contemporary marketing treats value as a ratio of the benefits compared with the costs. From the marketers' perspective, the benefits refer to the contribution their marketing programs bring to the company, and the costs are the necessary expenditures to achieve the benefits. It remains unclear, however, what the benefits and costs really are.

To reflect on this issue, let's work on an exercise. In Exercise 1.1, you will find six possible descriptions of value created by the marketing programs shown in Table 1.1. Please follow the steps to complete the exercise and determine the value of your marketing programs.

Exercise 1.1

1. Read each value description of your marketing program and select the one (can be more than one) that is important to you right now. Place a check to the left of that description in the "Your Choice" column.
2. Rank each of the statements in terms of importance to measuring the total value of your marketing program. In the "Your Rank," column, place the number 1 in the row of the item that you would consider the most important and continue numbering until the least important measure is ranked as 6.

(continued on next page)

3. As the third step, in the next column, "Measure Now," check the statements that define the categories you are actually measuring now. For example, if you are counting the number of customers reached and the spending on marketing programs, check the first item. Check all that apply.
4. In the next column, "Executive Rank," indicate how your senior executives would rank these data items in terms of what is valuable to them from 1 to 6, with 1 being the most valuable and 6 the least valuable.
5. In the "Percent Measured Now" column, indicate the percentage of your marketing programs measured annually now at each of the levels.
6. In the last column, "Percent Executive Expectation," indicate the percentage of marketing programs your senior executives would expect to evaluate at each category for each year.

Answers to these questions reveal interesting information. This will show the kind of marketer you are when it comes to measuring value, determining the status of the measurement system of your marketing programs, and identifying the gaps between your current practices and your executives' expectations. It also reveals the type of value you focus on and what type of value you are measuring.

Activity-Based Value

Consciously or unconsciously, some marketers choose option A. They measure the number of customers reached, new products launched, number of phone calls made, number of emails sent out, and number of tweets posted. Occasionally, they conduct surveys, facilitate focus group studies, and monitor the company website and social media to see customers' reactions and attitudes to their marketing programs (which is option B). At other times, they collect data about customers' knowledge of their programs, products, and services. This is usually the marketing

TABLE 1.1 What is the value of your marketing programs?

YOUR CHOICE	VALUE DESCRIPTION OF MARKETING PROGRAM	THE POSSIBLE MEASURES OF VALUE					
		YOUR RANK	MEASURE NOW	EXECUTIVE RANK	PERCENT MEASURED NOW	PERCENT EXECUTIVE EXPECTATION
	A. "Reach the largest number of customers with the least amount of cost."					
	B. "Customers are engaged, enjoy the marketing program, and see our offerings as interesting and valuable."					
	C. "Customers are learning the features, advantages, and benefits of our products and services to make purchase decisions."					
	D. "Because of the marketing program, customers take desirable action, try the product samples, and take steps to make a decision."					
	E. "Customers purchasing our products and services and have a positive impact on the profitability and growth."					
	F. "The organization has a positive return on the investment of marketing efforts, time, and the resources used."					

message (option C). Still, at other times, they monitor the actions customers take, such as comparing ratings with other products' ratings, requesting a sample, asking for a demonstration, or agreeing to a sales call (option D). Overall, marketers of this kind believe that the value of marketing resides in the effort itself. They focus on inputs, perceptions, and activities instead of outcomes and results. These input-oriented marketers argue that the outcome of their input is influenced by many external and internal environmental factors and that most of the factors are beyond their control. Therefore, they choose to focus on what is under their control, the design and launch of marketing programs.

These marketers are obsessed with the activities they conduct or the activities of the customers. Others simply enjoy and are proud of the activities they are conducting. They often boast about the large number of marketing programs they design, launch, and maintain. These marketers measure and show the value they create by counting the number of customers they are reaching. For example, in the advertising industry, agencies measure reach, frequency, and GRP (gross rating point) and report these numbers to clients as value creation. In marketing vocabulary, "reach" refers to the total number of individuals or households exposed, at least once, to a marketing program during a given period. A similar concept was developed for social media marketing. As an analytics metric, "social media reach" refers to the number of unique users who have come across particular content on a social platform such as Facebook, Instagram, or Twitter. Both are measures at the input level, similar to option A of our exercise.

A problem with this type of value measurement is that it does not align with executive expectations. As a study by the ROI Institute shows, 96 percent of CEOs want to see measures related to the business impact of marketing programs, especially the extent to which marketing programs help achieve growth of market share, revenue, and customer base. These measures correspond to option E of our exercise. Executives are least likely to care about the input and actually think these activities are a costly consumption of resources. Focusing on input and activities also contributes to the perception that marketing is all "fluff" and not a substantial contribution to real business results. It will hurt marketing's credibility because it shows a lack of accountability and does not create the mindset that marketing should be treated as an investment instead of a cost.

Result-Based Value

Result-based marketers are at the other end of the spectrum. These marketers recognize that marketing is about results, from generating sales revenue to acquiring new customers. Therefore, they measure and demonstrate the value of their marketing programs at the business impact level (option E). This is one step closer to meeting executives' expectations than the activity-based value demonstration. However, focusing only on results may create its own challenges, which include failure to show a chain of evidence and proof to support the claim that the financial and customer results are indeed due to the marketing effort. The business outcomes are inevitably under the influence of many factors, and most of these factors are beyond the control of the marketer. When there are multiple factors influencing the results simultaneously, the marketer needs to (1) show a chain of evidence and (2) isolate the effects of the marketing program (proof). Failing to do either will hurt the marketer's credibility.

For some executives, the impact is not enough. They want to know if the marketing campaign is worth it. This requires the monetary benefits of the marketing campaign to be compared with the cost of the campaign. Most of the impacts have been converted to money. The cost of the campaign must include all costs—direct and indirect. This comparison is the financial ROI calculation. It's the same way the CFO would calculate the ROI for a capital expenditure. This is option F in the exercise, and it's a fast-growing metric for marketing activities, programs, events, and campaigns. Much of this book is devoted to measuring success at the impact and ROI levels.

The New Definition of Value

Both the external challenges and internal pressures demand a new definition of value, guiding marketers to measure, improve, and demonstrate the contribution of their effort. The new definition of value should not be a single number. Rather, the new definition should comprise a variety of data points along the chain of impact. The new definition of value should focus on the key consideration of marketing, the target customers. Instead of treating customers as a commodity, we respect them by analyzing and understanding their reactions, facilitating their learning about the product or service, and enabling them to take proper action on our marketing programs. Value should be balanced with both activities and the outcomes created by these activities. Neither activity nor outcome suffices as a measure of value. We need both. Similarly, we need to balance the value measurement with both quantitative and qualitative data. We should measure the value we are creating with both financial and nonfinancial perspectives. The value definition should reflect both the tactical aspects of marketing, such as activity, and the strategic aspects, such as financial impact.

Concerns About Current Models

Over the years, marketing practitioners and researchers have developed a variety of approaches and tools to measure the value of marketing. These approaches and tools have helped marketers to a certain extent. However, due to the changing market conditions, shifting customer preferences, and intensified competition, the current practices are struggling to step up and meet the high expectations of executives by falling short in multiple areas. We don't mean to criticize any of the existing ROI models. They have served, and will continue to serve, useful purposes. But the economic climate, executive expectations, and funding formulas have changed. We must have an updated system to evaluate our marketing programs that deliver both financial and customer performance, serve multiple purposes, and contribute to organizational success in different ways. In this section, we will highlight several inadequacies of the existing ROI models.

The Current Models Define Value Too Narrowly

Many existing marketing ROI methodologies focus on profitability as the sole purpose of marketing efforts. Indeed, profitability is the lifeblood of company growth. However, as highlighted by Kaplan and Norton, financial measure itself is inadequate for guiding organizations through complex and competitive environments.[19] Instead, a comprehensive framework is needed to ensure sustainable growth and long-term success. The authors proposed four perspectives in their balanced scorecard framework, namely, financial perspective, customer perspective, internal business process perspective, and learning and growth perspective. Similarly, Zoltners, Sinha, and Lorimer also defined marketing and sales organizational success on four dimensions: (1) company results, (2) customer results, (3) sales activities, and (4) salespeople.[20] The authors argue that instead of narrowly focusing on a single dimension, companies should take a balanced view by managing all four dimensions in order to maintain sustainable growth and long-term competitive advantages.

The Current Models Lack Customer Focus

Marketing, first and foremost, focuses on customers. However, some existing ROI models in marketing fail to recognize the importance of the customer. They either ignore the customer decision-making process completely in their methodology or take customer purchases for granted. Some models even treat customers as commodities that a company can easily acquire and discard. It is surprising and detrimental for marketers to adopt such a mindset. After all, it is the customer purchase that drives short-term financial performance, and companies rely on customer satisfaction, loyalty, and lifetime value to sustain future growth. In all marketing strategies and programs, we should put customers at the core of our consideration. Lack of customer focus can be costly. There are plenty of examples of failures and mistakes in the marketplace due to inadequate attention paid to customer needs and preferences.

The Current Models Ignore Internal Marketing and Communication

An important aspect ignored by many evaluation models of marketing programs is internal marketing, which refers to the application of marketing concepts and strategies inside an organization. This application includes the promotion of the organization's objectives, products, and services to its employees, with the purpose of increasing employee job satisfaction, loyalty, and engagement with the organization's mission and goals. Internal marketing provides organizations with a variety of benefits. Research has shown that marketing management can be more effective and successful if employees of an organization are knowledgeable about its mission, goals, and offerings, understand who the target customers are, and can articulate the branding messages to customers. Companies like Southwest Airlines, Nordstrom, and Ritz-Carlton have been relying on internal marketing to ensure superb customer service. Engaged and well-trained employees can be the best and most trusted organizational ambassadors and brand advocates. They can positively influence target customers by demonstrating knowledge, skill, pride, and enthusiasm in ways that nobody else can. However, most current evaluation models either ignore the internal customers and stakeholders or take their support for granted.

The Current Models Lack a Chain of Evidence to Justify Value

Another concern associated with existing models is that many of them simply assume marketing programs create value but fail to provide adequate justification. This notion may be applauded by marketers but probably will not pass the scrutiny of CEOs and CFOs. To win credibility and support for funding, marketers need to justify the value they have created by building a chain of evidence. Just as in legal contexts, when prosecutors must establish an unbroken chain of custody, this process involves chronological documentation of data and facts to record the sequence of collection, analysis, and disposition of physical and electronic evidence. Similarly, marketers should strive to show value by presenting a logical flow of data that come from marketing projects and programs.

Table 1.2 shows such a chain of value. As you will notice, the first column of this figure lists the options we worked on in the exercise. In fact, these options correspond to data collected at the different levels that can be used to build a chain of value created by the marketing programs. Input data, at Level 0, measure the investment side of a marketing program. The next three levels, Levels 1, 2, and 3, measure data reflecting customers' decision-making process and can be used to demonstrate and justify the value creation process. Next, there is a consequence of that action, which is often a purchase. This is the business impact, Level 4. Finally, sometimes there is a need to see if the program is worth it, a comparison of the monetary benefits to the marketing program costs, the ROI, Level 5. By combining the data collected at the reaction, learning, action, and impact levels, we are able to build a chain of evidence to justify the value that our marketing programs create. Unfortunately, many of the existing models do not focus on the chain of value, which diminishes their ability to demonstrate the contributions of marketing programs.

The Current Models Lack an Emphasis on Attribution (Proof)

We implement external and internal marketing programs to improve performance measures such as sales revenue, profitability, market share, customer satisfaction, customer loyalty, and customer retention rates. Improvements of these important measures will certainly benefit the organizations that sponsor the marketing programs. One issue that almost always surfaces, however, is to show that an improvement is attributed to the marketing program, not something else. Marketing is a highly visible discipline. This means that the outcome data of many marketing programs are generally available to executives and stakeholders.

TABLE 1.2. Chain of value based on six levels of data

VALUE DESCRIPTION OF MARKETING PROGRAMS	LEVEL	MEASUREMENT FOCUS	TYPICAL MEASURES
A. "Reach the largest number of customers with the least amount of cost."	0 Input	Input into programs, including indicators representing scope, volumes, times, costs, and efficiencies	• Types of topics, content • Number of programs • Number of people • Hours of involvement • Costs
B. "Customers are engaged, enjoy the programs, and see our products and services as interesting and valuable."	1 Reaction	Reaction to the marketing programs, including their perceived value of the product or services and planned action of the customer	• Relevance • Importance • Usefulness • Valuable • Intent to take action • Motivation • Recommendation to others
C. "Customers are learning the features, advantages, and benefits of our offerings to make purchase decisions."	2 Learning	Knowledge gained, including learning how to develop concepts and how to use skills and competencies at work	• Knowledge • Capacity • Competencies • Confidence • Contacts

VALUE DESCRIPTION OF MARKETING PROGRAMS	LEVEL	MEASUREMENT FOCUS	TYPICAL MEASURES
D. "Because of the marketing program, customers take action, try the samples, and take steps to make a decision."	3 Action	Action by customers and the use of knowledge, skills, and competencies in the work environment	• Behavior change • Request for a demo • Trying a sample • Review of customer ratings • Actions completed • Barriers to actions • Enablers of actions
E. "Customers purchase our products and services and have a positive impact on the bottom line of the organization."	4 Impact	The impact of marketing programs and activities, expressed as business impact	• Market share • Revenue • Customer loyalty • Brand • Efficiency • Customer complaints • Customer retention • Customer satisfaction
F. "The organization has a positive return on the investment of marketing efforts, time, and the resources used."	5 ROI	Comparison of monetary benefits from the marketing to the marketing program costs	• Benefit-cost ratio • ROI (%) • Payback period

However, because the outcomes of most marketing programs are influenced by many factors simultaneously and most of them are beyond our control, executives may have reasons to doubt the extent to which the marketing programs drive results. For example, three months after Gold's Gym launched a social media campaign, membership applications nearly doubled in the month of January. Was the improvement caused by the social medial marketing program or other factors, such as New Year's resolutions or the recent completion of a road construction project in front of the gym? Without a proper attribution process, the results will not be credible.

The Current Models Assume Perfect Information and Static Environments

Bold assumptions are made by some existing marketing ROI models. For example, that it's possible to figure out most of the unknowns of a market in advance and marketers have all the information they need even before they actually execute the marketing program. These models also assume that business environments remain static as marketing programs are implemented and customers will behave exactly the same way for five to ten years. These assumptions probably held true some time ago, but not anymore, since the new reality of the business environment is far from static. More business leaders agree that we are operating in a world of VUCA, a term that originated in the US Army War College and stands for the volatility, uncertainty, complexity, and ambiguity of the world after the cold war. In many industries and sectors, the concept of VUCA is gaining popularity and relevance. All these factors mandate strategic and tactical changes to the current evaluation models of marketing programs.

The Current Models Lack a Focus on Process Improvement

Many evaluation efforts take place around the end of marketing programs, usually months or years after a marketing program is initiated. If the results show the program didn't work or the ROI was below expectation, it's too late to do anything about it. Therefore, every evaluation model should have a process improvement focus. When evaluation reveals disappointing results, the model should help marketers identify what changes need to be made. Even when results are satisfactory, the model should enable marketers to know how to improve the results. From marketing planning to implementation, the process can be lengthy and complex. Without a proper evaluation model, marketers will find it challenging to identify and address problematic areas. This focus on process improvement will also help overcome the greatest barrier to evaluation: the fear of the outcome. Marketers typically have a genuine and understandable fear that the program may not deliver the desired value and the shortcomings will be exposed at the evaluation stage. With process improvement as the focus for the model, marketers have the option to make necessary adjustments to deliver expected results before it is too late.

The Current Models Lack the Ability to Influence Investment and Funding

All marketing programs consume resources. No marketing initiative can succeed without adequate funding and support. It is in the marketers' best interests to show that their marketing programs are a valuable investment of organizational resources in order to secure future funding. With potential rivalry among different functions within an organization, fighting for future investment funding can be a confusing and even controversial matter. The challenge is to help executives and stakeholders see the value so that they can continue to fund the program. Evaluation models need to provide marketing managers and professionals with the capability to influence future investment and make the case for adequate funding. Figure 1.1 shows a logical process flow from evaluation of the program, to optimization of results, and eventually to increased future allocation of funds. Specifically, marketers take proper measurements to reveal value and issues, optimize ROI to improve both the process and results, and then make a strong case to secure funding for marketing programs.

FIGURE 1.1   Evaluation, optimization, and allocation

The ROI Methodology

In this book, we introduce the ROI Methodology to marketing professionals, students, and researchers. This methodology, developed by ROI Institute, addresses the eight concerns with current evaluation models and helps marketers in demonstrating accountability and securing funding. ROI Institute is a global center of excellence that focuses exclusively on the ROI Methodology. Jack and Patti Phillips, two of the coauthors of this book, founded ROI Institute with the mission to evaluate the results of complex but "softer" noncapital programs. From talent management, to leadership development, to technology and innovation, the ROI Methodology has helped both practitioners and researchers demonstrate the value their programs created in order to win both financial and nonfinancial support from stakeholders. During the past 25 years, the methodology has been adopted in more than 6,000 organizations across the world, including 85 percent of Fortune 500 companies and the United Nations. Meanwhile, ROI Institute executives have published more than 100 books and more than 400 ROI case studies showing how the method can be used in various applications. The ROI Methodology has been continuously improved and frequently updated since its creation. The model introduced in this book is the most up-to-date version for marketers and is inspired by design thinking principles. It can be used by marketers with or without strong statistical and financial backgrounds, as the process is user-friendly, with simple, logical, and sequential steps. The methodology has a solid theoretical foundation and has been tested empirically through widespread use. We will provide an overview of the ROI Methodology in Chapter 2 and explain the details, steps, techniques, and tools in subsequent chapters.

Final Thoughts

Marketers are under pressure to show value. This chapter defines value and makes the case for measuring, improving, and demonstrating value created by marketing programs to respond to executive requests and address the accountability issue. Current models are not working due to a variety of limitations. The marketing field needs a new evaluation model that is applicable for business marketing, consumer marketing, and internal marketing while also addressing concerns associated with current models. The new model is built on a solid theoretical foundation, has been empirically tested across industries and nations, and is user-friendly. It will enable marketers to explore new ways to measure, show, and improve value—and, most importantly, to secure funding and support.

2

How the ROI Methodology Works

Stones from other hills may serve to polish the jade of this one.

CHINESE PROVERB

National Investment Corporation (NIC) is a large financial service firm that provides investment and insurance products to customers nationwide. It was founded in the 1950s as an insurance company that primarily serves farmers in the Midwest. Today, it serves customers in 23 states, although the bulk of business, roughly 70 percent, still comes from customers in the Midwest. NIC's financial products include stocks and mutual funds, annuities, life insurance, home and auto insurances, long-term care insurance, and financial planning and trust services. For several decades, the company has managed to grow the business with a very successful marketing and sales strategy that emphasizes customer relationship management.

Richard has recently been appointed as the marketing director of NIC. After graduating with a marketing degree from college, Richard has worked a plethora of jobs in the insurance and financial service industries. Equipped with business acumen and personal selling skills, as well as marketing and management experience, Richard is confident that he will succeed in this new position.

However, the current situation at NIC is far from ideal. First, the sales revenue number has been flat. Specifically, the firm has seen its annual growth rate decreasing from 15 percent five years ago to less than 1 percent last year. Sales revenue per customer of NIC, an important measure of marketing and sales effectiveness, has been reduced below the industry average by 20 percent. In addition, records show that the number of customer complaints has increased to 120 per month, and most of them are related to customer service quality. Meanwhile, NIC's rate of staff turnover, roughly 30 percent, is much higher than the industry average, which is around 15 percent in this market.

Richard and his team conduct a series of analyses to explore the performance gaps, which reveal that one of the pain points is NIC's slow response time to customer requests. Customer surveys confirm this finding, as many customers cite slow response times as the main reason for their dissatisfaction with customer service. Richard and his team collect historical data from company records and conduct one-on-one interviews and focus groups to further understand this issue. These analyses point to a potential root cause, ineffective customer relationship management (CRM).

A task force made up of representatives from sales, marketing, finance, information technology, and training examined several solutions for improving relationships, including a variety of CRM software services. After comparing features and prices of multiple options, Richard chooses to implement a CRM service package with both on-site and cloud-based versions. The software package is called CRMNow!, which is designed to turn contacts into relationships and relationships into increased sales. It features a flexible customer database, easy contact entry, a built-in calendar, and a to-do list. CRMNow! enables quick and effective customer communication and is designed for use with customized reports.

Sales consultants of CRMNow! claim that they can help NIC with customer acquisition and customer retention, as well as improve customer profitability. Since NIC has never used such a service before, Richard decides to conduct a pilot study to assess the functionality and potential success of CRMNow!. Instead of purchasing the software for each of the 4,000 financial advisors, he is planning to implement the software for 60 financial advisors and test its effectiveness and efficiency. The implementation process involves a one-day meeting to teach the financial advisors how to use the software. The CRMNow! software will be demonstrated and used at the meeting. If adopting this software yields the appropriate return on investment, NIC plans on implementing the software and one-day training session for all its financial advisors throughout the company.

Richard has heard about the ROI Methodology but does not know the details of it. He is wondering whether and how this methodology may help him properly measure, evaluate, and demonstrate the value of his strategy, compete for funding and support for marketing, and ensure the best usage of NIC's resources.

Using Six Levels of Data to Measure Value

As discussed in Chapter 1, ROI in marketing builds its framework around customers' decision-making processes and evaluates the impacts on business outcomes through a chain of impact. These data examine the value creation process at different levels and represent the inherent richness of the ROI Methodology. Specifically, marketers collect and analyze data at the following levels using metrics that correspond to each level.

Level 0: Input

At Level 0, marketers measure the financial and nonfinancial resources invested into the marketing campaigns, projects, programs, and events. Typical metrics at this level include the types of projects, costs and expenditures, number of customers and participants, number of meetings, tweets posted, emails sent, mobile ads purchased, etc. In an internal marketing program such as the one launched by NIC in the story discussed at the beginning of the chapter, Level 0, Input, can be the number of participants (60 financial advisors), costs related to purchasing and installing the CRMNow! system, number of training sessions offered, number of hours involved in training, etc.

Level 1: Reaction

Reaction refers to the feelings experienced by customers or program participants in response to a stimulus or a situation. At this level, marketers measure the target segment's reaction to advertisements, products, services, information sessions, promotional messages, etc. In the case of NIC, the marketing director and his team should monitor the reactions of the financial advisors to the CRMNow! system and related training sessions. The extent to which the financial advisors find using the system to be relevant, important, and helpful to provide customer service can be treated as measures at the reaction level.

Level 2: Learning

Learning is the acquisition of information, knowledge, skills, or preferences through exposure to ads, social media promotions, training, and interactions with sales professionals. Although learning itself does not guarantee project success, it is an important determinant of customers' actions and, eventually, business outcomes. At this level, NIC needs to ensure that the 60 financial advisors have adequate knowledge and skills to use the CRMNow! system in their interactions with customers.

Level 3: Action

Action refers to what marketers expect the target audience to do with what they have learned. The actions may include customers' phone and email inquiries, company website visits, and usage of coupons and samples. Although still no guarantee of success, these actions generally have significant impacts on business outcomes. For internal marketing programs, this level measures the extent to which program participants apply what they have learned. In the example of NIC, Level 3, Action, refers to the financial advisors' application of the CRMNow! system to better serve customers. This involves the extent of use, frequency of use, and success with use. At this level, we also examine barriers to use and enablers of use.

Level 4: Impact

Impact measures the desired business outcomes that marketing projects and programs intend to achieve. Typical outcomes include increased sales revenue, profit, number of new customers, etc. The marketing team of NIC initiates the CRMNow! program to improve sales revenue, enhance customer satisfaction, reduce customer complaints, and, the hope is, reduce the staff turnover rate; all are metrics of the business impact at Level 4.

Level 5: ROI

At this level, we compare the monetary benefits of the business impact measures with the fully loaded program costs in order to calculate the ROI, which is the ultimate measure of value created by marketing. In order to calculate the ROI of its CRMNow! program, the marketing team of NIC needs to tabulate both direct and indirect costs related to implementing the CRMNow! system. Also, the annualized monetary benefit of the program would be calculated. This means that sales revenue, customer satisfaction, customer complaints, and staff turnover would be converted to money to develop the total benefits. The impact measures should be isolated to reflect the effect of the CRMNow! program, before converting the data to money. We will discuss the details of this approach in subsequent chapters.

As discussed in Chapter 1, the ROI Methodology can be used by all three types of marketing programs, including business-to-consumer

(B2C), business-to-business (B2B), and internal marketing programs. All six levels of data in the framework are applicable to the three types of marketing, but the metrics for each type of marketing may differ. The six levels of data and corresponding metrics are summarized in Table 2.1.

TABLE 2.1 Six levels of data for three types of marketing programs

LEVEL	MEASUREMENT CATEGORY	B2C MARKETING	B2B MARKETING	INTERNAL MARKETING
0 Input	Measures input into marketing campaigns including the number of programs, attendees, audience, costs, and efficiencies	A new TV commercial promoting a new product	Personal selling of a new service package	Salesperson attending sales skills training
1 Reaction	Measures customer or participant reaction to the marketing program including perceived value and planned action to make it successful	Consumers find the commercial interesting	Purchasing agents find the service unique	Salespeople find the training useful, relevant, and important to their success
2 Learning	Measures what participants learned in the program— information, knowledge, skills, and contacts (takeaways from the marketing program)	Consumers learn the benefits of the new product	Agents learn the new features of the service package	Salespeople learn how to use the new sales skills

LEVEL	MEASUREMENT CATEGORY	B2C MARKETING	B2B MARKETING	INTERNAL MARKETING
3 Action	Measures actions taken because of the marketing program—using information, requesting a proposal, trying a sample, changing behaviors, etc.	Consumers search online to find the new product reviews	Purchasing agents recommend the service package to managers	Salespeople use the sales skills when selling
4 Impact	Measures changes in business impact variables such as revenue, profit, customer loyalty, quality, and costs, linked to the marketing program	Sales of the product increase by 1 million units in 6 months	Profit of the service package reaches $750,000	Monthly revenue per salesperson increases by $60,000
5 ROI	Compares the monetary benefits of the business impact measures with the costs of the program	50%	25%	40%

Creating Alignment

Marketing is a central function essential to any organization. As a core business activity, marketing management is the process of planning, developing, and implementing strategies to serve the needs of the target customer segment and achieve organizational goals. Every year, marketers launch various programs and projects to improve individual, departmental, and organizational performance by leading and managing all facets of the marketing process. These marketing programs consume financial and human resources and are becoming increasingly costly. We need to take actions to make sure the programs are generating benefits that exceed costs and are absolutely necessary.

Research shows that one important reason for a program failing is lack of alignment. Good marketing programs address important business needs and satisfy business goals at different levels. It is critically important to align our marketing program's objectives with organizational goals to solicit support and resources and ensure success. The ROI Methodology uses an alignment model, also known as the V model, to help marketers achieve alignment for their programs. As shown in Figure 2.1, the model starts with examining needs on the left-hand side and ends with the value chain on the right-hand side; both sides of the model include Levels 1 to 5, discussed previously.

FIGURE 2.1 The Alignment Model

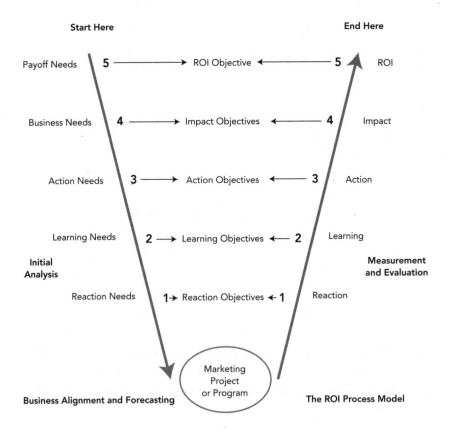

Payoff Needs

The first step in this alignment process examines the potential payoff of the marketing program and asks the following questions: Is this a problem worth solving or an opportunity worth pursuing? Is the marketing program worthy of implementation? What is the likelihood of a positive ROI? Marketers should consider both strategic payoff needs at the organizational level and tactical payoff needs at the functional level to ensure alignment.

Business Needs

The next step is to make sure the marketing program is initiated and implemented to address real business needs, for example, to improve sales, market share, customer loyalty, new account growth, product returns, or customer complaints. Although it is possible for an organization to face multiple business needs simultaneously, these business needs should be prioritized based on strategic considerations and weighed on their costs and potential benefits.

Action Needs

Next, examine the action needs, which are the behaviors that the customers need to adopt to satisfy the business needs defined previously. For example, if the sales are flat, what should the marketing team do to increase sales? What should the customers be doing? What should the sales team be doing? This step can be complex but intriguing. It is critical because it provides the connection linking the input of a marketing program to its intended results.

Learning Needs

After determining action needs, we next examine learning needs. Relevant questions of this step focus on assessing the information, skills, or knowledge that are needed to drive the desired actions defined in previous steps to now determine what can change. Every marketing program involves a learning component, no matter if it is a business-to-business, business-to consumer, or internal marketing program. The needed knowledge may be as simple as knowing where to buy a new product or may be as complicated as understanding how to install new equipment. Depending on the context, the learning can be either active or passive, conscious or subconscious, online or offline.

Reaction Needs

The final step involves examining reaction needs and ensuring external and internal customers find the marketing program and products and services interesting, important, or valuable so that they will want to learn more or take action. Reaction itself is not enough for program success, but it serves as the starting point and initial consideration of the alignment process.

NIC Case Study

Understanding the need for a marketing program builds a solid foundation for the marketing program to succeed. It also enables marketers to develop clear and specific objectives that are communicated to all stakeholders. These objectives should define success at each level and answer the question, "How will we know the needs have been met?" During and after marketing program implementation, we can measure and evaluate outcomes at each level and compare them with the objectives. In the case of NIC's CRMNow! system, the marketing director and his team may set the following objectives at different levels. The ROI (Level 5) objective is set as "20 percent," whereas business (Level 4) objectives can be set as "increasing sales with existing customers by 10 percent in six months and reducing customer complaints to below 20 percent in six months." In order to achieve the objectives at higher levels, NIC should conduct analyses to determine desirable action and learning needs. Based on these analyses, the action (Level 3) objective could be set as "more than 80 percent of the financial advisors who participated in the training program will use the CRMNow! system within one month," and the learning (Level 2) objective could be set as "90 percent of the financial advisors who participated in the training program understand the steps to use the system." To ensure proper learning, the NIC marketing team needs to carefully design the promotional message sent to the financial advisors. A reaction objective could be "95 percent of financial advisors find the training program of the CRMNow! system to be relevant, helpful, and important."

Using Design Thinking to Deliver Results

Design thinking is a very popular concept in innovation and, more recently, in marketing. Although the idea of design thinking emerged several decades ago, it gained popularity in the past years with books like *Change by Design* by Tim Brown with IDEO[1] and *Design Thinking for Strategic Innovation* by Idris Mootee.[2] As a human-centric and holistic approach, design thinking utilizes elements such as empathy and experimentation to arrive at innovative solutions. Instead of relying on historical data or instinct, marketers who use design thinking make decisions based on what customers want in the future by adopting an iterative process. After success is clearly defined, marketers quickly start with ideation and prototype based on the initial level of understanding, actively seek to understand users' needs by constantly acquiring new information, challenging old assumptions, and willingly redefining problems in an attempt to identify alternative strategies and solutions.

Design thinking is both a way of thinking and a collection of hands-on methods. It empowers the entire team to design for the definition of success, not just validate it. If we want better sales performance, everyone works on it. If we want more satisfied customers, everyone is focused on customer service. If we want to reduce customer churn rates, the focus is there for every stakeholder. With that success clearly and properly defined, the team works through a series of steps, guided by design thinking principles, to reach the desired success. In Box 2.1, we summarize 10 common design thinking principles. These universal design thinking principles inspired us to update the ROI Methodology and create a model to design for results, design for data collection, and design for more investment.[3] The first eight principles uniquely influence the 12 steps of the ROI Methodology. The steps and the design thinking principles used for each step are highlighted and described in Table 2.2.

Every system is perfectly designed to get
exactly the results it gets.
W. EDWARDS DEMING

Box 2.1   Design Thinking Basic Principles

1. A problem-solving approach to handle problems on a systems level
2. A mindset for curiosity and inquiry
3. A framework to balance needs and feasibility
4. A way to take on design challenges by applying empathy
5. A culture that fosters exploration and experimentation
6. A fixed process and a tool kit
7. A storytelling process to inspire senior executives
8. A new competitive logic of business strategy
9. A means to solve complex or wicked problems
10. A means to reduce risks

Idris Mootee. *Design Thinking for Strategic Innovation: What They Can't Teach You at Business or Design School.* Hoboken, NJ: Wiley, 2013.

TABLE 2.2 Designing for results

1. **Start with Why:** Align Programs with the Business • Alignment is the key • Is it a problem or opportunity? • Need specific business measure(s)	**Design Thinking Principle:** A problem-solving approach to handle problems on a systems level
	ISPI Standard 1: Focus on Results or Outcomes
2. **Make It Feasible:** Select the Right Solution • What are we doing (or not doing) that's influencing the impact measure? • How can we achieve this performance?	**Design Thinking Principle:** A mindset for curiosity and inquiry
	ISPI Standards 5, 6, and 7: Determine Need or Opportunity, Determine Cause, and Design Solutions Including Implementation and Evaluation
3. **Expect Success:** Plan for Results • Set objectives at multiple levels • Define success • Expand responsibilities	**Design Thinking Principle:** A framework to balance needs and feasibility
	ISPI Standard 2: Take a Systemic View
4. **Make It Matter:** Design for Input, Reaction, and Learning • Focus on the objectives • Think about ROI • Make it relevant • Make it important • Make it action-oriented	**Design Thinking Principle:** A way to take on design challenges by applying empathy
	ISPI Standard 8: Ensure Solutions' Conformity and Feasibility
5. **Make It Stick:** Design for Action and Impact • Focus on objectives • Ensure the application of the program • Design application and action tools • Collect data	**Design Thinking Principle:** A culture that fosters exploration and experimentation
	ISPI Standard 9: Implement Solutions
6. **Make It Credible:** Measure Results and Calculate ROI • Isolate the effects of projects • Convert data to money • Tabulate costs • Calculate ROI	**Design Thinking Principle:** A fixed process and a tool kit
	ISPI Standard 10: Evaluate Results and Impact

(continued on next page)

7. **Tell the Story:** Communicate Results to Key Stakeholders • Define audience • Identify why they need it • Select method • Move quickly • Consider one-page summary	**Design Thinking Principle:** A storytelling process to inspire senior executives
	ISPI Standard 4: Work in Partnership with Clients and Stakeholders
8. **Optimize Results:** Use Performance Improvement to Increase Funding • Measure • Improve • Fund	**Design Thinking Principle:** A new competitive logic of business strategy
	ISPI Standard 3: Add Value

(Revised from Patricia Pulliam Phillips and Jack J. Phillips. *The Business Case for Learning: Using Design Thinking to Deliver Business Results and Increase the Investment in Talent Development.* West Chester, PA: HRDQ and Alexandria, VA: ATD Press, 2017.)

Using the ISPI 10 Standards to Ensure Success

The International Society for Performance Improvement (ISPI) is a nonprofit organization that believes "being better matters." All the coauthors of this book have volunteered for and served in various leadership positions at the ISPI. For nearly six decades, this organization has been providing tools and strategies for effective and universal performance improvement and helping people and organizations make a difference. Members of the ISPI apply a systematic approach known as human performance technology (HPT) to improve performance at individual, organizational, and societal levels. The HPT approach assesses current performance status, identifies performance gaps and growth opportunities, and analyzes causes, before designing, developing, implementing, and evaluating performance improvement solutions. During the whole process, they follow the 10 ISPI standards as guidance.[4] We include the 10 standards in Box 2.2.

> ## Box 2.2   ISPI's 10 Standards
>
> **Standard 1.** Focus on Results or Outcomes
> **Standard 2.** Take a Systemic View
> **Standard 3.** Add Value
> **Standard 4.** Work in Partnership with Clients and Stakeholders
> **Standard 5.** Determine Need or Opportunity
> **Standard 6.** Determine Cause
> **Standard 7.** Design Solutions Including Implementation and Evaluation
> **Standard 8.** Ensure Solutions' Conformity and Feasibility
> **Standard 9.** Implement Solutions
> **Standard 10.** Evaluate Results and Impact

As you can see in Box 2.2, the 10 ISPI standards emphasize results, outcomes, and value add. The standards are consistent with the ROI Methodology, which also strives to measure, enhance, and demonstrate improved performance and value created by our programs and projects. Similar to the design thinking principles we discussed in the previous section, the ISPI 10 standards also influence the 12 steps of the ROI Methodology. Look again at Table 2.2, where we demonstrate the first eight steps of the ROI Methodology, the design thinking principles, and the 10 ISPI standards influencing them.

The ROI Process Model

One typical challenge facing many marketers is how to use an ROI model to measure and demonstrate value. Some professionals complain that although they understand the ROI in marketing concept in theory, they still do not know how to use it in practice. In this book, we show the step-by-step process of the ROI Methodology and provide tools, examples, and cases to support usage. As shown in Figure 2.2, the

FIGURE 2.2 The ROI Methodology

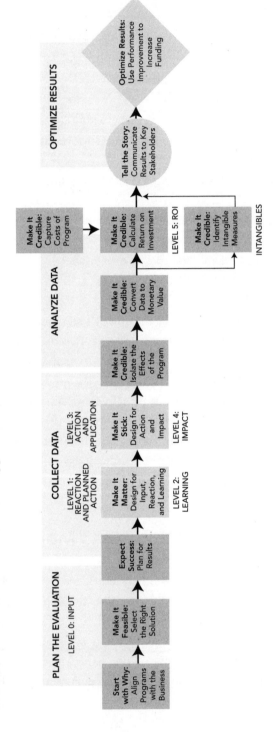

eight-step approach in Table 2.2 has been adjusted for the 12 steps with four phases:

Phase 1. Plan the Evaluation (Steps 1–3)
Phase 2. Collect Data (Steps 4–5)
Phase 3. Analyze Data (Steps 6–10)
Phase 4. Optimize Results (Steps 11–12)

Because of the importance of credibility in data analysis, Phase 3 now has five steps, each labeled with "Make It Credible" at the beginning of the step. We briefly introduce the process model in this section and discuss the details of the 12 steps in subsequent chapters.

Phase 1. Plan the Evaluation

The first phase of the ROI Methodology, "Plan the Evaluation," has three steps. "Start with Why" is the first step, which will be discussed in Chapter 3. This step focuses on aligning the marketing program with the organizational mission, goals, and strategies. The second step is "Make It Feasible," which involves selecting the proper solution to achieve the desired impact. The third step, "Expect Success: Plan for Results," defines success, sets objectives, and clarifies the roles played by the different stakeholders to achieve success. We will discuss Steps 2 and 3 in Chapters 4 and 5, respectively.

Step 1. Start with Why: Align Programs with the Business

We name the first step of the ROI process model as "Start with Why," because this step defines why we are pursuing the program. In this step, the design thinking principle is to "handle problems on a systems level," and the ISPI standard is "Focus on Results or Outcomes." Marketing plays a unique role in implementing organizational strategies. Marketers need to ensure that each aspect of the marketing program is indeed serving that purpose. Depending on the strategic choices made by top management and the challenges facing the organization, marketing programs may be used to improve sales revenue, profitability, and market share, or they may be used to secure new clients and reduce customer complaints. Marketing programs can also be internally oriented with goals like reducing product returns, improving customer response times, etc. No matter what the reasons are, marketers need to define, articulate, and communicate why we are pursuing the marketing program as the first step. For example, the marketing director of NIC chooses improving customer service and sales revenues as reasons why NIC needs the CRMNow! program.

Step 2. Make It Feasible: Select the Right Solution

In this step, the design thinking principle is "a mindset for curiosity and inquiry." There are three ISPI standards involved: "Determine Need or Opportunity," "Determine Cause," and "Design Solutions." Marketers need to conduct various analyses in order to identify problems and opportunities, explore cause, and design or select the most feasible solution to achieve the goals set in the first step. Should we modify the product or its package? Should we adjust the price? Should we target a different segment or try a different distribution channel? Should we launch a new social media campaign? No matter what solution you choose, the choice should be justified with analysis, evidence, and considerations of both expected impact and costs. In the case of NIC, the company chooses to implement the CRMNow! system and train financial advisors as the solution to reach the goals set in Step 1.

Step 3. Expect Success: Plan for Results

In this step, marketers set objectives at the impact, action, learning, and reaction levels, as highlighted in the alignment model. The design thinking principle is "a framework to balance needs and feasibility," and the ISPI standard is "Take a Systemic View." These objectives should be SMART, that is, specific, measurable, attainable, relevant, and time bound. This step defines success at the impact level so that all stakeholders will understand the roles they are expected to play and will work toward achieving action and impact objectives during the implementation process. Marketers monitor progress, compare with the objectives, and make necessary adjustments if one or more indicators are not on track. Revisions can be made throughout the process in order to ensure success. The objectives also help marketers plan the data collection, data analysis, and communication components, thus completing the "Plan the Evaluation" phase.

Phase 2. Collect Data

Data collection is central to the ROI Methodology. This phase uses two steps to verify success at various levels. Chapter 6, "Make It Matter," measures success at Levels 0 (Input), 1 (Reaction), and 2 (Learning). Chapter 7, "Make It Stick," involves data collection to measure success at Levels 3 (Action) and 4 (Impact). The data can be hard data, soft data, primary data, and secondary data, which are collected either internally or externally from online or offline sources. During this phase, marketers need to select the method or methods appropriate for the marketing program within the time and budget constraints.

Step 4. Make It Matter: Design for
Input, Reaction, and Learning

In this step, the design thinking principle is "a way to take on design challenges by applying empathy," and the ISPI standard is "Ensure Solutions' Conformity and Feasibility." The ROI in marketing is a customer-centric approach. We design solutions for a marketing program by considering customers' reaction, learning, and action as well as the impact of these lower-level factors on results and outcomes. The key is to enable internal customers to think what external customers think, feel what they feel, and be able to design the program accordingly to accommodate their needs. In the NIC example, it requires the marketing director to first consider what input is needed (who should be involved, for how long, and at what costs), how the 60 financial advisors will react to the CRMNow! system, and what the financial advisors need to learn to be successful with the CRM. This step focuses on making sure that the marketing program will be relevant, be important to the parties involved, and have adequate resources and support from the stakeholders to succeed.

Step 5. Make It Stick: Design for Action and Impact

The design thinking principle applied here is "a culture that fosters exploration and experimentation," and the ISPI standard is "Implement Solutions." In this process, marketers must follow through on the initial plans but, at the same time, be willing to adapt and update the plan with new information collected from customers. We need to explore what works and does not work by quickly moving forward with an iterative process of testing, learning, and validating. Essentially, this is transferring customers' attitudes and knowledge into action and business impact. During the process, we need to collect data, address enablers and barriers, and make sure the marketing program is operating smoothly. If data show that our marketing program is not making adequate progress, we should be willing to go back to previous steps and examine input-, reaction-, and learning-level indicators with newly acquired information about customers' actions. We also need to develop, test, and revise tools to measure, drive, and influence the success at the action and impact levels.

Phase 3. Analyze Data

This phase deals with analyzing data to build the credibility of our marketing programs. The design thinking principle for the steps in this phase is implement "a fixed process and a tool kit," which are the steps of the ROI Methodology. The ISPI standard is "Evaluate Results and Impact." Making it credible involves several steps including a critical but often overlooked step of isolating the effects of the marketing program. Isolating and pinpointing the amount of improvement directly related to the marketing program leads to increased accuracy and credibility of the ROI calculations. Chapter 8 provides more detail on this critical issue. The next step involves converting data to monetary values. Some measures are not converted to money and are left as intangible benefits. Chapter 9 provides more detail on these important issues. An important part of the ROI equation is the program costs. The final two steps in the analysis focus on the costs and the actual ROI calculation. More details on costs and ROI are presented in Chapter 10.

Step 6: Make It Credible: Isolate the Effects of the Program

An often overlooked issue in evaluation is the process of isolating the effects of the program. In this step, specific strategies are explored to determine the amount of outcome performance directly related to the project. This step is essential because many factors can influence sales and marketing data. The specific strategies of this step pinpoint the amount of improvement directly related to the marketing program, resulting in increased accuracy and credibility of ROI calculations. The following techniques have been used by program evaluators to tackle this important issue:

- Control group analysis
- Trend line analysis
- Mathematical modeling
- Participant estimates
- Manager or significant other estimates
- Senior management estimates
- Experts' input
- Customer input

Collectively, these techniques provide a comprehensive set of tools to handle the important and critical issue of isolating the effects of the marketing program.

Step 7: Make It Credible: Convert Data to Monetary Value

To calculate the return on investment, impact data are converted to monetary values and compared with program costs. This requires a value be placed on each unit of impact data connected with the program. Many techniques are available to convert data to monetary values. The specific technique selected depends on the type of data and the situation. The techniques include:

- Use the value add of output data as standard values.
- Use the cost of quality as a standard value.
- Convert time savings to wage and employee benefits (standard value).

- Calculate the value using an analysis of historical costs.
- Use internal and external experts to provide value.
- Search external databases for the value.
- Use participant estimates.
- Use manager estimates.
- Locate soft measures mathematically linked to easy-to-value measures.

This step in the ROI model is absolutely necessary to determine the monetary benefits of a program. The process is challenging, particularly with soft data, but can be methodically accomplished using one or more of these strategies.

Step 8: Make It Credible: Identify Intangible Measures

In addition to tangible, monetary benefits, the intangible benefits—those not converted to money—are identified for most programs. Intangible benefits include items such as:

- Enhanced brand reputation
- Improved organizational image
- Less team stress
- Increased customer engagement
- Improved quality of life
- Increased brand awareness
- Improved networking
- Enhanced patient satisfaction
- Improved service
- Fewer complaints
- Reduced conflicts

During data analysis, every attempt is made to convert all data to monetary values. All hard data—such as output, quality, and time—are converted to monetary values. The conversion of soft data is also attempted for each data item. However, if the process used for conversion is too subjective or inaccurate, and the resulting values lose credibility in the process, then the data are listed as intangible benefits with the appropriate explanation. For some programs such as green marketing, intangible, nonmonetary benefits are extremely valuable and often carry as much influence as the hard data items.

Step 9: Make It Credible: Capture Costs of Program

An important part of the ROI equation is the denominator, the calculation of marketing program costs. Tabulating the costs involves monitoring or developing all the related costs of the program targeted for the ROI calculation. Among the cost components to be included are:

- Initial analysis costs
- Cost to design and develop the program
- Cost of program materials
- Costs for the program team
- Cost of the facilities for the program, if applicable
- Travel, lodging, and meal costs for the customers and sales team members
- Sales team salaries (including employee benefits), if appropriate
- Facilitator costs, if appropriate
- Administrative and overhead costs, allocated in some convenient way
- Evaluation costs

The conservative approach is to include all these costs so the total is fully loaded.

Step 10: Make It Credible: Calculate Return on Investment

The return on investment is calculated using the marketing program benefits and costs. The benefit-cost ratio (BCR) is calculated as the program benefits divided by the program costs. In formula form, it is

$$BCR = \frac{\text{program benefits}}{\text{program costs}}$$

The return on investment is based on the net program benefits divided by program costs. The net benefits are calculated as the program benefits minus the program costs. In formula form, the ROI becomes

$$ROI\ (\%) = \frac{\text{net program benefits}}{\text{program costs}} \times 100$$

This is the same basic formula used in evaluating other investments, in which the ROI is traditionally reported as earnings divided by investment.

Phase 4. Optimize Results

The last and fourth phase of the ROI Methodology is reporting and optimizing results, with two critical steps: communicating results and making improvements. The reporting step involves developing appropriate information in impact studies and other brief reports and telling a powerful story to all stakeholders. Chapter 11 provides more details. The improvement step focuses on continuous improvement, optimization, and the process of using the results to increase funding for marketing programs in the future. Chapter 12 provides more details on performance improvement and optimization.

Step 11. Tell the Story: Communicate Results
to Key Stakeholders

In this step, the design thinking principle is "a storytelling process to inspire senior executives," and the ISPI standard is "Work in Partnership with Clients and Stakeholders." Marketing programs do not end when we have results in hand. Marketers must communicate to all stakeholders and let them know the success of the program. Even when the results are not ideal, marketers still need to communicate to stakeholders, using the data to show what needs to improve and what actions are needed to improve it. Storytelling is a powerful tool. It will be even more powerful when we are able to tell the story with data collected at different levels. The story will be more interesting and compelling to stakeholders when we are addressing their concerns associated with performance issues and showing how our marketing programs can help them achieve the goals they care about. We will be able to inspire senior executives and other key stakeholders to support marketing when we back up the story with proof and a chain of evidence that our program has made a difference and contributes to organizational success. We devote Chapter 11 to this critical step in the ROI process.

Step 12. Optimize Results: Use Performance Improvement to Increase Funding

The design principle used here is "a new competitive logic of business strategy," and the ISPI standard is "Add Value." The key here is to make sure that marketing programs are properly and continuously supported and funded. We need to use the performance improvement approach to analyze the results, continuously seek new value-adding opportunities, and improve and sustain performance in order to secure and increase funding. This should be done regularly regardless of whether improvements are made. It is a mandate when there is a lack of improvement. When a failure is identified, marketers can use the systematic approach of performance improvement to analyze the causes of this failure and design appropriate solutions to address them. Even with success, improvements are made to make marketing programs deliver even more value. The ultimate goals are to improve value, optimize the ROI, and secure allocation of more funds as we build the case for more investment. It is a novel way to integrate design thinking and performance improvement with the ROI Methodology. We design for the needed results, capture data to tell a compelling story, use data to improve the program and optimize ROI, and then make the case for more funding. We focus on these issues in Chapter 12.

Operating Standards and Philosophy

The ROI Methodology has been routinely used by thousands of organizations worldwide over the past 25 years. To ensure consistency across projects conducted in different industries and by different individuals, operating standards must be applied to develop ROI studies. We have developed 12 Guiding Principles, shown in Box 2.3, to detail how steps and issues of the process will be handled in a consistent and credible manner.[5] The 12 principles also provide a much-needed conservative approach to the analysis, which helps build credibility and secure buy-in and support from the target audience. We will discuss these guiding principles in subsequent chapters, as they are critical to all aspects of the ROI Methodology in marketing.

Box 2.3   The 12 Guiding Principles of the ROI Methodology

1. When conducting a higher-level evaluation, collect data at lower levels.

2. When planning a higher-level evaluation, the previous level of evaluation is not required to be comprehensive.

3. When collecting and analyzing data, use only the most credible sources.

4. When analyzing data, select the most conservative alternative for calculations.

5. Use at least one method to isolate the effects of a project.

6. If no improvement data are available for a population or from a specific source, assume that little or no improvement has occurred.

7. Adjust estimates of improvement for potential errors of estimation.

8. Avoid use of extreme data items and unsupported claims when calculating ROI.

9. Use only the first year of annual benefits in ROI analysis of short-term solutions.

10. Fully load all costs of a solution, project, or program when analyzing ROI.

11. Intangible measures are defined as measures that are purposely not converted to monetary values.

12. Communicate the results of ROI Methodology to all key stakeholders.

Final Thoughts

This chapter introduced the ROI Methodology for marketing. We briefly presented the chain of value based on data at different levels, the business alignment model, the 12 steps in the ROI process model, and the standards necessary to guide how the ROI Methodology works in practice. We also demonstrated how design thinking principles and the performance improvement standards influence the 12 steps of the ROI Methodology to add value and secure funding. We discussed the key aspects of each step and concluded the chapter with the 12 Guiding Principles of the ROI Methodology. The subsequent chapters will provide more details on the 12 steps of the ROI Methodology. We begin by taking a closer look at how to establish the business needs for our marketing programs in Chapter 3, "Start with Why."

PART II

The Details of the ROI Methodology

3

Start with Why: Align Programs with the Business

However beautiful the strategy,
you should occasionally look at the results.
SIR WINSTON CHURCHILL

Two management consultants gave a joint presentation at a marketing conference in Chicago. The topic was the application of the ROI Methodology in marketing. The audience consisted of marketing managers, scholars, and students. After briefly reviewing the theoretical foundation of the ROI Methodology, the consultants discussed the changing measurement system of marketing programs and highlighted the 12-step approach of ROI in marketing. They also discussed the challenges marketing professionals face while in the process of measuring, demonstrating, and improving the value of their marketing programs and how the ROI in marketing approach can help address the issues.

One marketing manager from the audience was particularly interested in the discussion and asked quite a few questions during the presentation. The consultants had a conversation afterward with her. It turned out that she was the product manager of iTalent, a software and social media firm based in Chicago, which provided an employee experience platform to organizations with remote and offsite workforces. The platform was mobile based so that employees could use their smartphones and tablets to connect with headquarters and employees in different geographical locations. The product was particularly useful for internal communication and engagement purposes, with employees working from home and other remote locations. After its launch into the market five years ago, the iTalent mobile platform had been adopted by dozens of clients in different industries. Recently, however, the iTalent team began to encounter issues and challenges with the clients.

According to the marketing manager, executives of several clients looked at the expenses associated with the mobile platform and thought that the budget was sizable. They asked to see the ROI of the iTalent mobile platform program implemented within their organizations. The iTalent marketing team members replied that they had not evaluated the product at the ROI level, but they had collected other data that could be used to indicate the value of the mobile platform. The consultants asked the marketing manager what type of data the team members had collected. She mentioned that they had been conducting a regular engagement survey. In addition, they had collected usage data indicating the types of online conversations employees had and how much time employees spent on their mobile platform. However, the executives of these clients insisted that they needed to see the ROI for expenditures this large and for a product that was designed to help their most valuable resource, the employees.

To offer help, the consultants asked the marketing manager a series of questions. These conversations led to a formal request from the iTalent company for the consultants to conduct a marketing ROI study for its mobile platform. The consultants agreed and began the process of evaluating the product. Their analyses showed that there were no financial measures connected to the product. Instead, iTalent had collected data on some very important intangibles measures such as team collaboration, job satisfaction, and engagement among employees. These measures remained as intangibles because it would be difficult to credibly convert them to money. Because of the lack of monetary benefits, it was decided not to push the evaluation to ROI. The impact of iTalent mobile could be expressed as intangibles, but not as ROI. Although these intangibles showed the product as valuable in improving internal communication and employee engagement, they failed to satisfy the executive request to see the return on their investment. Also, because of the lack of business impact data, the team at iTalent missed the opportunity to improve the product in their efforts to help clients drive business.

• • •

This story highlights the reasons marketing programs should start with "why." "Why are we doing this?" "Why should my boss support this?" "Why should our customers care?" The why can be one or more business measures linking to the value created by the marketing program. It emphasizes that not only should marketing teams show the value of a marketing campaign based on increases in sales and new accounts, but the teams should be prepared to show the client's ROI for buying your product. In this story, iTalent's customers do not purchase and implement the product just to provide their employees some fun. The customers purchase and implement the product to create a positive impact on their employees' productivity and quality of work and maybe some cost reduction. Although not all products and services should be evaluated all the way to impact and ROI, there are times when they should. The story of iTalent's mobile platform was one of those times.

Focusing on the Business Value

This chapter presents the first step of a 12-step process that will transform marketing programs into business-contributing processes. This step, "Start with Why," defines why we are pursuing the marketing program. In this step, the design thinking principle guiding us is to use "a problem-solving approach to handle problems on a systems level." Similarly, we have two performance improvement standards to guide this step. The first standard is "Focus on Results or Outcomes," and the other standard is "Determine Need or Opportunity." Following these standards, marketers should focus on results throughout their programs. Instead of predisposing to a set of solutions, marketers must help leaders of their organization define what goals they want to accomplish, what problems or issues they want to address, and what business needs they want to fulfill.

Whether you are conducting business-to-consumer, business-to-business, or internal marketing programs, business needs exist and can often be expressed in terms of sales revenues, profits, market shares, growth rates, and costs. Defining business needs clearly and early avoids inefficiencies and problems that usually permeate the marketing management process and produce disappointing results. This chapter explains the first two of the five levels of needs assessments embedded in the ROI evaluation framework: addressing payoff needs and defining business needs.

All marketing programs must begin with a clear focus on the outcomes and results they intend to deliver. These results must be specifically defined in terms of their contribution to the long-term organizational mission and short-term organizational goals. In both business and nonprofit organizations, executives want to see their organizational missions accomplished, goals achieved, and resources efficiently utilized. As an indispensable function of every organization, marketing plays a major role in achieving organizational goals, and marketing programs should serve as essential tools to deliver the business performance critical to the success of an organization.

However, due to a variety of reasons, many marketing programs fail. ROI Institute conducted and reviewed approximately 5,000 evaluation studies and found that the number one cause of program failure was lack of business alignment. Program failure leads to wasted resources and lost opportunities, which may put the financial future of the organization at risk and the careers of the marketers who design and deliver these marketing programs in jeopardy. The principal culprit is usually lack of business alignment from the beginning, when the marketing program is launched.

Aligning Marketing Programs with Business

Marketers are creative and full of new ideas or, at least, supposed to be. We always find it exciting to create marketing plans filled with new initiatives, programs, and campaigns using the latest technology and tools. At the same time, marketing programs are becoming increasingly costly, and it is an uphill battle to get an ambitious marketing plan and budget approved by top management. But don't place the blame on the CFO who rejected your budget. After all, she is charged with a daunting task to reach lofty revenue goals with a finite pool of money to spend on each line item. Our mission is to focus on helping the CFO to solve her problem, instead of becoming a problem. We need to show that marketing programs drive organizational goals and satisfy payoff needs.

Moeller and Landry, partners of Booz & Company, suggest aligning the organization around marketing ROI as one of the pillars of profit-driven marketing in their classic book.[1] According to the authors, aligning marketing programs with business provides at least three important benefits. First, business alignment ensures support from the organization and top executives. Second, business alignment helps focus on identifying the roles and responsibilities of marketing professionals in the process of marketing program planning and implementation. Third, business alignment motivates employees to achieve the intended objectives of the marketing programs. All three are critical to the success of marketing programs, ensuring sufficient contribution to organizational goals. In order to align marketing programs with the business, marketers need to carefully explore the relevance and importance of the proposed programs and their strategic and operational implications as well as the cost thresholds. But how do we achieve business alignment?

The Alignment Model

To understand alignment, let us review the business alignment model shown in Figure 2.1, which is repeated here as Figure 3.1. Following the first performance improvement standard, we focus on the outcomes and results of our marketing programs. Following the second standard, we work on determining need or opportunity and pay particular attention to the needs at different levels on the left-hand side of the model. In this book, we define needs as gaps in the current measures and the expected measures of data at different levels from reaction, learning, action, and business impact to payoff. We label these gaps as needs because they all need to be analyzed and improved.

FIGURE 3.1 The Alignment Model

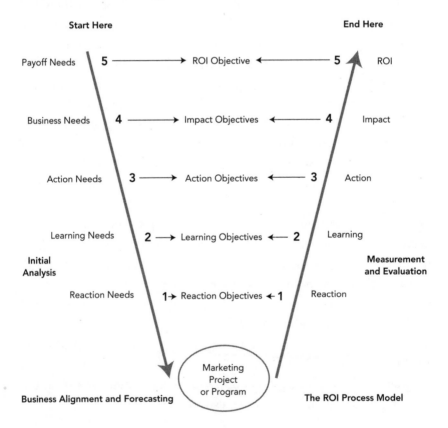

In this chapter and the next, we explore the left side of the model, beginning with payoff needs and progressing to reaction needs. In Chapter 5, we will focus on the middle of the model and explore the multilevel objectives derived directly from these needs. The right side of the model deals with evaluation of the marketing program and measurement of success corresponding to needs and objectives at different levels, which will be presented in Chapters 6 to 10.

Key Questions to Ask

In the next sections, we will analyze an organization's payoff needs and business needs for alignment purposes. Consider several key questions to ask (see Box 3.1) before, during, and after conducting the analyses. These questions should be asked up front because they are critical to make the case for proceeding with or without the analyses. They remind us of the important factors influencing business alignment during the analyses and help us review all aspects of the process after the analyses are completed to avoid ignoring any of them. Answers to the questions may even indicate there is no need for the marketing program. Understanding the implications of moving forward (or not) enables us to examine and reveal the legitimacy of our marketing programs, which helps when enlisting support from stakeholders.

Box 3.1 Key Questions to Ask About the Proposed Program

- Why is this an issue?
- What happens if we do nothing?
- Is this issue critical?
- Is this issue linked to strategy?
- Is this issue linked to goals?
- Is it possible to correct it?
- Is it feasible to improve it?

(continued on next page)

- How much is it costing us?
- Can we find a solution?
- Are there multiple solutions?
- Who will support the program?
- Who will not support the program?
- How much will the solution(s) cost?
- Is the program consistent with our mission?
- Is the program consistent with the strategy?
- Does the program help achieve the goals?
- How can we fund the program?
- Are some important intangible benefits involved?
- Is there a potential payoff (positive ROI)?
- Do we need to forecast outcomes, including ROI?

Payoff Needs

In this model, payoff needs represent gaps or opportunities for marketing to contribute to the organization by increasing revenue, improving profits, or doing other greater good such as building brand equity, while at the same time adding value to customers, clients, partners, and society in a cost-efficient way. Determining the potential payoff is closely related to the next step in the alignment analysis, determining the business need, since the potential payoff is often based on one or more business needs.

Marketing generally occurs on two dimensions within an organization, namely, strategic marketing and tactical marketing. Along the first dimension, marketing serves as a core driver of the firm's business strategy and represents a long-term, organizational-level commitment to enhance performance. In contrast, tactical marketing occurs primarily at the departmental or operational level, and focuses on product, price, place, and promotion functions of marketing to engage and serve customers. Although tactical marketing always needs to be consistent with and supportive of strategic marketing and both are naturally connected within a firm, it is meaningful to distinguish the tactical and strategic payoff needs of the firm for better alignment.

Tactical Payoff Needs

As suggested in the previous paragraph, tactical payoff needs are relatively obvious and related to the basic functions of marketing at an operational level. We estimate two factors in order to determine the payoff: the potential monetary benefit of improving an impact measure and the approximate cost of the marketing program. The monetary benefit may come from improved sales revenue, increased market share, new products introduced, new markets developed, improved salesperson productivity, enhanced customer satisfaction, or increased employee loyalty. These benefits can be translated into improved profit and added to the organization's bottom line. For nonprofit organizations, the "profit" may come in the forms of increased donations, memberships, grants, sponsorships, generated tuitions, etc., which financially benefit the organization.

In addition, the benefit may come from reduced or avoided costs. If, for example, a marketing program reduces customer complaints, shortens new product development time, or reduces product delivery errors, it will save costs related to remedies. Similarly, a public relations campaign may benefit the organization by avoiding damaging, negative word-of-mouth effects. Furthermore, internal marketing programs may reduce costs by lowering employee turnover or reducing unethical behaviors. These benefits can be calculated as monetary value using methods we will discuss in subsequent chapters.

We can then assess the payoff value of a marketing program by comparing the monetary benefits and costs of the program. Consider a marketing program designed to improve the profit of a new product. Based on appropriate analyses, the annualized profit improvement is $900,000. If the marketing program costs $400,000, then the ROI of the marketing program is

$$ROI\ (\%) = \frac{\$900{,}000 - \$400{,}000}{\$400{,}000} \times 100 = 125\%$$

This suggests that for every $1 invested in this marketing program, $1 is recovered plus another $1.25 is returned. In this particular case, the firm's tactical payoff need is to ensure the marketing program generates a positive return in a cost-effective way. This is an obvious payoff need, and there are many obvious needs that are usually problems worth solving, as shown below:

Obvious Payoff Opportunities

- Sales are flat, while competitors are increasing.
- The time to process a customer order has increased 30 percent in two years.
- Customer complaints are the highest in the industry.
- Website downtime is double last year's performance.
- Excessive turnover of sales talent: 35 percent above benchmark data.
- Very low market share in a market with few players.
- Inadequate customer service: 3.89 on a 10-point customer satisfaction scale.
- This year's out-of-compliance fines total $1.2 million, up 82 percent from last year.
- Excessive product returns: 30 percent higher than previous year.
- Excessive absenteeism in call centers: 12.3 percent versus 5.4 percent for industry.
- Net Promoter Scores are declining.
- Same-store sales are declining.

Strategic Payoff Needs

However, not all payoff needs are as obvious. For many marketing programs, marketing managers and professionals need to consider both the tactical and strategic payoff needs of their firms in order to properly align marketing programs with business.

As discussed in previous sections, marketers should take a systemic perspective by putting payoff needs assessment into the organizational context. These strategic payoff needs linked to long-term strategies and goals are less obvious and less likely to estimate as ROI numbers, but are equally important as, if not more important than, the tactical payoff needs. Box 3.2 shows examples of not-so-obvious opportunities. Sometimes the strategic payoff needs may be expressed, in the ROI Methodology framework, as intangible benefits, which include brand equity, brand image, customer trust, customer loyalty, employee loyalty, etc. We discuss several important concepts related to strategic payoff needs assessment in the following sections. These concepts define what an organization is, where it wants to be, how it plans to stay there long term, and what the major elements of organizational analysis are.

Box 3.2　Not-So-Obvious Payoff Opportunities

- Improve brand awareness.
- Win a customer service award from a consumer group.
- Provide empowerment opportunities for customers.
- Establish a project management office.
- Implement mindfulness sessions with sales team members.
- Conduct healthy living sessions for the community.
- Implement recycling in all communities.
- Create a green organization.
- Provide customer service awareness for all associates.
- Become a technology leader.
- Create a great place to work.
- Implement career counseling for the marketing team.
- Build capability for future growth.
- Create an engaged workforce.
- Conduct compliance sessions with all staff.

Mission and Vision

For alignment, marketers need to connect marketing programs with the organization's overall mission and vision. It is the responsibility of an organization's founders and top management to develop core values, define its mission, and choose general directions for the whole organization.[2] They also create a mission statement to articulate the firm's fundamental and unique purposes, or reasons for existence. By doing so, they set expectations for stakeholders both inside and outside the organization and answer the questions, "What business are we in and what business should we be in?" It is the responsibility of the organization's marketing professionals to ensure all their marketing programs are properly aligned with the organization's business and connect marketing programs with the organization's overall mission and vision.

Strategies

Strategy is a comprehensive action plan stating how the organization will achieve its mission and serve its fundamental purposes.[3] Executives state their expectations and lay out a road map for the whole organization using organizational strategies. Regardless of its size, an organization faces the challenges of limited financial, human, and technological resources. Simply put, we cannot be all things to all people. Executives therefore develop strategies that guide members of the whole organization to utilize the resources effectively and efficiently to achieve its mission.

Organizational Goals

An organization often converts its mission and strategies into long- and short-term performance goals and targets. These organizational goals are statements of an accomplishment of a task to be achieved by a specific time.[4] Organizations can pursue several types of goals, which include financial goals, activity-related goals, customer-related goals, talent-related goals, and social responsibility goals. These goals are important for the sustainable growth of both businesses and nonprofit organizations.

• • •

In summary, a good understanding of organizational mission, strategy, and business goals helps address the first issue of business alignment: payoff needs. Specifically, developing a marketing program that is consistent with the mission, supporting the strategy, and fulfilling the organizational goals are perfect examples of business alignment by satisfying an organization's strategic payoff need. To satisfy tactical payoff needs, we should assess the benefits and costs of a marketing problem in its own context, because value may differ from one organization to another. The second issue of business alignment is to pinpoint one or more business measures that need to improve. In order to understand this issue, we must discuss the business needs of the alignment analysis.

Business Needs

In order to ensure that payoff needs are fulfilled, we should determine specific business needs corresponding to and supporting the payoff needs identified. In this book, we use the term "business" to refer to both for-profit and nonprofit organizations, as well as educational institutions, NGOs, and government agencies. In all types of organizations, marketers develop programs and projects in order to accomplish the organizational mission and goals, as well as generate monetary value by improving productivity, processes, and efficiency by saving time, reducing errors, and lowering costs. All these achievements can satisfy business needs.

A business need is a gap represented by a business measure. Any process, item, or perception can be measured, and this measurement is critical to this level of analysis. If the program focuses on solving a problem, something clearly established in the minds of program initiators, the measures are often obvious. If the program prevents a problem, the measures may also be obvious. If the program takes advantage of a potential opportunity, the measures are usually still there. Otherwise, how will the opportunity be described? How will the value proposition be defined? The important point is that measures are in the system, ready to be captured for this level of analysis. The challenge is to identify the measures and to find them swiftly and economically. Developing measures for the business needs will not only provide appropriate measurement schemes, but also help assess the business situation.

The mission and strategies we discussed in previous sections set the strategic direction, but how do marketers know if they are making progress achieving the goals? Tracking marketing performance with marketing analytics and big data becomes the key to answering this important question. However, an endless array of data, complex models, and complicated statistical techniques may lead to paralysis by analysis, which traps marketers in a cycle of analysis. In reality, analysis does not have to be difficult. Multiple techniques are helpful to uncover marketing performance weaknesses and ignored opportunities.

Gap Analysis

Needs essentially are gaps between desired and actual performance states (see Figure 3.2). The gap suggests a need to do something, and the magnitude of that gap signifies the seriousness of the need. The gaps also indicate possible barriers of business measures or imply factors preventing an organization from taking advantages of opportunities.[5] To conduct gap analysis, marketers should consider both the organizational factors and environmental factors. The systemic approach to analyzing gaps involves the following sequential steps:

1. Identifying and analyzing desired and actual performance states
2. Identifying the gaps between the desired and actual performance states
3. Prioritizing the gaps[6]

A useful tool to identify desired and actual performance states and identify gaps is the marketing performance FACTs model.[7] We introduce this framework in the next section.

FIGURE 3.2 Marketing performance gap

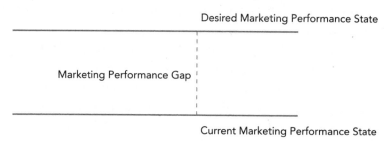

Marketing Performance FACTs Model

Traditionally, marketing professionals have been obsessed with the financial results of their marketing programs. Indeed, financial performance measures the extent to which a company's marketing function contributes to its bottom line. Outcomes such as sales revenue, profits, and market share are good indicators of financial performance and critical to organizational well-being. However, as highlighted by Kaplan and Norton, a financial measure itself is inadequate for guiding organizations through complex and competitive environments. Instead, a comprehensive framework is needed to ensure long-term success. Kaplan and Norton proposed four perspectives in their balanced scorecard framework, namely, financial perspective, customer perspective, internal-business-process perspective, and learning and growth perspective.[8] Similarly, Zoltners, Sinha, and Lorimer also defined marketing and sales organizational success on four dimensions: (1) company results, (2) customer results, (3) sales activities, and (4) salespeople.[9] The authors argue that instead of narrowly focusing on a single dimension, managers should take a balanced view by managing all four dimensions in order to maintain sustainable growth and long-term competitive advantages.

Why is a balanced view more desirable than a single-minded perspective? Imagine a company that has been trying to increase its sales revenue and market share aggressively. This year, its sales revenue grew by 20 percent over last year. You should be confident with the company's financial future, right? What if, however, you then find out that the company's customers are dissatisfied, its employees are overworked, turnover rates are high, and some salespeople have been engaging in unethical activities? Chances are this company will not have sustainable growth for too long.

Organizations behave like human bodies. Boosting short-term performance at the expense of other aspects of the body may deter overall health and long-term productivity. For example, it is well known that abusing anabolic steroids builds muscle fast and extreme dieting helps you lose weight quickly, but both will cause serious health problems. Similarly, focusing only on financial outcomes and ignoring other aspects of the marketing performance may cause disastrous results for the company in the future. Just like balanced nutritious diets and regular exercise lead to long-lasting health, balanced performance management leads to sustainable growth.

Along this line of thinking, we propose the FACTs framework for marketing performance assessment. As demonstrated in Figure 3.3, the FACTs framework consists of five components.

FIGURE 3.3   The FACTs framework

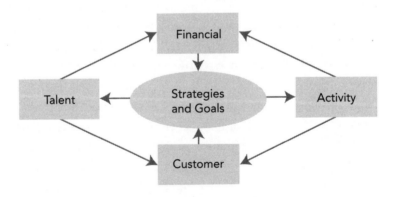

Specifically, this framework includes four critical aspects of marketing performance: financial performance, activity performance, customer performance, and talent performance. Additionally, there is a strategies and goals component, because performance becomes meaningful only when it is compared with the strategy you are implementing and the goals you are attempting to achieve. The four marketing performance dimensions reflect the outcomes of strategic implementation and goal achievement. The marketing performance FACTs specify the current state of marketing performance on four dimensions and discover desired performance from a strategic perspective, satisfying the first step of the gap analysis. Let us examine the five components below.

Financial Performance

The financial aspect of the marketing performance FACTs framework deals with the extent to which sales revenue, market share, and profitability goals are achieved. In addition, it measures the growth rate compared with that of the competition and the cost control compared with the industry average. For most marketing professionals, the financial dimension includes the most important measures of marketing success at both individual and organizational levels. From top management to individual salespeople, the financial measures are the most visible outcomes of marketing efforts and demand the most attention. This is understandable, as sales revenue and profits determine the success and even survival of many organizations.

Activity Performance

The activity aspect of marketing performance measures how an organization allocates its time and resources to ensure that the internal processes are of high quality and add value. It also measures how marketers allocate their time and resources to achieve financial and customer goals through marketing programs, campaigns, and initiatives. At the functional level, marketing engages in many activities. However, from the performance improvement perspective, not all marketing activities are qualified as performance. Marketing activity performance reflects both the marketing activity and, more importantly, the outcomes this activity generates.[10] For example, making a sales call is a marketing activity, whereas making a sales call *together with* generating valuable intelligence by revealing important customer preference changes is activity performance. Similarly, training salespeople is an activity, but training salespeople *together with* being able to enhance their selling skills is activity performance.

Customer Performance

The customer aspect of the FACTs focuses on customer relationship, customer satisfaction, and customer loyalty. It also measures customer retention, customer defection, and the numbers of existing and newly acquired customers. One unique characteristic that distinguishes marketing from other functions of the organization is the frequent interactions of marketers with their customers. In order to implement organizational and marketing strategies, marketers work hard to identify target customers and satisfy customer needs, initiate and maintain customer relationships, and bring new products to and seek feedback from customers. The outcomes of these customer-oriented sales efforts are measured as customer performance.

Talent Performance

Talent performance is related to an organization's employees, for example, marketing professionals, customer service representatives, salespeople, etc. Human resources are arguably the most valuable asset an organization possesses, because people are the ultimate drivers of organizational results and success. People are also the source of creativity and innovation. In the marketing management context, marketers are the initiators, dealmakers, and change agents of the marketing process. Marketing employees are the drivers of activity performance, customer performance, and financial performance. The talent performance of an organization is indicated by employees' job satisfaction, capabilities, organizational commitment, turnover rates, citizenship behaviors, etc. Identify the performance type for each of the examples in Exercise 3.1.

Strategies and Goals

The fifth element of the marketing performance FACTs framework is the organization's strategy and goal. As we discussed, it is in an organization's best interest to become a high-performing organization that has superior performance on all four dimensions simultaneously. However, due to the dynamic nature of marketing, it is quite common that an organization has one or even more dimensions of its marketing performance below par. In order to identify key performance gaps to focus on,

Exercise 3.1

Please identify the right performance type for each of the following:

A. Sales revenue increased by 30 percent last quarter.

_____

B. The social media marketing program answered questions related to a new product.

_____

C. Customer complaints decreased from 12 times per month to 6 times per month.

_____

D. Employee turnover of the sales team was only half of the industry average.

_____

Answers:
A. Financial performance
B. Activity performance
C. Customer performance
D. Talent performance

we need to compare the current performance level with the expected performance level implied by the strategies and goals. This effort identifies performance gaps and satisfies the second step of the gap analysis.

It is highly possible to identify multiple gaps. Considering both environmental forces and organizational strategies, marketers should be able to prioritize and focus on the performance gaps that matter the most. This is the third step of the gap analysis.

Aligning a marketing program with business involves building the marketing program to close performance gaps. We can use the marketing performance FACTs to identify such a performance gap. As discussed, we define the difference between the current performance level and the goal as a performance gap. Depending on the magnitude and importance of the performance gap, marketing managers may choose to focus on one or more key performance gaps. It is typical for an organization to set multiple goals, and one marketing program may address multiple performance gaps. Practice completing a performance FACTs analysis and a gap analysis with Exercise 3.2.

Exercise 3.2

Case Studies in Performance FACTs Analysis and Gap Analysis

Imagine that you are a marketing management consultant and you have been working with the following three clients to help them improve their marketing performance and identify opportunities to add value to the organization. Conduct a marketing performance FACTs analysis and a gap analysis for each of the three companies.

Company X is a manufacturer that recently launched a new product to consumers in a major US city. The marketing department used TV commercials to promote the product, and its ads were on four local TV channels during prime time. After three months, however, the new product achieved only 50 percent of its sales volume quota. The latest survey showed that 60 percent of the target audience saw the TV commercial, but less than 20 percent of the respondents were able to describe features and benefits of the new product. Additional studies showed that 90 percent of the customers who bought the product were satisfied with the product and were willing to repurchase.

Financial Performance: _____

Customer Performance: _____

Activity Performance: _____

Talent Performance: _____

Strategies and Goals: _____

Performance Gaps: _____

Company Y is a telecommunications provider that serves the Midwest market. Driven by a strong demand for its service, the company has been growing at a 25 percent annual rate in the past three years. Its market share reached a stunning level of 40 percent early this year. However, the company notices that the number of customer complaints has almost doubled from 15 complaints per month last year to 28 complaints per month this year, and only 60 percent of its customers are satisfied. The CMO of Company Y is a believer in excellent customer service and aims to make 100 percent of the customers happy and satisfied.

Financial Performance: _____

Customer Performance: _____

Activity Performance: _____

Talent Performance: _____

Strategies and Goals: _____

Performance Gaps: _____

Company Z is a medical equipment company that has dominated the blood pressure monitoring device market for nearly a decade. With a steady 20 percent market share and a healthy 3 percent growth rate in this relatively mature market, Company Z has earned the trust of both doctors and patients. In the past 10 years, the annual customer satisfaction index has consistently been over 95 percent. The company recruits graduates from universities and trains them to be professional sales representatives. However, in the past three years, the sales managers of

Company Z has noticed that 50 percent of the recruits leave the company in the first year after they join, either voluntarily or involuntarily. Similar companies in the same market are able to keep 80 percent of their new recruits.

Financial Performance: _____

Customer Performance: _____

Activity Performance: _____

Talent Performance: _____

Strategies and Goals: _____

Performance Gaps: _____

Answers:

For Company X, we have the following results of the FACTs framework:

Financial performance. The new product achieved only 50 percent of its sales volume quota.

Activity performance. The survey showed that 60 percent of the target audience saw the TV commercial, but less than 20 percent of the target audience were able to describe features and benefits of the new product.

Customer performance. The survey showed that 90 percent of the customers who bought the product were satisfied with the product and were willing to repurchase.

Talent performance. Not available.

Strategies and goals. To achieve the sales quota of the new product.

Performance gaps. Sales of the new product is only half of its goal.

For Company Y, we have the following results of the FACTs framework:

Financial performance. The company has been growing at a 25 percent annual growth rate in the past three years. Its market share reached a stunning level of 40 percent early this year.

Activity performance. Not available.

Customer performance. The number of customer complaints has almost doubled from 15 complaints per month last year to 28 complaints per month this year.

Talent performance. Not available.

Strategies and goals. To achieve 100 percent customer satisfaction.

Performance gaps. Only 60 percent of customers are satisfied while the goal is 100 percent.

For Company Z, we have the following results of the FACTs framework:

Financial performance. The company has a steady 20 percent market share and a healthy 3 percent growth rate in a relatively mature market.

Activity performance. Not available.

Customer performance. In the past 10 years, the annual customer satisfaction index has always been over 95 percent.

Talent performance. In the past three years, 50 percent of the recruits leave the company in the first year after they join.

Strategies and goals. To keep 80 percent of the new recruits in the first year.

Performance gaps. New employee retention rate is 50 percent, below the 80 percent goal.

The FACTs analysis paints a clear picture of the current marketing performance of an organization. It also highlights potential performance gaps. These gaps signal business needs and demand further attention. The FACTs analysis builds the foundation for subsequent steps such as examining causes, exploring solutions, and setting up objectives. We will discuss these steps in Chapters 4 and 5. When searching for the proper performance measures to connect to the marketing program and pinpoint business needs, we need to consider all the possible measures that could be influenced in the context of the marketing performance FACTs because many of the measures are interdependent.

For example, efforts to improve employee productivity may also increase customer satisfaction and profitability. Similarly, reducing product delivery time may lead to improved market share. Meanwhile, there may be an adverse impact on certain measures. For example, when employee job satisfaction decreases, service quality may suffer; or when pushing aggressive sales growth, customer satisfaction may deteriorate. Therefore, marketing program team members must prepare for unintended consequences and capture them as other data items that might be connected to, or influenced by, the program. The final decision whether to launch a new marketing program should be made by considering its overall contribution to the organization, both tactically and strategically.

Final Thoughts

"Start with Why" is the first step in the 12-step, results-based process. The "why" of programs includes both payoff needs and business needs. These needs are the strategic and tactical focuses of the business, that are critical to the organization, part of a strategy, or important to the management team. Before starting any marketing program, we must begin with a clear focus on the outcome. The outcome could be a problem to solve or an opportunity to improve. The result of the program must be specifically defined in terms of business needs and business measures so that the actual improvement in the business measures and the ROI can be clearly measured and calculated. Beginning with the end in mind also involves ensuring the marketing program aligns with the strategic payoff needs of the organization. Top executives want marketing programs to improve marketing performance measures that are critical to the long-term goals and strategies of the organization.

4

Make It Feasible: Select the Right Solution

Every problem has a solution.
You just have to be creative enough to find it.
TRAVIS KALANICK

M r. Wang and his friends really enjoyed their safari vacation in Africa. Their Phantom 3 Advanced drone made by Dji brought them shockingly close to the zebras, giraffes, hippos, elephants, and even lions. Although still preferring the taste of Jingzhou draft beer at home, they had to admit that the ice-cold Castle Lager certainly added an exotic flavor to this tour. They could not wait to bring the breathtaking pictures of Africa's wildlife back to families and friends in Handong. The fact that this vacation was financed by a bonus they had won from a recent performance improvement project contributed to the enjoyment as well. This was indeed a relaxing and well-deserved vacation.

Mr. Wang is the general manager of the Lincheng Branch of National Telecom, Inc. A project he and his colleagues conducted in 2018 more than doubled the market share of smartphones in an important market segment within six months. This project not only won an award from National Telecom but also demonstrated the value creation process of a marketing performance improvement project. It satisfied the payoff and business needs of the organization by delivering increased sales revenue, improved customer satisfaction, and intangible benefits of better brand equity and enhanced client relationships. This project showed that without significant additional resources invested, it is possible to improve marketing performance significantly with smart efforts and use of a proper methodology.

Lincheng is the fifth-largest city of Handong Province in Southeast China, which represents one of the high-potential markets of National Telecom. In 2018, Mr. Wang and his marketing team launched a marketing program to improve the branch's business performance. In order to ensure business alignment, they started the project with an organizational analysis by reviewing the corporate vision, mission, and goals. The corporate mission of connecting people with the world and the key organizational strategy to expand business scale required the Lincheng Branch to continually increase its market share and service level in the mobile phone market. After completing the organizational analysis, they conducted situation analysis and examined the environmental factors both inside and outside the organization at the world, workplace, work, and worker levels. These analyses revealed multiple marketing performance gaps, including a market share gap in the top 500 enterprises market.

With the help of consultants, Mr. Wang and his team conducted a key value chain analysis, an analytical tool developed by Sinotrac Consulting Company in Beijing. The analysis identified the relatively low "effective employee contact rate" as a measure for improvement. The effective employee contact rate measures the ratio of the number of employees effectively contacted by National Telecom's marketing team and the total number of employees in an organization. On average, the effective employee contact rate was only 20 percent, which was significantly below the 50 percent target. The key value chain analysis showed that closing this gap would help the Lincheng Branch achieve its market share goal of 20 percent. Mr. Wang and his team then conducted cause analysis using the behavioral engineering model (BEM) before considering multiple solutions to address this business measure and increase the effective employee contact rate. The cause analysis showed that the primary reasons for the low contact rate were (1) a lack of information about the organizational structure, employee characteristics, and needs, (2) a lack of resources and channels to communicate with the target employees, and (3) a lack of incentives to motivate channel partners for better coordination and cooperation. The team then designed a package of solutions, based on the causes, to close the gap.

To address the first cause, the team worked with salespeople to collect data and information regarding the organizational structure and employee characteristics. The team then developed a WeChat-based social media promotion method and trained the sales force to use it. In addition, the team worked with clients to embed National Telecom's product introduction into the clients' new employee onboarding process. Both solutions were designed to address the second cause. To address the third cause, the project team provided bonuses specifically designed for channel partners to motivate them to build good relationships with clients' gatekeepers. Implementing these solutions increased the effective employee contact rate from 20 percent to 55 percent in six months, which led to significant improvement of market share. From January to June 2018, the market share of National Telecom's mobile phone in the top 500 enterprise target segment increased from 11 percent to 25 percent, significantly exceeding the goal of 20 percent.

• • •

In the last chapter, we discussed the strategic and tactical payoff needs of an organization along with the importance of uncovering the business measures that define those needs. After discovering the "why," the next step is to design or select the proper solution or solutions to address the issues, close the gaps, and take advantage of the opportunities. In this chapter, we will focus on the steps of cause analysis and solution selection. Solution selection is a serious matter. Choosing a wrong solution will not solve the problem or improve the performance but will waste resources and perhaps tarnish the image of the marketing function. In that sense, a wrong solution is worse than no solution. Even if the senior executive requests a specific marketing program as a solution, it is the marketers' responsibility to ensure that the solution is appropriate because the marketing team will be eventually evaluated on the success or failure of the program. The design thinking principle of this step is "a mindset for curiosity and inquiry." We use two performance improvement standards to guide our analysis. Specifically, in this chapter, we conduct analysis to (1) "Determine Cause" and (2) "Design Solutions."

As marketers, we have quite a few tools available in our toolkit to make a difference. To increase sales revenue, we may develop new products, modify pricing strategies, choose additional distribution channels, or conduct digital and social media marketing promotions. Alternatively, we may target different customer segments, modify positioning statements, and choose new differentiation strategies. Further, we may train the members of our staff to improve their productivity, change their working habits, or equip them with new tools, resources, skills, and knowledge. Additionally, we can modify compensation schemes and evaluation policies to motivate salespeople. All of these may serve as solutions, but which of them should we select? Without a good understanding of the situation, the best answer we can provide is that we do not know.

Before selecting any major solutions, we need to conduct various analyses to identify opportunities, define problems, and explore root causes. No matter which solution we choose, the choice should be justified with evidence and considerations of both expected business impact and the costs of the solution. In the story of National Telecom, the organization chose to implement solutions focusing on the business needs identified by the key value chain analysis in order to close the gaps and satisfy the strategic payoff and business needs. These solutions generated positive results and added significant value to the organization.

Action Needs

With marketing performance gaps identified and business needs defined, the next step is determining what actions are needed to improve the business measures targeted by our marketing programs. By definition, a marketing program is a set of activities carefully designed and coordinated to achieve objectives at different levels. Action measures describe the extent to which customers, employees, sponsors, or others adopt new behaviors, change existing behaviors, and take desirable actions as expected by a marketing program:

- In the business-to-consumer context, action measures could refer to the extent to which consumers download a new smartphone app, try out new running shoes, or visit a retail store because of a new TV commercial.
- In the business-to-business context, action measures could refer to the extent to which an organizational buyer sends requests for proposals (RFPs) or adds the organization to its approved vendor list due to recent promotional efforts.
- In the internal marketing context, action measures could refer to the extent to which employees apply the new skills they learned and knowledge they acquired in everyday work, after attending a training session.

In all three scenarios, the action measures themselves are not business outcomes. However, without these action measures, marketers are unlikely to achieve the desired business outcomes. On the other hand, although the action measures are no guarantee of marketing program success, they certainly build a solid foundation upon which success can occur. Analyzing and understanding the action measures establishes a chain of impact to assess the effects of our marketing program on business results.

As discussed in Chapter 3, we treat action needs as gaps in the current and expected levels of activity performance of a marketing program. In the process of designing marketing programs to improve and demonstrate value, the action needs of the target audience deserve attention and scrutiny. Specifically, analyzing action needs enables us to understand what caused the business measures to miss their marks and not be where they should be.

Analytical Techniques

One approach to assessing action needs is to use one or more analytical techniques as listed in the Box 4.1. Details of these techniques can be found in many references.[1]

Box 4.1   Diagnostic Tools

- Key value chain analysis
- Statistical process control
- Brainstorming
- Problem analysis
- Cause-and-effect diagrams
- Force-field analysis
- Mind mapping
- Affinity diagrams
- Simulations
- Benchmarking
- Diagnostic instruments
- Focus groups
- Probing interviews
- Job satisfaction surveys
- Engagement surveys
- Exit interviews
- Observations
- Nominal group technique

Some of the techniques listed in the box are data-driven, and others are based on subjective assessments of managers and researchers. No technique is superior under all conditions, but some are more appropriate than others under certain conditions. Marketers may consider using multiple methods for better analysis outcomes.

Learning Needs

Action needs uncovered in the previous step always require a learning component. Customers and others must learn what to do to take action. In the business-to-consumer context, consumers do not download our new smartphone app, probably because they are not aware of this app or simply do not know where or how to download it. In the business-to-business context, the organizational buyers do not send us RFPs because they have not learned the unique benefits of the offering. Similarly, in the internal marketing context, when sales teams fail to apply a new skill taught at a training session, the reason may be they do not know how to use the skill in their work environment.

In marketing, we use learning to inform, to motivate, to teach, or to change the attitude and behavior of a target audience. The target audience, based on the contexts, could be consumers, organizational buyers, or employees and partners. In some cases, learning is supporting another solution such as a promotion campaign. In other cases, learning itself becomes the principal solution, as in learning new product knowledge, new selling skills, new technology, or a new system. Sometimes, learning can be a minor solution and often involves simply understanding the product, service, pricing, market position, or benefits. Additionally, learning can be the starting point of a major positioning campaign to build brand equity. In summary, we do not always need a learning solution, but it is safe to say all solutions in marketing have a learning component.

Reaction Needs

The final level of needs analysis of the alignment model is based on reaction, which is the starting point of an information processing process. As Steve Jobs mentioned, the marketplace is very crowded and noisy, as so many competitors are trying to get customers' attention. If our marketing program does not generate a positive reaction to get people's attention, we do not stand a chance for them to learn who we are, take action, and have them purchase our products and services. Box 4.2 shows the typical reaction needs from the perspective of the audience, who can be the consumers, customers, and participants of our marketing program. These stated needs define the parameters of a marketing program in terms of its value, necessity, and convenience. Some of the attributes such as "cool," "fascinating," and "interesting" are more related to business-to-consumer marketing programs because consumers tend to rely on subjective and emotional attributes to make decisions. Organizational buyers tend to use objective attributes such as "informative" and "compatible" with current systems. For internal marketing programs such as sales training, participants prefer programs that are "meaningful," "useful," and "easy to use."

Box 4.2   Typical Reaction Needs

Customers need this program to be:

- Relevant
- Important
- Valuable
- Useful
- Meaningful
- Easy to use
- Beneficial
- Convenient
- New
- Cool
- Fascinating
- Compatible
- Interesting
- Informative

Determining Causes

Cause analysis serves as the bridge between the gaps identified and the solutions that will eliminate the gaps. It determines why the gaps exist. Just as a doctor needs to diagnose before prescribing, marketers need to identify root causes of a gap before selecting a solution. Too often, marketers are overly confident in their own diagnostic ability and move directly to solutions after identifying gaps and opportunities. This practice may create problems because the gaps are simply symptoms, and the same symptom may be caused by multiple causes. Solutions based on wrong causes will not solve the problems but will cost resources. Without a solid understanding of causes, the choice of solution is flawed. A systemic approach is therefore needed to conduct cause analysis. We can use the following steps to conduct a cause analysis:

1. **Generate as many potential causes as possible.** Potential factors and drivers exist in the environments affecting the outcomes of our marketing programs. There are also human factors influencing execution and implementation of the programs. Generating as many potential causes as possible ensures that we examine many sides of the problem and increase the chance of finding the true, root causes.

2. **Classify the causes by determining where they originate.** The causes may be external or internal, related to strategies or tactics, or occurring during planning or implementation stages. Figure 4.1 shows a framework of the 12 Elements of Marketing Performance Causes. This framework originates from Rothwell's environment model, which categorizes the environmental forces into four levels.[2] The world, workplace, work, and worker environments influence the outcomes of marketing efforts by either sustaining or obstructing actual marketing performance.

FIGURE 4.1 The 12 Elements of Marketing Performance Causes

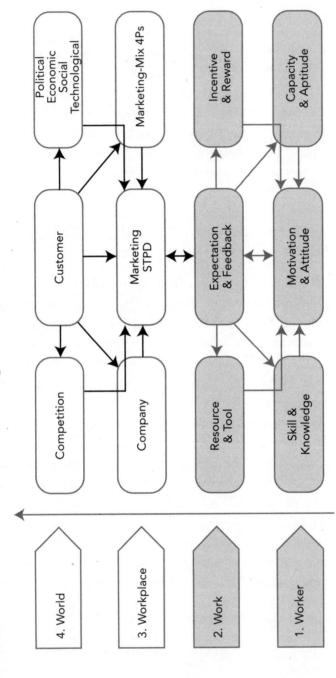

- At the world level, there are three components: factors related to customer, factors related to competition, and factors related to political, economic, social, and technological (PEST) forces. Out of the three components, the customer is the key consideration because the customer is always at the core of marketing strategies and programs. All three components are beyond the control of marketers, but they all have significant impact on marketing programs and therefore deserve attention.

- At the workplace level, the three components are factors related to marketing strategy development. The first component is company, which includes factors such as vision, mission, and goals. The second comprises factors related to marketing segmentation, targeting, positioning, and differentiation strategies (STPD), as well as the four marketing-mix elements of product, price, promotion, and place (distribution), or the 4Ps. Out of the three components, the marketing STPD strategies should be the focus. They are the marketers' responses to the factors at the world level. They must be consistent with the mission and goals of the organization and provide guidance for developing the marketing-mix strategies.

- Both the work- and worker-level factors are related to marketing strategy implementation. The six components originate from Thomas Gilbert's behavioral engineering model; these components are modified by Chevalier and Binder to be more manager-friendly.[3,4,5] The model contains six cells. The three cells at the work level: resource, expectation, and incentive, represent the system. The other three cells are at the worker level, representing individuals' skill, motivation, and capacity. We will discuss details of the BEM analysis in the next section.

3. **Prioritize the causes according to their impact.** Although the effects of the causes may differ from situation to situation, the higher the levels are, the stronger the effects they have on the

marketing programs. In general, the macro factors such as economy, competition, and government regulations have tremendous impact across the board, but they are out of the control of marketers. We need to carefully consider their effects and adjust our marketing strategies accordingly. The priority of cause analysis also differs with positions and the responsibilities of the marketers who conduct the analysis. For marketing managers and product managers, strategy planning should be considered before strategy implementation. However, if you are a manager who is in charge of marketing strategy implementation, for example, a sales director or a customer service director, you need to first consider the work-level factors such as setting proper expectations, providing appropriate resources, and offering incentives before considering individual factors such as employee knowledge, skill, motivation, and capacity.

4. **Determining and verifying root causes.** Various tools are available to determine the root causes of business and action gaps. Common tools used by performance consultants and marketers were presented earlier in Box 4.1 and include interviews, observations, surveys or questionnaires, focus groups, and analytical approaches. In addition, marketers may verify causes by discussing the concern with colleagues and stakeholders and by asking who, what, when, where, why, and how questions.

> *If you pit a good performer against a bad system,*
> *the system will win almost every time.*
> GEARY RUMMLER AND ALAN BRACHE

Causes Related to Strategic Planning

Many organizations use a strategic marketing process to allocate marketing-mix resources in order to reach target markets.[6] The planning phase of the process involves analyzing external and internal environments in order to determine the STPD strategies and the marketing-mix elements, the 4Ps. Typically, professionals who are responsible for the strategic planning phase have titles such as marketing director, marketing manager, product manager, etc. In many industries, these professionals are treated as representatives of the marketing function.

In Figure 4.1, the top two levels correspond to the strategic planning phase. The three world-level components—competition, customer, and the PEST—are external and beyond marketers' control. At the workplace level, the first component is company, which includes the organization's vision, mission, and corporate goals, and is also beyond marketers' control. In order to accomplish marketing objectives, marketers need to focus on the components under their control, the STPD and marketing-mix components, but at the same time pay attention to the components beyond their control. In other words, instead of worrying about factors beyond their control, marketers should focus on adjusting their STPD strategies and making marketing-mix decisions as responses to the changing factors beyond their control.

Causes Related to Strategic Implementation

After developing the marketing program, the next step is to implement it. The implementation phase of the process puts the plan into action and executes strategies to reach desired goals. This phase involves obtaining financial and human resources, defining tasks, and executing marketing programs. Professionals who are responsible for the implementation phase have titles such as sales director, sales manager, distribution manager, promotion manager, client manager, account manager, etc. In Figure 4.1, the bottom two levels correspond to the strategic implementation phase of the marketing program.

The six components of these two levels are from the BEM. According to the model, the six components (or factors) are significant influencers on the job performance of individuals who implement marketing programs. Researchers and managers agree that the magnitude of the influence on job performance is generally higher for factors at the work level than those on the worker level. One study conducted in the United States showed that 75 percent of job performance is influenced by the work-level factors, whereas 25 percent of job performance is influenced by those at the worker level.[7] These numbers are generally stable across industries and job positions. Table 4.1 demonstrates a cause analysis tool focusing on factors related to each of the six components of the behavioral engineering model.

TABLE 4.1   Cause analysis for marketing implementation

EXPECTATION & FEEDBACK
• Individuals' performance goals are properly set, and roles are clearly defined.
• Managers' performance expectations are clearly communicated.
• Clear and relevant information is provided to describe the work process.
• Individuals are given relevant and timely feedback about their performance.
RESOURCE & TOOL
• Financial and human resources are properly deployed to do the job.
• Individuals have the promotional materials, tools (such as computers and customer database), and time needed to do the job.
• Overall physical and psychological work environment is conducive to performance.
• Support from leaders and external experts is available to do the job.
INCENTIVE & REWARD
• Financial incentives such as compensation, reward, and bonus are properly set.
• Nonfinancial incentives such as recognition are properly set.
• Job enrichment and career development opportunities are available.
• There are negative consequences for poor job performance.
SKILL & KNOWLEDGE
• Individuals have the necessary knowledge (such as product knowledge) to do the required job activities.
• Individuals have the necessary skills to do the required job activities.
• Individuals have the ability to accomplish the required job activities.
• There are learning and training opportunities to enhance the necessary skill, knowledge, and ability to do the required job activities.

CAPACITY & APTITUDE
• Individuals have the intelligence (including emotional intelligence) to learn and do what is needed to perform the required job activities successfully. • Individuals have the traits and personalities that match the required job activities. • Individuals have the educational background and experience needed to perform the required job activities. • The capacity and aptitude of individuals match the characteristics and requirements of the job.
MOTIVATION & ATTITUDE
• Individuals have the desire and willingness to expand the effort required by the job activities (including effort, direction, intensity, and persistence). • Individuals have the appropriate role perceptions (including role accuracy, role conflicts, and role ambiguity). • Individuals are committed to the job and demonstrate organization commitment and citizenship behaviors. • Individuals have a positive attitude toward customers, managers, coworkers, and the work.

Determining Solutions

After identifying gaps and conducting cause analysis, we are now ready to develop solutions. Marketers should develop their solutions according to the causes and with a focus on closing the gaps or taking advantage of the opportunities. We recommend the following four-step approach to systematically determine solutions.

Step 1. Generate Potential Solutions

The term "solution" refers to solving a problem or exploiting an opportunity in order to improve marketing performance and help the organization achieve its strategic goals. It typically involves taking conscious and deliberate actions that facilitate a change according to the causes identified in order to address the gaps and needs revealed at different levels. Depending on the specific causes, marketers may choose solutions associated with the planning phase or implementation phase. They may modify a strategy or change a technique. They may choose a single solution to solve a problem or a package of solutions to address different aspects of the problem. Marketers need to consider the following principles when generating solutions.

Solutions Are at Different Levels

As demonstrated in Figure 4.1, marketers may choose solutions at different levels. Specifically, marketers may choose strategic solutions at the workplace level, the work level, and the worker level. If the causes identified are primarily at the world level, such as changes in competition intensity, customer preference, technological breakthroughs, or governmental regulations, then first consider solutions related to the STPD. Marketers may need to target a different customer segment or change their positioning and differentiation strategies. The STPD strategies may also be appropriate if there are changes associated with the organization. For example, if the company develops a new organizational goal after acquiring another organization, then it is possible for marketers to adopt different segmentation strategies. If, on the other hand, marketers determine that the STPD strategies are appropriate, then they may choose solutions related to the marketing-mix elements, including the 4Ps.

If the causes identified are primarily at the work and work levels, we may conclude that the issues occurred during the implementation phase. As discussed in previous sections, the factors may be related to one or more of the bottom two levels of Table 4.1. As shown in Table 4.2, there are potential solutions corresponding to each factor. This list is by no means a comprehensive one, but it is a starting point for solution development. Please note that some solutions appear more than once because they may serve multiple purposes.

Solutions Should Be Selected at the Highest Level First

As we discussed in the cause analysis section, the impact of each factor differs. Some factors are significantly more powerful than others. Those issues causing most of the problem therefore demand the most attention and perhaps even the most resources. They are also the highest priority, because if we take proper actions, they are much more likely to generate positive results with little or no additional investment. Generally, the

TABLE 4.2 Potential solutions for marketing implementation

EXPECTATION & FEEDBACK
• Goal and quota setting • Leadership program • Coaching and feedback • Sales contest
RESOURCE & TOOL
• Designing a territory • Setting up a call center • Adding new salespeople • Developing a new product brochure
INCENTIVE & REWARD
• Commission • Bonus • Recognition • Sales contest
SKILL & KNOWLEDGE
• Training • Job aid • Coaching • Recruiting and hiring
CAPACITY & APTITUDE
• Recruiting and hiring • Changing organizational structure
MOTIVATION & ATTITUDE
• Coaching • Job rotation • Job enrichment

higher the level is, the more powerful a factor is. For example, changing the STPD strategies of a firm will have much stronger effects on marketing performance than changing the 4Ps of the marketing-mix elements. Similarly, changing one or more of the factors at the work level, for example, providing resources and tools, will be easier and more likely to generate positive results than changing employees' attitude, which is at the worker level.

When a Higher-Level Solution Is Selected,
Changes Must Be Made at Lower Levels

The higher-level solutions generally refer to the strategic actions taken at the workplace level, and the lower levels are actions at the work and worker levels, as shown in Figure 4.1. For example, if marketers determine that the right solution is to target a new customer segment, then after adopting this strategy, marketers need to change the product packaging, modify price, or even choose different distribution channels. In addition, marketers need to work with sales management to set goals, provide resources and tools, and change incentives, all three at the work level. Further, marketers may need to train salespeople and equip them with new product knowledge or selling skills to serve the new segment, which occurs at the worker level. However, when a lower-level solution is selected, it is not necessary to make changes at higher levels. For example, when a sales manager decides to have a sales contest program to motivate her sales force, marketers do not have to modify their marketing strategies as long as the strategies are appropriate.

Step 2. Match Solutions to Needs

The most important and difficult part of the process is to match the solutions to the needs at different levels for different causes of the problem. This task is both art and science. We recommend the following principles for marketers to follow that will ensure alignment.

Some Solutions Are Obvious

Some causes are obvious as they point directly to a solution. If consumers prefer purchasing your product online, then making the product available online is the obvious solution. If salespeople need updated marketing brochures for their sales calls, then updating marketing brochures is an appropriate solution. Certainly, there are still design issues to attend to, and we will discuss those issues in the next several chapters, but the solutions themselves are relatively obvious in these situations. Consider the following case.

Case in Point   An inbound call center of a large manufacturer was trying to improve its marketing performance.[8] Representatives of the call center provided technical support, handled repair inquiries, and answered billing and general questions for current and prospective customers over the phone and online through live chat. However, managers were not satisfied with the representatives, and the focal gap was on customer performance. Specifically, less than 70 percent of the customers who called the center were satisfied, whereas the managerial expectation was at least 85 percent customer satisfaction. Managers conducted a top-performer benchmarking analysis and found that the actions of top performers differed from the actions of average representatives. Top representatives had much higher numbers on the following measures than the average representatives:

1. The number of times a representative mentions the customer's name during conversations
2. The number of times a representative is able to provide a target date for problem resolutions
3. The number of times a representative answers questions by following the call scripts from the training manual

Based on these results, managers quickly developed an internal marketing solution consisting of training, coaching, and incentives. The call center achieved its customer satisfaction goal within three months after the solution was implemented.

Solutions Can Come as a Package

In marketing, more than one solution typically exists for any problem. The solutions can come in different sizes and sometimes may come as a package. When you are able to solve the same problem using different solutions, you see the beauty of marketing creativity. However, this can be a challenge when you are facing a full range of possibilities and dealing with all levels of complexity with the solutions. For example, if your customers have expressed a need for better service quality, the solution could range from improving the physical shopping environment, to changing the shopping process, to providing prompt service, to training employees to be more responsive or show more empathy. Some programs are more expensive than others, and their effectiveness varies.

Additionally, we need to note that when we choose a high-level strategic solution, changes may be needed downstream. For example, if we decide to target a different customer segment, we need to make appropriate changes to the positioning statements, product package, pricing policy, distribution channels, and promotional messages accordingly. This way, the solution is an integrated package instead of a single item. It is also helpful to understand what would be considered an acceptable solution, recognizing that not addressing the issue at all—in other words, taking no action—is one solution option. No matter which solution we choose, or do not choose, the considerations should focus on benefits, costs, and, eventually, values and contributions of the different options.

Some Solutions Take a Long Time

Although some issues respond to a short-term fix, such as training salespeople to be more effective in closing a deal, others take a long time to rectify. For example, if consumers are reluctant to purchase because of the public image of the organization (bad word of mouth, recent negative events, tarnished brand reputation, etc.), it could take a long time to repair the situation. The solution to rebuild brand equity would have to start at the top of the organization and go throughout the entire organizational process. Another example could be that an organization recognizes a new growth opportunity and decides to reposition its brand. The repositioning solution could take months, if not years, to take effect and change the perceived brand image in consumers' mind.

Step 3. Select Solutions for Maximum Payoff

After matching solutions to needs, the next step is to make sure that we select solutions with maximum payoff. Specifically, we need to consider two major issues that can affect that payoff: the cost of the solution and the monetary benefit from the implementation. As discussed in previous chapters, we define value as the ratio of benefit and cost. To achieve maximum payoff, we need to consider both benefits and costs. From the cost perspective, the smaller the cost, the greater the potential value and payoff. From the benefit perspective, the greater the benefit, the greater the potential payoff.

Step 4. Verify the Match and Ensure the Success of the Solution

After identifying possible solutions, marketers must verify that a match exists between the need and the solution. It is often helpful to review the needs identified at different levels and return to the source of input (focus groups, employees, etc.) to affirm that the solution meets the need. Marketers may want to review the strategic payoffs and business needs to ensure the solutions are aligned with them. During the process of initial implementation of the solution, obtain feedback to see whether the solution is indeed a fit as expected. Early feedback can prompt adjustments that need to be made or, in worst-case scenarios, suggest abandonment of the solution altogether. Taking corrective measures, if the solution is not working toward the early objective, can avoid a big surprise at the end of the implementation process. In addition, marketers may analyze the feasibility and workability of the solution by examining resources available and employees' skills. Both employee involvement and managerial support are important to ensure the success of the solutions.

Final Thoughts

This chapter focused on the second step of the 12-step ROI in marketing process, "Make It Feasible: Select the Right Solution." The overall objective of making it feasible is to ensure we have the right solution based on analyses to address the payoff and business needs identified in the previous chapter. By examining needs at the action level, marketers can conduct cause analysis to determine the right solutions to close gaps and take advantage of the opportunities. Alignment is needed at all levels during the process. We provide tools and processes for marketers to understand the problem or opportunity, making sure the solution is feasible, workable, and appropriate. It is critical to avoid mismatch, because a wrong solution wastes resources, creates resentment, and misses opportunities to add value. Marketers need to pay serious attention to employee and manager involvement, adoption, and support of their programs to ensure success of the solution. Marketers must be on the right path to deliver value. This path includes clearly defined business needs and proper solutions to meet those needs.

5

Expect Success: Plan for Results

"Would you tell me, please, which way I ought to go from here?" said Alice.
"That depends a good deal on where you want to get to,"
said the Cheshire Cat.
"I don't much care where—" said Alice.
"Then it doesn't much matter which way you go," said the Cheshire Cat.
LEWIS CARROLL IN *ALICE'S ADVENTURES IN WONDERLAND*

Green Food Networks (GFN) is a manufacturer of consumer packaged goods.[1] The company's product lines include meal products, grain snacks, breakfast cereals, and baking products. One popular item offered by the company through retailing chains nationwide is Green Delights Desserts, a microwavable cake mix contained in a plastic cup. This delicious, warm, indulgent dessert can be ready in minutes using the microwave, without time-consuming preparation and cleanup. The Green Delights Dessert comes in different flavors such as hot fudge brownie, molten chocolate cake, caramel cake, peanut butter fudge brownie, fudgy chocolate chip cookie, cinnamon swirl cake, and lemon swirl cake. After picking up the product from a store or ordering it online and having it delivered, consumers can simply add water, stir, and microwave it and then enjoy their warm and delicious treat in minutes. The delicate balance of taste and convenience makes Green Delights Desserts especially popular among young professionals, college students, and families with little kids.

Abby is the product manager of Green Delights Desserts, and she never stops thinking how to improve the marketing performance of her great product. One area she pays particular attention to is the alignment of her positioning and promotional strategies with the company's mission and long-term goals. As implied in its name, Green Food Networks cares about the environment and emphasizes the importance of reducing its environmental impact through green technologies. One initiative among GFN's efforts to be a good corporate citizen is to trim solid waste generation continuously. As shown in GFN's "Five Year Social Responsibility Report," which was recently made available, the company has been making progress. In five years, GFN has reduced its solid waste generation rate by 24.5 percent, just half a percent shy of the 25 percent goal.

This report inspires Abby to consider her own product, the Green Delights Dessert. Working with GFN's package engineers, she realizes that the bowls used by the product are made entirely of polypropylene, which is sourced from petroleum. An alternative way is to create new bowls using calcium carbonate, a material that occurs naturally in the form of chalk or limestone.[2] The material has been widely used in many industries including pharmaceutical, agriculture, and construction, but it will be the first application in retail food packaging if Abby gives a green light. The factors considered for this decision include the costs and benefits. On the benefit side, the new packaging material, calcium carbonate, is safe, is in abundant supply throughout the world, and does not influence the recyclability of the finished bowl. If adding the right amount, the new bowls look almost the same, although the finish will be slightly less glossy. Abby and her team are also pleased to discover that the new bowls are just as sturdy as the earlier bowls and even perform slightly better in the microwave. On the cost side, the calcium carbonate is 50 percent more expensive than polypropylene as a food package, if Abby can find the right supplier to develop the new packaging.

However, packaging, as part of the product strategy, is just half the story. Abby expects that if the target consumers of Green Delights Dessert know how environmentally friendly the new package is, they will respond positively to the new initiative, which may potentially boost sales and profit. At the same time, informing and educating consumers will take time and resources. Abby works with her team to design a promotional program that will use social media to accomplish these purposes. In order to ensure success, Abby and her team develop an action plan and set objectives using the multilevel framework we discussed in previous chapters.

- At Level 0, Input, the marketing team chooses two cities in the Midwest as test marketing sites. The cities have demographic characteristics and economic conditions that make them representative of the national market. Abby and her team also carefully design the promotional aspects of the marketing program and set proper objectives for the reach (number of customers reached) and frequency (number of times an average consumer is exposed to the message) of the campaign.
- They set the objective at Level 1, Reaction, that at least 90 percent of consumers in the test markets exposed to the packaging message will feel it to be interesting, favorable, relevant, and important.
- At Level 2, Learning, the team sets an objective to ensure at least 50 percent of consumers will be able to describe the benefits of the new packaging materials one month after the new promotion program is launched.
- The Level 3, Action, objectives involve the consumers' behaviors. The team expects that 30 percent of consumers who learn about the benefits of the new packaging will try the free samples and coupons available online and in the stores.
- The team tentatively sets the Level 4, Impact, objective to be a 50 percent increase in the sales revenue of Green Delights Desserts with the new packaging within three months.

- The team also sets a Level 5, ROI, objective of a 25 percent minimum return on the initiative.

Three months later, the test marketing generates amazing results. The sales of the newly packaged Green Delights Desserts have more than doubled. Survey and observational data show that most of the objectives set at the lower levels have also been achieved. After isolating the effect of the initiative, the ROI of the marketing program is estimated to be 350%. Today, all flavors of the Green Delights Desserts are equipped with the new bowls made of calcium carbonate, reducing plastic use by 15,000 pounds per year. In addition to increased sales revenue and profitability, the marketing program creates tremendous intangible benefits for Green Food Network as more consumers see GFN as a socially responsible company that cares about the environment.

• • •

The best way to predict the future is to create it.
PETER DRUCKER

The previous chapters introduced two steps: the first, to ensure that our marketing programs are aligned with the business measures, and the second, to ensure that we have selected the right solution to achieve the desired results. In this chapter, we directly address designing for the results we need at the business impact and even ROI levels. Many organizations implement marketing programs without clearly defining the expectations at the appropriate levels of success. They may have vague ideas about what they would like to accomplish. However, without clearly defined objectives at different levels, marketers may not know what exactly they must do to ensure the success of their marketing programs. Without knowing what to do, it is difficult for marketers to understand their roles in implementing a marketing program and the reasons for doing so. Setting clear expectations up front takes the mystery out of what is expected.

Case Studies

To illustrate how objectives can help to drive success, here are two variations to drive sales with a new product.

A B2B Marketing Case: Blake Engineering (Part A)

Blake Engineering Company (BEC) is a global corporation that develops, manufactures, and markets products for professional customers in the construction and building maintenance industries.[3] The company relies on its sales force to sell products to business customers. After the marketing department chooses the customer segments to target, decides on pricing, and designs promotional messages, the BEC sales force implements the marketing strategies in the field. The BEC salespeople work independently in their own assigned territories, carry multiple products, and are responsible for all new product launches. This business model has proved effective in generating sales revenue as salespeople demonstrate the features and benefits of BEC's products, answer customers' questions, handle product delivery, and collect payments. The sales force's effort is especially critical during new product launches because customers are typically hesitant to purchase a new product due to uncertainty and the perceived risks associated with adopting an innovative product.

Recently, BEC added another new product to its portfolio, which is a new-to-the market demolition tool with superior features that will potentially benefit builders and contractors. To ensure the success of this new product, the marketing team at BEC begins a marketing program to launch the product to target customers through the company's sales force. As part of the process, BEC's marketing managers demonstrate the new product to the sales force during internal meetings prior to launch. Marketing managers also present the new product's technical features to the sales force, along with marketing strategies and supporting resources, in a series of prelaunch sales meetings, both online and offline. Additionally, the company makes new product knowledge available online for the salespeople to engage in self-learning. BEC does not provide product-specific bonuses that are directly linked to the sale of the new product. Instead, the company adds the new product to the regular portfolio of all products for the sales force. The BEC compensation plan for its sales force includes volume quotas for sales of all products collectively and incentives for exceeding quota. Based on territory potential and historical sales data, the company assigned each salesperson a unit volume goal (i.e., quota) for this new product. Although there is no direct incentive, salespeople are aware that BEC will publicize the sales performance ranking of this new product regularly through internal communications in sales meetings. The BEC marketing managers set the objectives for five levels, which are shown in Box 5.1.

Box 5.1 Objectives of BEC's New Product Marketing Program

Level 1: Reaction Objectives

After the initial sales call, BEC's target customers will:

1. Perceive the new product to be relevant to their work.
2. Perceive the new product to be important to their business.
3. Perceive the new product to be value added in terms of time and funds invested.
4. Rate the salespeople as effective.

   A rating of 4 out of 5 on a 5-point scale is desired.

Level 2: Learning Objectives

Within one month of the new product launch, the target customers contacted by the BEC sales force should acquire knowledge related to the new product. Target customers should be able to:

1. Name five of the seven features of the new product.
2. Describe at least three advantages of the new product compared with the competition.
3. Explain two benefits of the new product to their work.
4. List three of four benefits of the new product to their organizations.

Level 3: Action Objectives

Within three months of the new product launch, the target customers will:

1. Schedule a product demonstration.
2. Organize a buying center with participants from different functions to finalize the purchase.
3. Begin negotiating delivery schedules and payment terms with the BEC sales force.
4. Recommend this new product to other customers outside of their own organization.

Level 4: Impact Objectives

Within six months of the new product launch, BEC should realize improvements in at least three specific measures in the following areas:

1. At least 20 percent of target customers will purchase the product.
2. Sales growth of the new product will reach $2,100,000.
3. Ten percent of referred customers will purchase.
4. Customer satisfaction with the new product is 4.1 out of 5 on a 5-point scale.

Level 5: ROI Objective

The ROI value should be at least 25 percent.

Six months after the new product's marketing program was implemented, most BEC salespeople accomplished their sales volume quota, and the project generated a positive ROI of 185%. This case highlights the importance of setting expectations for success early. The salespeople knew that success was necessary and possible at the reaction, learning, action, and impact levels. Marketers set objectives to push the marketing program through the different levels to the ROI level. They then designed and built tools into the different levels to facilitate inducing the desired actions among customers and documented the impact. This process ensures that both the marketing managers and sales professionals expect success. The multilevel objectives take away the mystery about what this marketing program should achieve.

• • •

However, not all marketing programs succeed in the first attempt. Sometimes, when we fail to accomplish the objectives at one or more levels, adjustments are necessary and important. The following case highlights such a scenario and demonstrates how to set objectives for an internal marketing program.

An Internal Marketing Case:
Blake Engineering (Part B)

Three months after the new product launch, the BEC marketing managers collected data to monitor the progress of the sales force. The results were not as rosy as they expected. At the reaction level, it turned out that less than 20 percent of the target customers had a favorable reaction toward the new product. In fact, 70 percent of the customers had never heard of this new product. Additionally, less than half of the 20 percent of customers who had favorable reactions acquired sufficient product knowledge, and less than 5 percent of the target customers in total had taken actions to purchase the new product. Considering the dismal prospect of the new product, the BEC marketing managers and sales executives conducted investigations jointly to identify the causes of these poor performance measures.

The analysis showed that the main reason was due to the BEC salespeople not spending enough time and attention on selling the new product. Further analysis showed that many salespeople did not have enough confidence in selling the new product because they lacked sufficient new product knowledge and selling skills to sell the new-to-the-market demolition tool.

To address these issues, the BEC marketing managers, together with BEC's human resource department, designed a training course to specifically improve salespeople's product knowledge and selling skills. This internal marketing program was intended for the entire sales force of over 1,000 salespeople nationwide, but the top executive team suggested that the marketing managers first show the business value of the program before implementing it across the entire organization. The marketing managers agreed and worked with training professionals to make sure that the training program was aligned with the business needs, in this case, the sales of the new product. The team developed objectives at five levels and created data collection tools and ensured the tools were built into the training program. BEC selected 25 salespeople as the initial participant group and made efforts to ensure that this group was representative of the entire sales force by considering factors such as performance rating, tenure, job roles, etc. The five-level objectives of this internal marketing program, including ROI, are shown in Box 5.2.

Box 5.2 Objectives of BEC Internal Marketing Program

Level 1: Reaction Objectives
After completing this training program, the participants will:

1. Perceive the training program to be relevant to the job of the sales representative.
2. Perceive the training program to be important to the performance of the sales representative.
3. Perceive the training program to be a good use of time.

(continued on next page)

4. Rate the training program as effective.

5. Recommend this training program to other sales representatives of BEC.

Level 2: Learning Objectives

After completing this training program, the participants should be able to:

1. Identify customers who are most likely to purchase the new product.
2. Uncover customers' unique needs related to the new product.
3. Communicate the new product's benefit effectively.
4. Present the new product's value professionally.
5. Handle customers' objections effectively.
6. Gain commitment from customers.
7. Acquire resources to support the new product's success.

A rating of 4 out of 5 on a 5-point scale is desired.

Level 3: Action Objectives

One month after completing this training program, the sales representatives should:

1. Complete an action plan focused on selling the new product.
2. Adjust the plan as needed after receiving feedback from customers and managers.
3. Identify customers who are most likely to purchase the new product.
4. Uncover customers' unique needs related to the new product.
5. Communicate the new product's benefit effectively.
6. Present the new product's value professionally.
7. Handle customers' objections effectively.

8. Gain commitment from customers.

9. Acquire resources to support the new product's success.

A rating of 4 out of 5 on a 5-point scale is desired.

Level 4: Impact Objectives

Within three months after completing the training program, sales representatives should:

1. Sell the new product to two clients.

2. Contribute $15,000 in sales growth of the new product.

3. Achieve desired customer satisfaction with the new product sold.

Level 5: ROI Objective

The ROI value of this internal sales training program should be at least 25 percent.

• • •

These two cases reinforce the importance of setting expectations for success early. For both cases, the objectives were set to push the marketing programs through the different levels all the way to the business impact and financial ROI levels. There is no guarantee that a marketing program will succeed in its first attempt. The good news is that marketing programs can be adjusted and modified to drive success when data at the lower levels are available. Or as shown in Part B of the BEC case, marketers may choose to add internal marketing programs in order to drive the success of their business-to-business programs. The marketers expected success, and the sales executives expected success as well, and the participants were willing to deliver success. There was no mystery about the desired result of these marketing programs.

Defining the Success of Marketing Programs

It is helpful to review the critical exercise we worked on in Chapter 1 that involved measuring the value of marketing programs. Table 5.1 provides a list of statements similar to those in the exercise presented in Table 1.1. If you have already competed the exercise in Chapter 1, you will understand that these statements correspond to the different levels of the chain of impact of a marketing program. The typical conclusion from this exercise is that the marketing team needs to define the success of its marketing programs carefully, comprehensively, and consistently.

FIGURE 5.1 Levels for possible definition of success

THE POSSIBLE MEASURES	
VALUE DESCRIPTION OF MARKETING PROGRAM	LEVEL
"Reach the largest number of customers with the least amount of cost."	0 Input
"Customers are engaged, enjoy the marketing programs, and see our offerings as interesting and relevant."	1 Reaction
"Customers are learning the features, advantages, and benefits of our offerings to make purchase decisions."	2 Learning
"Because of the marketing program, customers take desirable action, try the product samples, and make steps toward purchase."	3 Action
"Customer purchases are driving important business measures and having a positive impact on the profitability and growth."	4 Impact
"The organization has a positive return on the investment of marketing efforts, time, and the resources used."	5 ROI

The new and balanced definition of marketing program success should be comprehensive. Instead of narrowly defining success as either the lower levels or higher levels, the new definition covers both. The lower levels consider the target customers, viewing them not as a commodity, but as individuals who can react to, learn about, and take actions based on the marketing programs. The higher levels consider the business impact and financial outcomes of the marketing programs, which are highly relevant to business needs, organizational goals, and executive expectations. By focusing on both, marketers are able to measure and demonstrate the chain of evidence through which marketing programs achieve financial goals by influencing target customers. This new definition covers both the input and output of the marketing programs, considers both the activities and outcomes, and reflects both tactical and strategic aspects of marketing. Using this new definition, marketers are able to demonstrate the value they create with the marketing programs so that executives and stakeholders will recognize marketing as an investment, not a cost.

Sneak Preview: Designing for Success at Each Level

The new definition of marketing program success implies that marketers should design their marketing programs based on the levels presented in Table 5.1. Defining success on all levels demonstrates the chain of impact that must occur as customers react, learn, act, and have a business impact. It starts with Level 0, Input, and reaches Level 4, Impact, and even Level 5, ROI. Table 5.2 lists important issues for marketers to consider when they design each level for results, summarizing the topics around which designing for marketing success should occur. We explore these issues in more detail in the next two chapters.

A wise man will make more opportunities than he finds.
FRANCIS BACON

TABLE 5.2 Designing for results

LEVEL	DESIGN ISSUES
0 Input	Who, what, where, when, how, how long, how much it costs
1 Reaction	Awareness, interests, attention, important, necessary, perceived risk, relevant, intent to learn more, intent to take action
2 Learning	Action oriented, benefits, features, pricing, advantages, attitude changing, easy to understand, motivating, confidence inspiring
3 Action	Timing, ease of taking action, frequency, usefulness, inhibitors, enablers
4 Impact	Financial, activity, customer, talent, business alignment
5 ROI	Efficiency, effectiveness

Level 0: Input

Many marketers believe that an important factor in determining the success or failure of a marketing program is to identify and focus on the right types of customers. To ensure the success of a marketing program, marketers need to involve the right people in the program at the right time with the right amount of content at the lowest costs possible to achieve the desired results. Marketing programs are likely to fail when they miss the mark with the target audience and the timing, sometimes with too much content and too much cost.

Level 1: Reaction

It is important to attract the attention of the target customers and create the desired reaction with marketing programs. The focus here is on the customers. Will they pay attention to the message of our marketing program? Will they see the content as relevant, important, necessary, easy to understand, and useful—something they intend to learn more about and to use? A good understanding of these issues will help marketers design the features, location, message, content, examples, activities, communication styles, and all the other elements that will motivate customers to process information, use the content, and make decisions.

Level 2: Learning

Much consumer behavior is learned, and learning is a critical component of consumer decision-making. The content of a marketing program is the message and it must be action oriented, relevant, easy to understand, engaging, and motivating to ensure it leads to desirable actions. The benefits, features, pricing strategy, and advantages are covered. Marketers may facilitate learning through either experience or reasoning. Business customers and participants of internal marketing programs learn primarily through reasoning. The marketing program must provide them with the confidence and determination to take proper actions. These issues drive many design activities.

Level 3: Action

Learning itself is not enough to ensure that customers will take desirable actions and internal participants (sales team) will apply what they have learned. Marketers may design their marketing program accordingly, to ease the action or increase persuasion so that customers are eager to act. Research shows that when customers find a product or service to be useful and easy to use, and when they have the capability to use the product, they are more likely to adopt it. For internal marketing programs focusing on either knowledge or skill, participants should know when they should use it, how often they should use it, and how they should identify success. Attention should be paid to limit the various inhibitors and enhance the enablers that support actions. The idea is that marketers must design their programs to induce appropriate actions in order to achieve desirable results. Stephen Wendel's book, *Designing for Behavior Change*, is an excellent reference for specific techniques and issues.[4]

Level 4: Impact

Ideally, the desired impact of a marketing program should be clearly understood from the beginning and throughout the whole implementation and evaluation process. The desired impact is actually the focus of the first step, as we introduced in Chapter 3. To achieve impact, marketers must choose the right solutions, as illustrated in Chapter 4. For all marketing programs, marketers must clearly understand business alignment and see a direct line of sight from the activities they are conducting to the impact measures. They should collect data at both lower and higher levels to understand their connections. As discussed in previous chapters, the business impact of marketing programs should be related to one or more dimensions of the FACTs framework, namely, enhancing financial, activity, customer, and talent performance. Many design issues will influence the impact requirements.

Level 5: ROI

Marketers do not need to calculate the ROI for all marketing programs. However, it is helpful to think about ROI from a design perspective, even if the ROI is not calculated. ROI has two key components, an impact component and a cost component. The impact component measures the business impact of a marketing program that can be converted to monetary benefits, whereas the cost component measures the cost of doing it. In other words, the impact component measures the effectiveness of a marketing program, and the cost component measures the efficiency. In the design phase, we focus on achieving greater impact and keeping the costs low in order to keep the ROI on track.

> *The essence of being human is*
> *that one does not seek perfection.*
> GEORGE ORWELL

Setting Marketing Program Objectives at All Levels

An important part of the third step is to set objectives at all levels. As shown in Table 5.3, objectives must be set for achieving a proper reaction from customers, ensuring customers have acquired the information they need, taking actions as expected, improving business impact measures, and receiving the expected ROI. Objectives can be powerful if we set them appropriately to provide direction, focus, and guidance. Setting objectives at all levels keeps business alignment on track during the project.

TABLE 5.3 All levels of objectives

LEVELS OF OBJECTIVES	FOCUS OF OBJECTIVES
1 Reaction	Defines the specific level of reaction to the marketing program as it is revealed and communicated to the customers, consumers, participants, and stakeholders
2 Learning	Defines the specific levels of knowledge, information, and skills needed by the marketing programs for customers, consumers, participants, and stakeholders to learn in order to make the marketing program successful
3 Action	Defines the specific measures and levels of action, application, and implementation needed to ensure success
4 Impact	Defines the specific business measures that will change or improve as a result of the marketing program's implementation
5 ROI	Defines the specific return on investment from the marketing program, comparing costs against monetary benefits from the program

Reaction Objectives

In today's environment, it is difficult to get customers' attention, as the market is becoming increasingly crowded. For any marketing program to be successful, customers must pay attention to the message and react favorably, or at least not negatively, to it before they can process the information. Reaction objectives are necessary to gain attention and maintain proper focus. For internal marketing programs, such as training, participants need to perceive the program to be relevant, timely, and important to their job. Typical reaction objectives for consumer marketing, business marketing, and internal marketing programs are presented in the boxes below.

Box 5.3 Typical Reaction Objectives for Consumer Marketing Programs

At the end of the program, consumers should rate each of the following statements at least a 4 out of 5 on a 5-point scale:

- The product highlighted in the program was relevant to me.
- The message of this program was interesting.
- The product highlighted in this program was valuable for me.
- The product highlighted in this program was important to me.
- The product highlighted in this program was desirable to me.
- The program had useful information.
- The program contained new information.
- The program represented an opportunity to make life more enjoyable.
- I will recommend the program to my family and friends.
- I want to learn more about this program.

Box 5.4 Typical Reaction Objectives for Business Marketing Programs

At the end of the program, consumers should rate each of the following statements at least a 4 out of 5 on a 5-point scale:

- The product highlighted in the program was relevant to my organization.

- The message of this program was informative.
- The product highlighted in this program was valuable for my organization.
- The product highlighted in this program was important to my organization.
- The program will make my organization more effective.
- The program had useful information.
- The program contained new information.
- The program will make my organization more productive.
- I will recommend the program to my colleagues.
- I want to learn more about this program.

Box 5.5   Typical Reaction Objectives for Internal Marketing Programs

At the end of the program, participants should rate each of the following statements at least a 4 out of 5 on a 5-point scale:

- The program was organized.
- The facilitators were effective.
- The program was valuable for my work.
- The program was important to my success.
- The program was motivational for me.
- The program had practical information.
- The program contained new information.
- The program represented an excellent use of my time.
- I will recommend the program to my colleagues.
- I want to know more about this program.

Learning Objectives

Every marketing program will involve some type of learning. In the consumer and business marketing cases, that includes awareness of a new product or service, improved features and benefits of a product, and updated information about a brand. It's the marketing message. In the internal marketing cases, that includes major skill-building solutions, new product knowledge, and new technology implementations. In all these situations, the learning component is significant and enables customers and participants to take proper actions. Learning objectives are important, because they deliver relevant information, target the customers who will make the decisions, communicate expected outcomes from the learning, and define the desired competence for participants of the internal marketing programs. We highlight typical learning objectives for consumer marketing, business marketing, and internal marketing programs in the boxes below.

Box 5.6 Typical Learning Objectives of Consumer Marketing Programs

One month after the consumer marketing program:

- Ninety percent of the consumers surveyed recall the marketing program from memory.
- Seventy percent of the consumers surveyed recall the product name from memory.
- Fifty percent of the consumers surveyed can describe at least one attribute of the new product.
- Forty percent of the consumers surveyed are able to describe at least one benefit of the new product.
- Thirty-five percent of the consumers surveyed are aware of at least one information source of the new product.
- Thirty percent of the consumers surveyed are aware of at least one purchase option of the new product.
- Twenty-five percent of the consumers surveyed have a more positive attitude toward the brand.
- Twenty percent of the consumers surveyed are more satisfied with the brand.
- Ten percent of the consumers interviewed are able to use the new product.

Box 5.7 Typical Learning Objectives of Business Marketing Programs

One month after the business marketing program:

- The buyer's purchasing managers are able to describe three features of the new equipment highlighted in the marketing program.
- The buyer's purchasing managers are able to describe at least one benefit of the new equipment highlighted in the marketing program.
- The buyer's purchasing managers are able to describe the manufacturing capacity of our company.
- The buyer's purchasing managers are able to describe the quality control procedure of our company.
- The buyer's purchasing managers are able to describe the terms drafted in the contract.
- The buyer's engineers are able to describe the specifications of the new equipment highlighted in the marketing program.
- The buyer's engineers are able to describe at least three quality criteria of the new equipment highlighted in the marketing program.
- The buyer's finance managers are able to describe the payment options for the new equipment highlighted in the marketing program.
- The buyer's finance managers are able to describe the delivery schedule for the new equipment highlighted in the marketing program.
- The buyer's training department is able to describe the training manual for the new equipment highlighted in the marketing program.

> ## Box 5.8   Typical Learning Objectives of Internal Marketing Programs
>
> After completing the internal marketing program, participants will be able to:
>
> - Name the six pillars of the division's new marketing strategy in three minutes.
> - Successfully complete the sales management simulation in 15 minutes.
> - Identify the six features of the new product policy.
> - Demonstrate the use of each new software routine in the standard time.
> - Use problem-solving skills, given a specific customer inquiry.
> - Determine whether a customer is eligible for the delivery schedule.
> - Score 75 or better in 10 minutes on a quiz about the new product.
> - Demonstrate all five customer-interaction skills with a success rating of 4 out of 5.
> - Explain the five categories for the value of diversity in a work group in five minutes.
> - Document suggestions for a sales contest program.
> - Score at least 9 out of 10 on a customer service policy quiz.
> - Identify five new technology trends explained at the sales conference.

Action Objectives

All marketing programs should have action objectives. Action objectives emphasize behaviors, tasks, activities, or applications. Marketers need to define the actions expected from their programs. In both consumer and business marketing programs, the objectives should be the actions directly related to or important antecedents of purchases. They should also involve specific milestones of customer decision-making, reflecting the actions desired from the marketing programs.

In internal marketing programs, the actions taken by participants are also known as applications since the desirable outcomes of internal marketing programs are that participants apply what they have learned from the program to their daily work. These action objectives are critical, because they describe the expected outcomes in the intermediate area between learning what is necessary and the actual impact that will be achieved. The box below shows typical action objectives for internal marketing programs and the key questions to ask at this level.

Box 5.9 Typical Action Objectives of Consumer Marketing Programs

Typical action objectives when consumer marketing programs are implemented include:

- At least 30 percent of the target consumers will actively seek new product information on the company website within 30 days.
- At least 20 percent of the target consumers will actively seek new product information through phone inquiry within 30 days.
- At least 10 percent of the target consumers will actively seek information about our new return policy through interacting with store salespeople within 30 days.
- At least 2,000 target consumers will download the free app designed for this new service package within 30 days.
- At least 1,000 target consumers will use the free samples of the new product within 30 days.
- At least 10 percent of the target consumers will post messages about our brand name on social media apps within 30 days.
- At least 15 percent of the target consumers will react to our posts on social media apps with emotional responses (emojis) within 30 days.

(continued on next page)

- At least 5 percent of the target consumers will send us private messages about our product on social media apps such as Facebook, Instagram, Twitter, etc., within 30 days.
- At least 1,500 target consumers will sign up for our weekly promotional newsletter this month.
- At least 5 percent of the target consumers will respond to our promotional emails this month.

Box 5.10   Typical Action Objectives of Business Marketing Programs

Typical action objectives when business marketing programs are implemented include:

- Within 90 days, 15 percent of target customers will add our company to their vendor lists.
- Within one month, 20 percent of the purchasing agents from target customers will actively seek new product information through phone inquiry.
- Within two months, 10 percent of target customers and clients will invite our salespeople to make an on-site presentation about our new product.
- Within one month, 20 percent of the purchasing agents from target customers will actively seek the return policy of our product from our salespeople.
- At least 15 target customers will start pilot programs on our new system within six months.
- At least 10 target customers will start a free trial of our new software within three months.
- At least 20 percent of target customers will respond to our promotional emails this month.

- Within three months, 10 percent of the purchasing managers of target customers will submit purchasing proposals for executive approval.
- Within three months, 20 percent of the purchasing managers of target customers will add our new product to their database.
- By November, at least 100 clients will seek information on the implementation procedure or financing options of our new product.

Box 5.11   Typical Action Objectives of Internal Marketing Programs

Typical action objectives when internal marketing programs are implemented include the following:

- The average 360-degree leadership assessment score for sales managers will improve from 3.4 to 4.1 on a 5-point scale in 90 days.
- At least 95 percent of high-potential sales employees will complete individual development plans within two years.
- At least 99.1 percent of CRM users will be following the correct sequences after three weeks of use.
- Within one year, 10 percent of employees in the shipping department will submit documented suggestions for reducing sales costs.
- Employees will routinely use problem-solving skills when faced with a product quality problem.
- Employees will take steps to engage team members each day.
- Compliance discrepancies will cease within three months after the zero-tolerance policy is implemented.

(continued on next page)

- In the next six months, 80 percent of the sales team will use one or more of the features of the sales incentive plan.
- Within 60 days, 50 percent of the conference attendees will follow up with at least one contact from the conference.
- By November, the pharmaceutical sales reps will communicate adverse effects of a specific prescription drug to all physicians in their territories.
- Managers will initiate three workout projects within 15 days.
- Sales and customer service representatives will use all five interaction skills they learned with at least half the customers within the next month.

Typical questions for action objectives that should be asked at this level include:

- What new or improved knowledge will be applied to the job?
- What is the frequency of skill application?
- What specific new task(s) will be performed?
- What new steps will be implemented?
- What new procedures will be implemented or changed?
- What new guidelines will be implemented?
- Which meetings need to be held?
- Which tasks, steps, or procedures will be discontinued?

Impact Objectives

All marketing programs should have impact objectives. These objectives can be expressed in terms of the key business measures that should be improved as the action objectives are achieved. The impact objectives define the marketing performance at individual, departmental, and organizational levels that should be connected to the marketing programs. They place emphasis on achieving bottom-line results and ensure business alignment throughout the marketing programs. Marketing impact objectives should contain data that are easy to understand and easily collectible. They should be based on results, be clearly worded, and specify what the organization and stakeholders want to accomplish as a result of the marketing program. They should also be relevant and well known to the target audience of the marketing program. For all marketing programs, the impact objectives should reflect the four types of marketing performance, namely, financial performance, customer performance, activity performance, and talent performance, as suggested in the FACTs framework. We show examples of impact objectives for marketing programs in the box below.

Box 5.12   Typical Impact Objectives of Marketing Programs

After program completion, the following conditions should be met:

- The market share of the brand should rise by one point during the next calendar year.
- After nine months, the average number of customer complaints should be reduced from three per month to no more than two per month in the Midwest sales region.
- Turnover of key account salespeople should be reduced to 10 percent in nine months.
- The average number of new accounts should increase from 300 to 350 per month in six months.
- Job satisfaction of call center associates should increase by 20 percent within the next calendar year.
- The profit quota should be achieved in the third quarter of this year.
- Employee complaints should be reduced from an average of three per month to an average of one per month at the central bank.
- By the end of the year, the average number of product defects should decrease from 214 per month to 150 per month at all extruding plants in the Midwest region.
- Sales expenses should decrease by 10 percent in the fourth quarter.

(continued on next page)

- There should be a 10 percent increase in sales revenue of the newly launched product during the next two months.
- The score of customer loyalty index should increase by 15 percent in six months.

ROI Objectives

The fifth level of objectives for marketing programs is the ROI (return on investment). The ROI objectives define the minimum or expected payoff of a marketing program and compare its cost with the monetary benefits of the marketing program. Consistent with the traditional financial ROI, we express the comparison as a percentage by multiplying the fractional values by 100 percent. The ROI calculation in formula form is

$$\text{ROI (\%)} = \frac{\text{net program benefits}}{\text{program costs}} \times 100$$

In this formula, net benefits are marketing program benefits minus total program costs, where total program costs include both direct and indirect costs for conducting the marketing program. The interpretation of this formula is, essentially, the same as that for capital investment. For example, when an organization launches a new product, the ROI of the product launch is calculated by dividing the annual earnings of the new product by the investment in the product launch. The annual earnings are comparable to net benefits (annual benefits minus the cost), whereas the investment is comparable to total and fully loaded costs. A program ROI of 50% means that for every $1 invested, the marketing program not only recovers $1 but also generates an additional $0.50. An ROI of 150% indicates that after the invested dollar is recovered, the marketing program generates a return of $1.50.

Using the ROI formula, we are able to place our marketing program investments on a level playing field with capital investments. By using the same formula and similar concepts, we ensure the ROI calculation of our marketing programs is easily understood by CEOs, CFOs, and other key management and financial executives, who regularly use ROI with other investments. But what is the best ROI objective for a marketing program? Due to the uniqueness of each challenge and complexity of each organization, no generally accepted standards exist to answer this question. We recommend the following four strategies to establish an acceptable ROI objective for a marketing program:

- The first strategy is to set the ROI value at a breakeven point by setting the ROI objective at zero. A 0% ROI represents the point where the benefits equal the costs. The rationale for this approach is an eagerness to recapture the cost of the program so that the program can pay for itself and is not a financial burden to the organization. This is the ROI objective recommended for many nonprofit, charitable, and public-sector organizations, with the philosophy that the organization is not attempting to make a positive return from a particular marketing program, but is striving to maintain financial health and stability. In addition, a 0% ROI may create benefits through intangible measures. Intangible measures are outcomes connected to the program that are not converted to monetary values but still benefit the organization. This can be especially useful when a company tries to strengthen its brand equity or build product awareness in the early stage of a product life cycle.
- The second strategy is to let the executives, managers, clients, or program sponsors set the minimum acceptable ROI value. In this scenario, the individuals who initiate, approve, sponsor, fund, or support the marketing program establish the acceptable ROI. Every program has individuals who are responsible for approving, funding, and supporting it. These individuals can be executives, sponsors, or even donors, and they may be willing to offer the acceptable value. This practice links the expectations of the financial return of a marketing program directly to the minimum expectations of the individuals who approve and sponsor the program.
- The next strategy sets the ROI objective by using the same values used when investing in capital expenditures, such as equipment, facilities, and new companies. For most markets in developed nations, the ROI objective is usually around 15 percent because

the cost of capital is relatively low in North America, Europe, and most of the Asia-Pacific area, including Australia and New Zealand. Marketers in developing nations and other areas of the world may choose a different ROI objective more appropriate for the cost of capital in their markets.

- Finally, a fourth strategy is for marketers to choose a minimum ROI objective reflecting a higher standard, with the target value above the percentage required for other capital expenditures. Because the marketing ROI process is relatively new and often involves subjective input such as estimations, choosing a higher ROI objective ensures a conservative and reliable process. A typical ROI objective using this strategy may be in the range of 20–30 percent.

Collectively, all levels of objectives inform the stakeholders and help them better understand the marketing program. With this important issue in mind, complete Exercise 5.1.

Exercise 5.1

Instructions: For each objective listed below, indicate the level of evaluation at which the objective is aimed: Level 1, Reaction; Level 2, Learning; Level 3, Action; Level 4, Impact; Level 5, ROI. Be sure to use the lead-in to the sentence before each objective.

OBJECTIVE	EVALUATION LEVEL
After completing the marketing program, customers (participants) should:	
Improve sales revenue by 20 percent in six months.	
Initiate at least three new product development ideas in 15 days.	
Achieve an average cost reduction of $20,000 per project.	
Increase the use of interactive selling skills in 90 percent of business-to-business sales calls.	

OBJECTIVE	EVALUATION LEVEL
Achieve a 2:1 benefit-to-cost ratio one year after the new product quality program is implemented.	
Be able to identify the five features of the recently launched new product.	
Increase the external customer satisfaction index by 25 percent in three months.	
Address customer complaints with the five-step process in 95 percent of complaint situations.	
Perceive the new social media marketing message to be interesting.	
Achieve a product knowledge test score average of 75 out of a possible 100.	
Conduct a performance review meeting with key account sales professionals to establish performance improvement goals.	
Provide a 4 out of 5 rating on the appropriateness of the new ethics policy.	
Decrease the time to recruit new account managers from 35 to 20 days.	
Complete marketing action plans in three months.	
Perceive the new compensation and incentive plan as influencing their intent to remain with the organization.	
Be involved in the career enhancement program at a rate of 15 percent of all employees.	
Decrease the amount of time required for product managers to complete a new product development project.	
Achieve a post-test customer service knowledge score increase of 30 percent.	
Use the new digital marketing app daily, as reflected by an 80 percent score on an unscheduled audit of use.	
Submit ideas or suggestions for improvement in the first year (10 percent objective).	

Answers are found in Appendix A.

Final Thoughts

This chapter shows what must change in three categories. First, the definition of success for marketing programs must change. The new definition involves setting objectives at all levels. Second, marketers need to recognize that designing for business results involves design thinking at each level. Specific actions designed to achieve the desired outcomes must be taken at each level. Third, expectations for customers, participants, and stakeholders must be created with objectives at each level. The objectives define success at the levels of reaction, learning, action, and impact. The objectives at Levels 3 and 4 are powerful, as they highlight the benefits created by the marketing program that matter to all the stakeholders. The objectives at Levels 0, 1, and 2 are also important because they demonstrate the path from input to outcome. When necessary, the data at the lower levels and those at the higher levels can be used to calculate an ROI, which measures the value of the marketing programs. Developing objectives at all levels, although it may be time-consuming, provides much more focus for the marketing program and helps marketers ensure that business results are created and delivered.

6

Make It Matter: Design for Input, Reaction, and Learning

There is only one winning strategy. It is to carefully define the target market and direct a superior offering to that target market.

PHILIP KOTLER

iosearch Pharmaceutical Incorporated (BPI) is a pharmaceutical company headquartered in New Jersey with sales offices all around the nation. For decades, BPI has been focused on research, manufacturing, and marketing of both prescription and over-the-counter consumer medication. Almost 50 percent of BPI's revenue comes from its hospital sales force operating in the US market. Salustatin is BPI's statin product, which effectively reduces cholesterol levels in the blood with no major side effects. It has been one of the best sellers on the market for three years. Similar to other prescription medications, this statin product is prescribed by physicians when patients have certain indications of heart disease. The competition for medication products in the statin market is fierce. BPI faces substantial challenges from a major pharmaceutical powerhouse that prevented the organization from achieving market share goals and reaching sales potential with Salustatin. A marketing research study was conducted, and the following conclusions came from the report:

- The prescribing physicians are key to achieve market share, because they determine which product to prescribe based on their belief in the effectiveness and safety of the product.
- Physicians are not well educated about Salustatin, do not understand the benefits of it, and do not believe it to be superior in treatment effectiveness and safety.
- The primary promotion from BPI toward the physicians is through sales calls. However, salespeople's messages are not consistent and lack scientific support regarding the benefits of Salustatin.
- Although the physicians' current attitude toward Salustatin is not favorable, they are open to receiving new information related to the effectiveness and safety of the product. Research shows that promotional efforts may be necessary and effective to change the physicians' attitudes.

This report confirmed the BPI marketing director's belief that the target customers were the prescribing physicians and revealed a significant gap at the learning level, as many of them did not understand the benefits of Salustatin. Based on these analyses, the BPI marketing director worked with Salustatin product managers and launched a Salustatin Promotion Program (SPP). With a series of physician seminars as a crucial element of this program, the goals of SPP were to educate physicians, change their attitude, and improve sales performance. These educational seminars demonstrated the clinical trial results and disseminated the scientific findings related to different statin drugs to target physicians. During the seminars, there were discussion sessions led by doctors from local hospitals and researchers from top medical schools. As the sole sponsor of the physician seminar events, BPI was able to promote its Salustatin product during the seminars. BPI salespeople followed up with phone calls and social media messages after the seminars. They also set up face-to-face meetings with the physicians to further discuss the seminar topics and answer questions, with the goals to change physicians' prescribing behaviors and boost sales numbers of Salustatin.

In order to assess the value of this marketing program, as a pilot study, BPI randomly selected 220 physicians who attended the one-day education event and invited them to share their reactions to the seminar. On a 5-point scale, the reaction data were summarized as following:

Relevance of information	4.2
Important to practice	4.0
Usefulness of presentation	4.8
Discussion and Q & A	4.1
Overall rating	4.3

The pharmaceutical industry is highly regulated. Although objectives were set at learning and action levels, marketers of BPI were not able to collect data at these levels due to the sensitive nature of the situation. However, the marketers were able to compare business impact data before and after the marketing program, a measure at Level 4. After isolating the effects, the annualized benefits of the program were estimated to be $657,695. The total program cost was $326,000. Using the ROI formula, the BPI marketers calculated the ROI of the SPP, which yielded a 101.7 percent ROI.

This result implied that BPI made nearly $1.02 for every $1 it invested in marketing the SPP program after recovering the dollar. This investment was considered highly efficient. In addition to the monetary value, the BPI marketing program would have positive long-term effects on brand reputation, customer satisfaction, and employee loyalty. All of these are important intangible benefits.

• • •

After selecting the right solutions in Chapter 4 and setting objectives at different levels in Chapter 5, our next steps focus on designing the contents of our program and implementing the solutions to accomplish the objectives. The process of designing for results involves two chapters. This chapter deals with the fourth step of the ROI Methodology, "Make It Matter," and in Chapter 7, we will discuss Step 5, "Make It Stick."

Design Marketing Programs with Results in Mind

An undeniable fact is that most marketing programs are expensive, and a related fact is that resources are scarce. Marketers should do their best to ensure the success of the marketing programs so that desired organizational goals will be achieved and scarce resources will not be wasted. However, according to studies, more than half the marketing programs implemented fail to achieve the objectives set for the programs.[1] To improve the success rate of marketing programs, marketers need to design the programs with the desired results in mind.

The alignment model, discussed previously, can be a useful framework for this purpose. It demonstrates both objectives and results at all levels throughout the life cycle of a marketing program. From input to reaction, through learning and action, to impact and ROI, designing for results across the levels ensures that sufficient attention, tools, templates, and processes are in place to achieve those results. Additionally, marketers need to prioritize the objectives at different levels. Because the business impact objective at Level 4 is the most important measure desired by executives, it deserves more attention. Marketers should have the expected business impact measures in mind when developing, implementing, and evaluating their marketing programs.

Design Input for Results

As we discussed in Chapter 2, the measures at Level 0, Input, include the number of marketing programs, number of attendees, audience, costs, timing, duration, channel, venue, efficiencies, etc. In fact, there are many additional variations and breakdowns within these measures. We cover the most important ones in this section.

Target Audience

The first question marketers need to ask regarding their marketing program is who should be the target audience, because the target audience is critically important for delivering impact and ROI. As Philip Kotler and Kevin Keller put it, "Carefully defining your target market and focusing on it is the only winning strategy in marketing."[2] For consumer and business marketing programs, this is the issue of targeting strategy. Targeting strategies should involve segmenting the market (that is, the customers) into different groups based on certain characteristics, selecting the most desirable group, and focusing on it. Ideally, the target segment has been chosen and clearly defined in the solution development stage. However, there is a possibility that it has not, and so a wrong customer segment might have been chosen. We know a segment is wrong when customers inside this segment do not appreciate our product as expected, they are not willing to pay the price, or there is no cost-efficient way to reach them. If so, then marketers may face risks that will potentially hurt the success rate and damage the value to be created by their marketing programs.

The Needs of Customers and Participants

Marketing is about discovering and satisfying customer needs, which are the tangible and intangible benefits customers need, want, and desire when purchasing products and services. Although customer needs should have been the focus of marketing analysis and solution development in previous steps, it can still be a persistent problem for some programs. In the process of designing input for results, we have to make sure that participants really need the program. As big data and marketing analytics become increasingly popular, organizations have more insight related to customers' needs. Meanwhile, social media marketing and digital marketing both enable customers with genuine needs and strong desires to approach the organization in order to receive beneficial products and services. Both external customers and internal participants realize that if they are involved in a program that they do not need, it adds to the costs with little or no benefits. For customers and employees, this is a waste of their time and energy. For organizations, it wastes resources and minimizes the ROI. Box 6.1 is a case study in point.

Box 6.1   Case Study: Google Glass

The failure of Google Glass is an example of a hyped technology that failed to deliver value due to an ill-defined target audience and misunderstood customer needs.[3] When the innovative product was launched, even its marketers disagreed upon where Google Glass would be used. One group of marketers thought that Google Glass could be chosen by people who would wear the glasses as a fashionable device, while another group thought it should be worn by people who needed them occasionally for specific purposes. No serious market research was conducted to identify and find the target customers, and no measures were taken to validate customers' needs. The marketers assumed that Google Glass would sell itself and the right people would find and accept the funny-looking device. Although this product was meant to provide two functions, taking quick pictures and surfing the internet, no target segment was clearly defined to pay the $1,500 price.

Media Channels and Place

In marketing, a media channel or promotion channel refers to the specific medium by which a message is conveyed to its intended audience. The media could be traditional promotional channels such as TV, radio, newspapers, magazines, and billboards, or they could be online channels such as social media sites including Facebook, Twitter, Instagram, LinkedIn, etc. To better design for results, marketers need to consider the offerings and the messages and to what extent they align with particular media in order to make the selection. The selected media should offer marketers the best influence on the targeted audience with reasonable costs. Further, these media channels should be desired by the customer due to their convenience and usability and, more importantly, be preferred by the organization based on effectiveness and efficiency considerations.

Timing and Duration

The timing and the duration of a marketing program represent other important opportunities that can have effects on both the program benefits and costs. Timing refers to when to begin implementing a program, whereas duration refers to how long the program should last. Because of seasonality, retail sales of many products vary by the month of the year and reach their peak as holiday shopping kicks in. Timing should reflect this seasonality. Marketers also need to consider the life cycle of their products. For both customer marketing and internal marketing programs, the duration refers to the amount of time devoted to the program. Duration can be a relevant and sometimes tricky decision with regard to the benefits, costs, effectiveness, and efficiency issues. If the duration is too short, the program may not have enough influence or impact on the customers or the participants. This may ultimately lower the monetary benefits and reduce effectiveness and the ROI of the program. On the other hand, if the duration is too long, it adds to the cost of the program, also reducing the ROI. Duration should be optimized and set from the perspective of maximizing the ROI.

Conclusion

As we have discussed, many types of input issues can have significant effects on either the effectiveness or efficiency of a program. Marketers must properly manage input throughout the process, and this effort involves a variety of individuals performing system checks to make it work. We show in Table 6.1 a checklist of the input items that can influence the success of customer and internal marketing programs with the right resources at the right time.

TABLE 6.1 Examples of input items

THIS MARKETING PROGRAM MUST BE:	PARAMETER
Conducted to cover at least 50,000 potential customers	Volume/staffing
Conducted with at least 100 participants per month at each of the six sales districts	Volume/staffing
Implemented as a pilot project only	Scope
Contained in the new product testing market only	Scope
For sales staff only	Audience/coverage
For large customer accounts (>$1 million in annual sales)	Audience/coverage
Initiated by the date of the new product launch	Timing
Completed by September 1	Timing
Conducted in less than three months	Duration
Completed with no more than three hours in a meeting	Duration
Within 3% of each sales region's budget	Budget/costs
Less than $1,000 in cost per customer	Budget/costs
Designed at a ratio of no more than 10 hours per 1 hour of content.	Efficiency
Devoted to advanced selling negotiation skills	Content
Focused on new attributes of the service package	Content
Originated based on thorough market research and analysis	Origin
Implemented to support new products recently launched	Origin

THIS MARKETING PROGRAM MUST BE:	PARAMETER
Implemented with social media and digital marketing	Delivery
Conducted at a resort on the Gulf Coast	Location
Implemented in the Midwest market only	Location
Implemented without disruption of work	Disruption
Seamless with customers	Disruption
Integrated with existing online ordering systems	Technology
Using a virtual project management tool	Technology
Implemented with no more than 50% outsourcing	Outsourcing

Design Reaction for Results

Consumer purchase decision-making is a complex process influenced by many factors. The process starts when customers, including both individual consumers and organizational buyers, realize that they have a need or problem, or they see an opportunity. For consumers, this can be as simple as finding an empty milk carton in the refrigerator or realizing that the family car is not driving smoothly. For business buyers, this can be discovering that inventory is low or realizing that the current customer relationship management system is not powerful enough to serve the new market segments. After recognizing the problem, consumers will engage in an information search, and a marketing program may provide the information they need. Processing this information will lead to consumer perception, which is a meaningful picture of our offerings created by consumers in their mind. This perception is a cognitive interpretation of our market offering, and customers may have feelings about it. When we feel something, we often react. To react means to say, feel, or do something in response to what we perceive and how we feel.

In ROI marketing terminology, reaction is the first-level response and outcome measurement our marketing program receives from the customers. It holds much value since it is the first indicator directly from the target audience that determines the success or failure of the marketing program. Whether the reaction is positive or negative demonstrates the extent to which target customers or participants will process the information the marketing program provides and engage in learning its content. With data collected at the reaction level, we are able to shed light on the potential for program success and identify potential roadblocks. For example, when consumers develop a positive reaction toward the green lizard with a Cockney accent, they are more likely to learn more about the benefits of GEICO's insurance policies. On the other hand, McDonald's 2017 TV commercial that featured a boy asking his mother about his dead father created extremely negative reactions among the audience.[4] The firm had to apologize for the upset caused by the ad's perceived exploitation of child bereavement and take action to withdraw the ad. For both consumer marketing and internal marketing, an adverse reaction toward the program is a good indicator that customers and participants will not process the information and engage in learning. Box 6.2 reports on other programs that elicited negative reactions.

Box 6.2   Case Study: Failures

Thousands of new products fail every year and cost American businesses billions of dollars. Research reveals that both marketing and nonmarketing factors contribute to new product failures, and some of them are related to consumers' reaction toward a marketing program.[5] Three prime examples are:

- **Avert Virucidal tissues.** This product by Kimberly-Clark contained vitamin C derivatives, which were claimed to be scientifically designed to kill cold and flu germs when users sneezed, coughed, or blew their noses into the tissues. This product failed because consumers were frightened by the "cidal" in the brand name because they connected it to words like "suicidal." This word association created negative reactions that prevented consumers from learning the product's benefits.
- **Hey! There's A Monster in My Room spray.** This product, with a bubble-gum fragrance, was designed to rid scary creatures from a kid's bedroom. However, many

children found the brand name to be scarier than their fear of a monster because it implied that the monster was still hiding in the bedroom somewhere. The negative reaction toward the product eventually led to its failure.

- **Fingos.** General Mills' Fingos was a sweetened cereal flake about the size of a corn chip. The company expected consumers to snack on them without milk. However, most consumers failed to see the product's superior benefits when compared with snacks such as popcorn and potato chips. Their reaction to Fingos was primarily insignificant. Fingos failed because consumers' reaction was not strong enough to induce behavioral changes, as most consumers did not want to try the product.

Topics to Measure

While having the right reaction is critical, not all marketing managers pay enough attention to it. Taking the reaction for granted or completely ignoring the early indicators of customers' reaction may cost more to correct in a later stage. Box 6.3 shows potential topics that we may use to capture reactions in consumer and business marketing programs.

Box 6.3 Topics of Reaction for Consumer and Business Marketing Programs

- Relevant	- Convenient
- Important	- New
- Valuable	- Cool
- Useful	- Fascinating
- Meaningful	- Compatible
- Easy to use	- Interesting
- Beneficial	- Informative

Similarly, for internal marketing programs, as shown in Box 6.4, we may divide the topics into experience and content. The experience is what makes participants feel good about the program, which may include service, comfort, surroundings, communications, facilities, and the coordinator. However, experience topics have limited effect on the outcomes of the internal marketing program, because the content of the program is more important than the experience. Therefore, the focus should be on content questions such as relevance to your situation, importance to your success, and intent for use.

Box 6.4 Topics of Reaction for Internal Marketing Programs

▪ Ready	▪ Powerful	▪ Intent to use*
▪ Useful	▪ Leading edge	▪ Learning environment
▪ Necessary	▪ Just enough	▪ New information*
▪ Appropriate	▪ Just for me	▪ Overall evaluation
▪ Motivational	▪ Efficient	▪ Content
▪ Rewarding	▪ Easy/difficult	▪ Delivery
▪ Practical	▪ Service	▪ Facilities
▪ Valuable	▪ Relevant*	▪ Facilitator
▪ Timely	▪ Important to success*	▪ Recommend to others*

Usually correlates with action and application.

Measuring Reaction

We can measure reaction on a 4-, 5-, 7-, or 10-point scale. The idea is to keep it simple, limit the number of questions, and use forced-choice questions with space for comments. In the past, marketers used survey or phone interviews to collect data. Today, more and more organizations use technology to measure reaction by facilitating data collection, analysis, and reporting. Depending on the nature of a marketing program, the measurement of reaction could occur before, during, or after the program. The timing of data collection can be interesting because reactions often change. Even before the marketing program, customers may have a perception about our product, service, or brand. This initial reaction may change when they are exposed to the marketing program. Comparing the changes in reaction can be interesting and useful and reveal important insights.

Using Reaction Data

The reaction data can be used to identify what is working and what is not, so that we can make adjustments in order to ensure proper learning will be induced. On a typical scale, we may use upper and lower numbers as markers for action. For example, on a 5-point scale, the upper number could be 4 and the lower number could be 3. We can then explore what causes a reaction to go beyond 4 and what causes it to drop below 3. The reasons could be related to the target audience, the content, the media, the facilitator, or the program coordinator if it is an internal marketing program. Changes can be made to address the reasons identified. The important point is to monitor the reaction data that link to learning and even action data. Occasionally, especially for internal marketing programs, we may use reaction data to forecast improvement in business impact measures, including the ROI. In Chapter 13, we will discuss how to forecast ROI using reaction data.

Design Learning for Results

Every marketing program involves learning, and much consumer behavior is learned. A part of designing for results is to make sure that the marketing programs are designed for proper learning. For consumer and business programs, learning involves the acquisition of information about a product, a service, a brand, an organization, or a concept. It's usually the marketing message. For internal marketing programs, learning includes the acquisition of knowledge and skills. When customers know the marketing message from a marketing program, they are more likely to take desirable actions, which will have positive impacts on business results. Similarly, when participants acquire proper learning from an internal marketing program, they are more willing to apply the knowledge and skills in their daily work, resulting in enhanced productivity and improved job performance. Several areas need attention.

Two Types of Learning

For consumer marketing programs, learning refers to the behaviors that result in either repeated experience or reasoning. Consumers learn which information to rely on for assessing products and services, which evaluative criteria to use when comparing alternatives, and how to make purchase decisions. There are generally two types of learning relevant to consumer marketing. The first type is behavioral learning, which is a process of developing automatic responses to a situation built upon repeated exposure to it. For this type of learning, marketers can use the same brand name to induce repeat purchase. Examples include the different products of Tylenol and the different beers of Budweiser. Brand loyalty, which is a favorable attitude toward a brand, leads to automatic purchase through behavioral learning.

The second type of learning is through thinking, reasoning, and mental problem solving. Known as cognitive learning, this type of learning involves establishing connections between brands and benefits through advertising, personal selling, social media marketing, or other promotional approaches. For example, Colgate Visible White established a connection between its brand and teeth stain removal by repetition in its advertising messages such as "One Shade Whiter Teeth in One Week." Similarly, after continuous marketing efforts, McNeil Consumer Healthcare successfully linked Tylenol 8-Hour brand to the idea of pain relief.[6]

Three Ways to Change Attitude

An important concept in the process of consumer learning is attitude, which is defined as "a learned predisposition to respond to an object or class of objects in a consistently favorable or unfavorable way."[7] From marketing theories, attitude is defined as a function of the belief about the extent to which a brand has certain attributes and the perceived importance of those attributes. In order to induce proper actions, marketers often need to change customers' attitudes toward their brands, products, or services through learning. There are three approaches commonly used by marketers in both consumer and business marketing programs:[8]

1. **Changing beliefs about the extent to which a brand has certain attributes.** Through promotion and communication efforts, marketers can change a consumer's subjective perception of how a brand or product performs on different attributes. For example, Hellmann's successfully convinced consumers that their mayonnaise had higher omega 3 content (a nutrient essential to human health) than they originally thought.

2. **Changing the perceived importance of attributes.** The fact that a product has certain attributes does not mean these attributes are important. Sometimes, marketers invest to change consumers' perceived importance regarding an attribute in order to change their attitude. For example, freshness is an attribute of drinks such as cola. However, few consumers considered freshness an important issue when choosing drinks until Pepsi spent about $25 million on advertising and promotion to educate consumers on the importance of this attribute. Afterward, as indicated by a consumer survey, 61 percent of cola drinkers believe freshness is an important attribute.

3. **Adding new attributes to the brand.** The third approach to change consumers' attitude is to educate the consumers that the brand actually has new attributes that they were previously unaware of, essentially adding new attributes to consumers' perception. For example, Colgate-Palmolive spent $100 million to educate consumers that its Colgate Total toothpaste has a new antibacterial ingredient, triclosan. Consequently, the Colgate Total toothpaste is now a billion-dollar global brand.

Data Collection Methods for Input, Reaction, and Learning

Among the methods of data collection, the following are especially relevant and useful for measuring input, reaction, and learning.[9]

Interview and Focus Groups

The principal way to collect data for a marketing program is asking people directly, such as in interview and focus group studies. The interview can be conducted by a single researcher with one respondent. This method enables marketers to ask in-depth questions and probe for additional ideas using follow-up questions. Using this method, General Mills was able to identify the causes of a new product failure by exploring customers' concerns at the reaction and learning levels. The interviews can be conducted face-to-face and online.

The focus group is another technique used to ask people questions. Focus groups involve 6 to 10 customers sharing their ideas, opinions, and attitudes toward the firm's brands, products, and competitors in an informal session led by a discussion leader or moderator.

Interviews and focus groups can be used to collect data at input, reaction, and learning levels for consumer, business, and internal marketing programs.

Observation

The second way to collect primary marketing data is observing people. Observation is a data collection method for obtaining facts and figures by watching how people behave. It is a useful tool for both consumer marketing and internal marketing programs. This method can generate data at the input, reaction, and learning levels. For example, Procter & Gamble observed consumers in India using its Gillette shavers and noticed that many Indian consumers shaved with a small cup of cold water, which caused the blades to clog. Using this information, the company introduced a razor with an easy-rinse single blade. Similarly, IKEA noticed that customers stopped shopping when their shopping carts were full. As a result, IKEA places additional shopping bags throughout their stores. Observation data can also be collected through a mechanical approach, for example, the national TV ratings collected by Nielsen. Recently, marketing researchers have started using neuroscience approaches such as brain scanning, eye tracking, biometric monitoring, and facial coding to observe responses to nonconscious stimuli. Results of these studies have been used to improve product quality, packaging, and advertising messages. Observation is also commonly used by managers and researchers to identify gaps and opportunities for improvement and to evaluate outcomes of internal marketing programs.

Other Data Collection Methods

Surveys and questionnaires are common data collection methods in marketing. They come in all sizes, ranging from short surveys to detailed instruments. Marketers can use them to obtain subjective data about participant reaction and learning, as well as to document business performance data for use in a projected impact study or ROI forecast.

Testing is important for measuring learning, especially in internal marketing program evaluations. For an internal marketing program such as sales training, improvement in test scores shows the change in skill, knowledge, or capability of the participant that can be attributed to the program.

Another technique for measuring learning is simulation. This method involves using a procedure or task that simulates application situations in the program. Participants try out their performance in the simulated activity. Another simulation process is the case study, which relies on documented real-life situations to illustrate the desired success.

Integrated Marketing Communications for Input, Reaction, and Learning

In marketing, integrated marketing communication (IMC) is an important concept. It ensures that all forms of communications and messages are carefully linked together to obtain organizational goals.[10] For marketing programs, integrated marketing communication means integrating all the communication and promotional tools, so that they work together in harmony to accomplish marketers' objectives set at different levels. IMC is important throughout the life cycle of a marketing program. A chain of communication immediately begins when initiating and designing a program. Marketers can use one or more of five promotional alternatives, known as promotional elements, to communicate with customers. The five promotional elements are advertising, personal selling, public relations, direct marketing, and sales promotion, which can be used for various communication tasks and as appropriate for different situations.[11]

Final Thoughts

We addressed the effectiveness and efficiencies of marketing programs through a design approach in this chapter. "Make It Matter" covers designing for success at the first levels of the ROI Methodology: input, reaction, and learning. We collect data at these levels with a focus on examining each measure or potential measure and making adjustments to ensure success. Each adjustment will add value, increasing monetary benefits, decreasing costs, or both. An important part of the process is to design for increasing the impact, which is converted to monetary benefits, or for reducing the cost of the programs. This is how to maximize the ROI, even in the early stages of marketing program implementation.

The chapter also focused on what to measure for input, reaction, and learning, how to collect data at these levels, and how to communicate to customers, participants, and stakeholders. We will continue the discussion of design for success in the next chapter with the focus on the action and business impact levels.

7

Make It Stick: Design for Action and Impact

*Better to return home and weave a net
than stand by water and desire the fishes.*

CHINESE PROVERB

alaxy Sports is a high-tech company that manufactures and markets sports wearables and apps in the United States and beyond. The company develops action cameras, mobile apps, and video-editing software for amateur and professional athletes who love to experience and share great moments of sports. Founded about 20 years ago by a group of sports enthusiasts, Galaxy has become one of the major players in the rapidly growing industry. At the beginning, Galaxy offered cameras that captured images using 35-mm film that needed to be processed at a pharmacy or photography studio. Later on, the company replaced its film cameras with digital cameras that generate both digital photos and VGA videos. Today, the company offers a variety of products equipped with audio capabilities, wide-angle lenses, and time-lapse features. Its product lines also include smartphone apps, video-editing tools, and Wi-Fi remote controls.

Since it was founded, Galaxy Sports has been investing heavily into new product development and relying on profits from the new product sales to recover the investment, covering the costs related to new product developments and fueling future new product projects. Recently, the company launched a 360-degree video camera. This product has multiple features that are superior to many of the competing brands in the marketplace. Galaxy Sports executives are hoping that this product can succeed in the marketplace and strengthen the company's leadership in the industry. Kelly is the product manager, and she has been working on the product from concept generation all the way to new product launch. Market research has indicated that this product has a great potential to satisfy unfulfilled needs of target customers, and Galaxy Sports has invested millions of dollars into it.

However, three months after its launch to the market, the 360-degree video camera has not been selling as expected. Kelly and her team are not satisfied with the performance of the new product, and the sales revenue has not grown fast enough. The current sales revenue is growing at a rate of only 15 percent per month, far below the expected 30 percent monthly growth rate. As an experienced product manager, Kelly knows that sales revenue is a significant measure of financial performance at Level 4, and growth rate is a critical measure for new product success, especially in the early stages of a product's life cycle. To better understand the situation, Kelly works with a performance consulting firm to identify the causes. The data and analysis show that although some customers have positive reactions toward the new product (Level 1) and even have learned some of its features (Level 2), very few customers are taking action (Level 3). Specifically, only 5 percent of customers who learned the new product features took action by either downloading the app or responding to social media promotion. In addition, the new product website traffic has been low, indicating very few customers are visiting the website and searching new product information.

Kelly decides that the key to the success of her 360-degree video camera is to convince more customers to take action. Therefore, she designs multiple solutions to address the issues with the assistance of the performance consulting firm. Based on survey research and suggestions from the performance consultants, she develops an integrated marketing communication (IMC) strategy by focusing on the following attributes:

1. **Perceived usefulness.** The research has identified that target customers are struggling to understand the benefits provided by the 360-degree video camera. To address this issue, the new promotion highlights the product features that make the product useful for customers. For example, the 360-degree action camera has a waterproof feature that is particularly useful for people who love surfing and enjoy sharing the moments on social media. Additionally, the clear lens cap that comes with the product is useful for protecting the lens when shooting intense action.

2. **Perceived ease of use.** It is clear that some customers are, to a certain degree, intimidated by the perceived sophistication and complexity of the new product. The new IMC strategy demonstrates the fact that, for most customers, the 360-degree video camera is easy to use. Through content marketing and digital marketing messages to target customers, Kelly and her team demonstrate how easy it is to use the new dynamic image stabilization feature of the camera for both still photos and videos. The messages also highlight the feature that provides all images captured by the camera to be automatically backed up through cloud connectivity, with very few skills needed.

3. **Self-efficacy.** According to research, self-efficacy refers to individuals' belief in their abilities to execute actions successfully and serves as a critical predictor of their actual actions. To induce desirable actions, Kelly and her team strive to increase target customers' self-efficacy to use the 360-degree camera. Videos created using the new product are uploaded to YouTube and Instagram, and many users are sharing their success stories. Research shows

that watching similar people succeed and hearing their success stories motivates customers to believe that they can do it too.

Kelly understands the importance of attitudinal changes prior to behavioral changes, so she uses surveys and interviews to carefully monitor the attitudinal changes of customers before and after the new IMC promotion. In addition, Kelly and her team use sponsorships as a critical component of their marketing program. They maintain a roster of over 100 athletes from a wide variety of sports who serve as champions and ambassadors for the Galaxy Sports brand and new products.

After launching the marketing program, Kelly and her team utilize multiple instruments to measure and evaluate the effects of the program at different levels and pay particular attention to measures related to action at Level 3. Specifically, they monitor website traffic and smartphone app downloads, in addition to questionnaire data collection. They also analyze how people watch their YouTube and Instagram videos and how customers respond to Galaxy Sport's Twitter and Facebook messages. All these measures are significantly improving and will, Kelly hopes, lead to increased sales revenue and growth rates.

Influence Actions to Achieve Business Impact

Most marketing programs break down at Level 3, Action. As shown in the opening story, when customers do not take action after we implement a marketing program, business impact does not materialize. When employees do not take action after attending an internal program, the knowledge and skill they have learned will have no influence on job performance. When there is a lack of action, marketing programs fail to generate benefits, and financial and human resources have been wasted. Figuring out exactly why no action has been taken can be a daunting task because there can be many barriers and enablers simultaneously influencing success, although some may be more notable and influential than others. The challenge is to identify, understand, and address these barriers and enablers before, during, and after our marketing program.

Making it stick, discussed in this chapter, is an important step in the ROI Methodology that focuses on customers' actions and their impact on business performance. This chapter offers tips for marketers to design for success at the action and impact levels. Specifically, we review various factors identified by research in the past decades, discuss their implications for our marketing programs, and provide tools and techniques for marketers to use to design their marketing programs for results.

Factors Influencing Customer Action

For decades, marketing managers and researchers have been engaging in studies focusing on factors that influence customers' behaviors. During this process, ideas have been borrowed from social psychology, from industrial and organizational psychology, and from the literature on management. Notable models and frameworks in this arena include the theory of reasoned action (TRA), the theory of planned behavior (TPB), and the theory of adoption model (TAM). These theories have been tested in various contexts and have gained considerable empirical support over the past decades. The following factors have emerged from the literature as the most significant and reliable predictors of customers' actions.

Attitude

Customers' attitude refers to their favorable or unfavorable predisposition toward a subject, which could be the product, service, promotional message, brand, or organization. Customers must find the product or service important or valuable to them. According to research, customers develop positive attitudes when they positively evaluate the most important attributes related to the subjects in question.[1] In contrast, when they negatively evaluate salient attributes related to a subject, their attitude will be negative. As predicted by the theories, positive attitude leads to strong behavioral intention and actual behavior. For example, when a customer has a positive attitude toward a product, he or she is more likely to seek more information about it, to discuss it with other people, and to try it out or even purchase it than people who have a negative attitude toward it.

In the previous chapter, we discussed three strategies to change consumers' attitude toward a brand. Specifically, we can change the perceived strengths of an attribute, change the perceived importance of that attribute, or add new attributes to consumers' minds. When consumers have a more positive attitude toward a brand, they are likely to take action to try and purchase (Level 3), thus improving sales revenue and profit (Level 4). These goals can be achieved by using advertising, personal selling, social media marketing, and other promotional approaches, as they can positively influence consumer reaction (Level 1) and learning (Level 2).

Attitude is also important for internal marketing programs such as training. When employees have a positive attitude toward an internal marketing program, they are more likely to engage in actions to participate, learn, and apply the contents. The attitude comes from a cognitive process as employees evaluate the most important attributes of the internal marketing program. Managers and program facilitators may use the same three strategies to change employees' attitude toward an internal marketing program by using announcements, brochures, flyers, meetings, and intranet communications. When these communication efforts create a positive reaction (Level 1) and learning (Level 2), employees develop positive attitudes, which lead to desirable actions (Level 3) and outcomes (Level 4).

Subjective Norm

Also known as normative pressure, subjective norm is a social pressure to perform or not to perform a behavior. Subjective norm plays an important predictive role in both TPB and TRA.[2] Its validity has been tested and confirmed in hundreds, if not thousands, of empirical studies. In marketing, strategies using subjective norm include relying on endorsements from opinion leaders and celebrities and on referrals from family members, peers, and friends. In an internal marketing program, it is critical to get managers' support and endorsements for the program because employees are more likely to comply with manager expectations.

Self-Efficacy

As discussed in the opening story, self-efficacy is an important predictor of one's behavior. When customers have more confidence in their abilities to successfully use a product, they are more likely to spend time and effort searching for information and exploring and trying the samples. For internal marketing programs, employees with increased self-efficacy are more likely to transfer and apply the skills they learned to work-related applications. From academic research and managers' experience, we know that self-efficacy can be improved in multiple ways. We may increase and improve an individual's self-efficacy by using verbal persuasion and by creating opportunities for individuals to have successful experiences, to learn from others' success, or to mimic their role models' behaviors.

Perceived Usefulness

A particularly relevant attribute for new product sales is customers' perceived usefulness of the product. As discussed in the opening story, this construct measures the extent to which customers perceive the new product to provide useful benefits to make their life easier, more enjoyable, and more productive.[3] Because adopting a new product always involves changing behaviors (Level 3), it takes effort to convince the customers that the change will lead to desirable outcomes. Marketers need to consider this in the process of designing content and promotional materials. It is also a powerful influencer of employee actions in internal marketing programs. When employees find an internal marketing program, such as sales training to be useful, they are more likely to take actions based on what they learn from the program. Sometimes, organizations utilize bonus and sales contests to increase the perceived usefulness of an internal program in order to induce desirable actions.

Perceived Ease of Use

Another relevant attribute for new product adoption is perceived ease of use. TAM defines this as the extent to which an individual believes that using the new product would be free from effort with less difficulty and barriers.[4] When customers believe a technology or a product is easy to use, they are more likely to try it. Otherwise, they may hesitate. As demonstrated in the opening story, marketers may use content marketing to convince customers. This can be accomplished through creation and distribution of content, including videos, web pages, white papers, podcasts, infographics, etc., for the specific audience of target customers. In internal marketing programs, managers may use templates, job aids, and tools to make the process of learning and the adoption of new skills and new knowledge easier, thus improving the perceived ease of use and facilitating desirable actions.

Implications for Marketers

These research findings provide meaningful insight to marketers in the process of designing, implementing, and evaluating marketing programs. This helps marketers identify appropriate strategies to influence and induce customers' action, both directly and indirectly, in order to achieve business impact. Additionally, these implications guide marketers in designing and choosing tools and techniques for various tasks in this process. Relying on the research finding, marketers may choose to influence customers' actions directly by changing their attitude toward and perceptions about the marketing programs. Alternatively, they may influence target customers indirectly by utilizing sponsorships, opinion leaders and significant others, or managers and executives if it is an internal marketing program.

The Alignment Model

The process of designing, implementing, and evaluating marketing programs means we have to manage many moving parts. During the process, it is important not to get lost in the details. As discussed in previous chapters, the alignment model (Figure 7.1) helps marketers achieve business alignment for their programs.[5] We will use the opening story as a case to demonstrate the components of and process to develop alignment.

FIGURE 7.1 The alignment model of a consumer marketing program

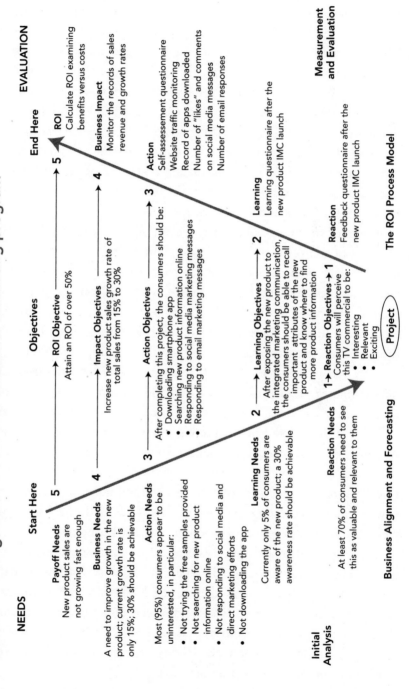

As shown in Figure 7.1, the situation of Galaxy Sports creates a payoff need, because the benefits derived from the 360-degree action camera sales revenue are not enough to recover the investment, as noted in the upper-left corner of the model. Also, on the left-hand side, we can see a business need, as the current sales revenue is growing at a rate of 15 percent, which is far below the expected 30 percent growth rate. Further analyses show several action needs, because 95 percent of consumers lack enthusiasm toward the new product. The lack of action may be explained by the fact that only 5 percent of consumers are aware of the existence of the new product, indicating there is a learning need. The marketers at Galaxy Sports believe that to ensure the effectiveness of their marketing program, the camera needs to be seen as relevant and valuable by the consumers.

As stated in the opening story, Galaxy Sports designs a marketing program to address these needs in an effort to improve the new product sales performance. Specifically, it launches an integrated marketing communication strategy highlighting important attributes of the new product. As shown in Figure 7.1, the company sets objectives at five levels corresponding to the five levels of needs identified. After launching the marketing program, Galaxy Sports utilizes multiple instruments to measure and evaluate the effects of the program at different levels. It uses questionnaires to measure the reaction and learning of the marketing program, Levels 1 and 2 data, respectively. To measure action at Level 3, which is the focus of the marketing program, the company monitors website traffic and smartphone apps downloads, in addition to questionnaire data collection. The Level 4 data of business impact are collected through monitoring records of sales revenue and the growth rate of the new product. Calculating the ROI generates data at Level 5 and completes the alignment model of this consumer marketing program.

The alignment model can also be used in business marketing programs. Figure 7.2 shows the alignment model of a distributor that is actively developing a new market in the Midwest through company salespeople. Marketing executives feel that there is a payoff need because the rate of new customer acquisition is too low. They also identify needs at the business impact, action, and learning levels as well as the reaction level, listed on the left-hand side of the model.

FIGURE 7.2 The alignment model of a business marketing program

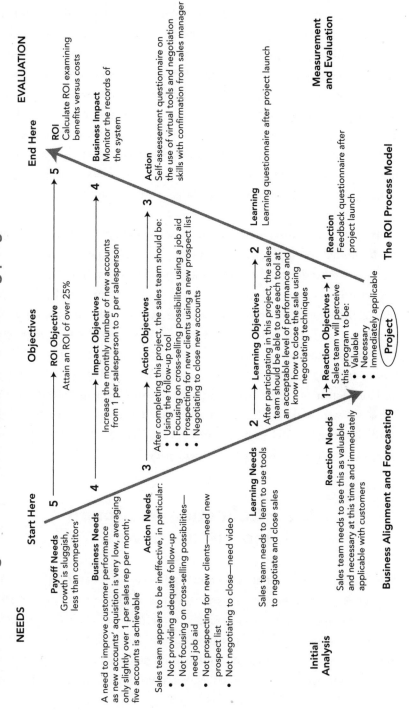

169

The marketing directors of a distributor conduct analyses and find that most of the salespeople lack the tools for negotiating and closing deals. Additionally, they find that the prospect database used by salespeople is incomplete and outdated. They design a solution to address the issues by providing tools, job aids, and updated databases. To ensure that salespeople will take action to use the tools and job aids (Level 3), the distributor develops objectives to achieve desirable reactions (Level 1) and facilitate learning (Level 2). These objectives are highlighted in the middle column of the model. The marketing directors also use a variety of methods to collect and evaluate data, as shown on the right-hand side of the alignment model.

Both cases we discussed demonstrate the benefits of using the alignment model for marketing programs. The alignment model enables marketers to understand the issues and problems clearly so that gaps and opportunities can be identified. These help marketers justify the initiation of the marketing program, secure funding, and enlist support from executives and stakeholders. Further, the alignment model helps marketers understand needs and set objectives accordingly at different levels. Understanding the needs and setting objectives will facilitate the design and development of the best solutions. It also will help marketers communicate with stakeholders from other departments in the organization. The alignment model provides an opportunity for marketers to review progress and make adjustments if necessary.

Data Collection for Action and Impact Levels

It is helpful to review data collection methods for measuring action and impact level data before discussing issues related to making it stick. Choosing appropriate data collection methods is critical throughout the program cycle.[6] As we discussed in the last chapter, some methods are suitable for collecting and measuring reaction and learning data. In this chapter, we explore data collection methods for action and impact, which can be used to confirm the effectiveness of the marketing program. Data collection may also reveal areas where the program is not working as planned, thus enabling marketers to take corrective measures for improvement in order to make it stick. In Table 7.1, we list several of the most commonly used data collection methods and the levels of data where they are used.

TABLE 7.1   Collecting action and impact data

METHOD	LEVEL			
	1	2	3	4
Surveys	✔	✔	✔	
Questionnaires	✔	✔	✔	✔
Observation	✔	✔	✔	
Interviews	✔	✔	✔	
Focus groups	✔	✔	✔	
Tests		✔		
Simulations		✔		
Action planning			✔	✔
Performance contracting			✔	✔
Marketing performance monitoring			✔	✔

Questionnaires and Surveys

The questionnaire is the most common method of data collection, whereas surveys are a specific type of questionnaire that captures attitudes, beliefs, and opinions. As discussed in the previous chapter, we can use questionnaires to measure customers' reaction and learning. We can also use questionnaires to obtain subjective information about customer actions, business results, and even ROI analysis. To control for potential bias likely to be associated with the results collected from questionnaires and surveys, it is important to ensure an adequate response rate. For more detail and many useful tips on how to increase and achieve desired response rates, please see our book *Survey Basics*.[7]

Observation

In addition to collecting data at the input, reaction, and learning levels as we discussed in Chapter 6, observation can be used to collect action data at Level 3. For example, marketers from Fisher-Price frequently use observation to monitor children's interactive actions with the toys the organization designs and promotes. The company even has a Fisher-Price Play Lab to accomplish such a task. Observation is also commonly used in internal marketing programs to monitor the extent to which employees use a precise sequence of actions or apply the learned skills as expected after a program.[8]

Interviews

Interviews are another helpful data collection method, which can be used to collect Level 3 data that may be difficult to obtain through questionnaires, observations, or other methods. Interviews may also be used to uncover success stories that can communicate evaluation results. To ensure the effectiveness of this method, interviewers must be skilled in interviewing a variety of individuals and using the probing process to uncover barriers to and enablers of actions and explore success stories.

Focus Groups

Similar to interviews, focus groups are helpful when direct and in-depth feedback is needed. As discussed in Chapter 6, focus groups can be used to collect data at the input, reaction, and learning levels. Additionally, this method can be useful when collecting data at Level 3. It is especially useful when marketers are interested in the following tasks:

- Gauging the overall effectiveness of a marketing program to drive actions
- Identifying the barriers to and enablers of actions that would prevent a successful implementation
- Isolating the impact of the marketing program from other influences

Monitoring Marketing Performance

One of the more important methods of Level 4 data collection is monitoring the organization's business records. Marketing performance data are available in every organization to report impact measures, such as sales revenue and profit, new accounts, product returns, sales cycle time, customer complaints, customer satisfaction, and loyalty. As emphasized in Step 1, "Start with Why," the key is to start with a business impact measure connected to one of the four dimensions of marketing performance. We can then compare it with the actual results of the marketing program. The business impact measures need to be converted to monetary values and isolated for the effects of our marketing programs before calculating the ROI. We will discuss these steps in the next chapters.

Final Thoughts

This chapter focused on Step 5 of the 12-step ROI marketing model. Because many marketing programs fail at Level 3, we explored factors influencing customers' actions. Equipped with this understanding, marketers can choose optimal strategies, tools, templates, and job aids to induce desirable actions and achieve business impact objectives. We reviewed and discussed the alignment model because it connects the needs, the objectives, and the results, which help marketers monitor each stage of their marketing program and make it stick. We also reviewed and compared data collection methods for data collection at different levels. The model, tools, and methods enable marketers to contribute to organizational success through value-creating marketing programs.

8

Make It Credible: Isolate the Effects of the Program

If you cannot show your direct contribution to the business, you have no credibility.

JEFF BEZOS

entech Incorporated is a high-tech company offering software products to customers. The organization operates in the areas of manufacturing, agriculture, pharmaceuticals, building and construction, mining, oil and gas refining, waste and water treatment, and transportation. Additionally, Gentech provides software engineering consulting services to government facilities, data centers, telecommunication companies, utility works, and large hospitals. It serves customers nationwide in seven sales regions through both direct sales force and distribution channel partners. Founded more than 20 years ago by a group of engineers, Gentech has established itself as an industry leader in the marketplace. However, the recent marketing performance of Gentech is far from satisfactory. In the past three years, Gentech has been consistently losing new customers. Last year, the company lost 22 percent of its new customers, and the average customer satisfaction score has reached a new low of 3.2, on a 5-point scale. The number of customer complaints is increasing, and many customers say that the products and services Gentech provides fail to meet their needs. Meanwhile, both the sales revenue and profit margin of Gentech have been shrinking.

The marketing department of Gentech decided to conduct analyses to better understand the issues. The team examined sales records and customer satisfaction data, collecting data from employees through interviews and surveys. The data showed that the total sales revenue of Gentech has been steadily declining over the years, and most sales regions have been struggling to achieve their sales revenue quotas. Sales associates typically do not analyze the customers' situations and requirements and invest no effort into understanding customers' needs when matching the best products to meet those needs. They simply sell what they want to sell.

After this analysis, the marketing department worked with Gentech's learning and training department to test the sales force's knowledge of new products. The results were disappointing, with the average score achieved by the sales associates reported at only 34 out of 100. The highest score was only 62. Not surprisingly, many sales associates were having trouble explaining the features, benefits, and applications of new products.

Basing its next step on these analyses, the marketing department asked Gentech's learning and training specialists to design an internal marketing program. One goal of the program is to improve the sales associates' new product knowledge and the ability to match customers' needs with the proper products. The marketing department also developed tools and job aids for sales associates to better answer customers' questions regarding price, packaging, software implementation, and product warranty. The internal marketing program was implemented in the seven sales regions with the help of regional sales managers. Implementing the program was not easy. The team of trainers had to travel to different sales regions, coordinate with different departments, and deliver the training courses both online and in the classroom. Understanding the importance of this internal marketing program, all trainers worked hard and persisted. After wrapping up all training sessions, they were eager to evaluate the outcomes and results of the program.

The results were mixed at best. Although both the sales associates' test scores and customer satisfaction ratings had increased, the improvements were not significant. Depending on the extent to which regional sales managers were involved, some regions achieved better results than others. Despite this fact, most sales associates who attended the training sessions were satisfied with both the content and the instructors. Still, the number of customer complaints only decreased slightly. In fact, the training team found that the only remarkable change after the internal marketing program was that the total sales revenue of Gentech had increased by 20 percent, a value measured in millions of dollars.

The members of the learning and training team summarized these data in their report and highlighted the sales revenue growth as an important contribution of this internal marketing program. They also emphasized the 20 percent revenue growth as an example of the value creation of their program during their presentation to the Gentech marketing director. The marketing director looked at the PowerPoint slides and made a blunt comment: "Guys, although I am pretty sure your program has created value, the 20 percent revenue growth is probably not part of it." The director paused and then continued. "You may not have heard, but in the past several months, Gentech has been trying to accelerate growth. The 20 percent revenue increase was primarily caused by our startup firm acquisitions."

• • •

It is exciting to see positive results after a program is implemented. Increased sales revenue, improved customer satisfaction, and enhanced employee productivity are all good reasons to be celebrating. Indeed, reporting improvements in marketing performance measures is an important step in our program evaluation, and we should publicize the value created by the program as much as we can. However, before we do all that, we need to ask ourselves one question: "How much of this improvement was the result of our marketing program?" Although the positive changes in impact measures may, in fact, be linked to our marketing program, other factors unrelated to the program may have contributed to the improvement as well. If we fail to answer this question with accuracy and confidence, then we are not addressing this issue. Consequently, the results of our marketing program will lack credibility, and our reputation will be in question.

As discussed in previous chapters, it is critical to isolate the effects of marketing programs from influences of other factors, sometimes significant factors, before we analyze the business impact and estimate the ROI. In this chapter, we explore useful techniques for isolating the effects of a marketing program.

The Importance of Isolating the Contribution

Marketing does not function in a vacuum. In almost every marketing program, multiple factors influence the business impact measures targeted by the program. It is not only important but also imperative to determine the effects of the program, regardless if they are positive or negative, large or small. Without an appropriate step to isolate the effects of the marketing program from other influences, we cannot validate our program's success or, on the other hand, learn from it if the results are not satisfactory. If we attribute the change in the business impact measure entirely to our marketing program, we run the risk of overstating the effects of the program. It is reasonable and legitimate for executives, managers, colleagues, and other stakeholders to question the validity of our conclusion. Their concerns may further jeopardize our ability to compete for funding and support in the future. The pressure is on us to demonstrate the effects of our marketing programs when compared with other potential factors.

Two Preliminary Issues

As highlighted in marketing journals and discussed in previous chapters, the relationship between marketing efforts and performance can be difficult to estimate. It is more challenging to prove the cause-and-effect relationship between our marketing programs and the business performance measured afterward. The estimation process needs to be transparent, to be easy to understand, and to demonstrate itself with a reasonable degree of accuracy. To achieve these goals, we need to first review two important preliminary issues.

Reviewing Chain of Impact

The first issue we review deals with the chain of impact discussed previously. As many of you recall, this framework measures and evaluates the effects of a marketing program at multiple levels. The desired results of a marketing program are typically at the business impact level (Level 4 data), and they should be derived from the actions induced by the program (Level 3 data). Successful actions of the marketing program should stem from customers learning new information and learning to do something different and necessary (Level 2 data). Successful learning usually occurs when customers react favorably or at least pay attention to the content of the marketing program (Level 1 data). The proper reaction can only be realized if the right people are targeted, contacted, and involved in the marketing program at the right time with the right frequency through the right channel (Level 0 data). This preliminary evidence facilitates the step of isolating the effects of a marketing program.

From a practical standpoint, if a marketing program targeted and involved the wrong people (Level 0 mistake), created an adverse reaction (Level 1 mistake) and no learning (Level 2 mistake), or induced no actions afterward (Level 3 mistake), we cannot conclude that any business impact improvements (Level 4 results) were caused by the marketing program. Although it is not required to collect data at all levels for all marketing programs, we do see that, without improvements detected at previous levels, making a connection between the ultimate outcomes and the marketing program is difficult or impossible. Using the chain of impact and data collected at lower levels, marketers have opportunities to establish a chain of evidence that helps establish a direct connection and pinpoint the extent to which their marketing programs have created improvement and value.

Identifying Other Factors

The second preliminary issue that deserves attention, before discussing the methods of isolating the effects, concerns the various factors that may potentially influence the outcomes. Theoretically, as a first step in isolating a program's impact, we should identify all the major key factors that may have contributed to the impact improvement. Practically, this may prove to be difficult because the list of potential influencing factors tends to be lengthy and the total number of relevant factors may be unknown. However, according to the Pareto principle, also known as the 80/20 rule, a minority of factors causes the majority of outcomes, and it is indeed possible to identify these significant factors. Further, this step communicates to interested parties that the marketing program is not the sole source of improvement and that other factors may have influenced the results. Consequently, we share the credit for improvement among several possible factors and multiple sources and are likely to garner the respect of the stakeholders.

Quantitative Isolation Methods

Multiple methods are available to isolate the effects of a program. Some are more credible than others, but none of them is perfect. Marketers need to carefully consider the conditions under which one method is more appropriate than others and be ready to pursue multiple methods to tackle this important issue. In the next sections, we will present two categories of isolation methods, with the most credible approaches presented first.

We discuss several quantitative isolation methods in the following sections, which include experimental design with control groups, trendline analysis, and statistical modeling.

Experimental Design with Control Groups

Many people agree that the most credible approach for isolating the impact of a marketing program is an experimental design with control groups. This approach involves the use of an experimental group that implements the marketing program and a control group that does not. The two groups are ideally from similar markets and with similar characteristics and should be as similar in composition as possible. If feasible, customers and participants for each group should be randomly assigned. The idea is to ensure that both groups are subjected to the same external and internal environmental influences. Thus, any difference in marketing performance between the two groups can only be attributed to the effects of the marketing program.[1]

We demonstrate the experimental design with a control group in Figure 8.1A. As shown in this figure, we implement a marketing program in the experimental group, but not in the control group. For both groups, we measure marketing performance twice. The first measurement is taken before the marketing program is implemented in the experimental group, and the second time is after. Since the only difference between the two groups is the marketing program, by comparing the marketing performances, we can measure the effects of the program.

As illustrated in Figure 8.1B, a simplified version of the experimental design suggests that the control group and experimental group do not necessarily require pre-program measurements. Measurements can be taken during the marketing program and after the marketing program.

FIGURE 8.1A Use of a control group

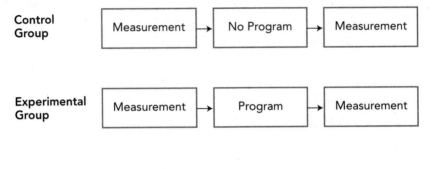

FIGURE 8.1B Use of a control group (simplified version)

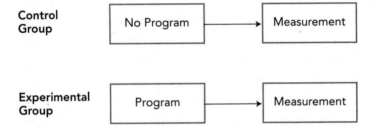

If we have enough reasons to believe that the starting points of the two groups' marketing performance are similar, we can simply compare the difference in marketing performance between the two groups measured after the program and indicate the amount of improvement to be directly related to the marketing program. The simplified version is appropriate when we have historical data to back up our assumption or when we are comparing the sales performance of a newly launched new product, where the starting points for both groups are close to zero.

Figure 8.2 shows the experimental and control group comparison for an internal marketing program conducted by Samsung (China) and Sinotrac Consulting Company to improve new product sales performance. Before the internal marketing program was implemented, both groups had similar average monthly sales performance at roughly 200 units per group. After the internal marketing program implementation, an average salesperson in the experimental group, the group that received training, was able to sell 215 units per month. However, an average salesperson in the control group, the group that did not receive training, was able to sell 205 units per month. Since the groups were similar in all the other characteristics, we can conclude that the difference in success between the two groups was primarily attributed to the internal marketing program.

FIGURE 8.2 Experimental versus control group

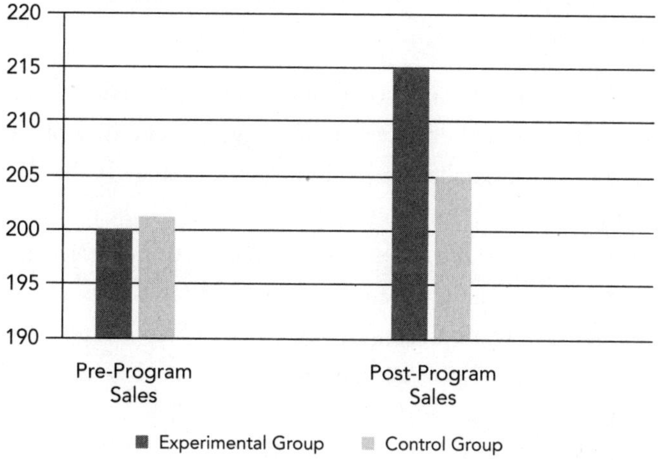

Trend Line Analysis

Another quantitative technique for isolating the effects of marketing programs is trend line analysis. Using this approach, we draw a trend line based on previous performance data to project the future. Then, when the marketing program is fully implemented, we compare the actual marketing performance with the trend line projection. When there is an improvement in marketing performance beyond what the trend line predicted, we attribute it to our marketing program. The trend line analysis is by no means a precise one. However, this process can provide a credible analysis of the marketing program's impact, especially when the experimental design with control group approach is not possible. To use the trend line technique, two conditions must be met:

- First, the trend would have continued on the same path if we had not implemented the marketing program. In other words, we assume that the trend that had developed prior to the marketing program would have continued without the marketing program.
- The second condition is that no other new variables or influences enter the process during the marketing program implementation and evaluation period. The keyword here is "new," which means that the trend has been established with the existing factors, and no additional influences have entered the process beyond the marketing program.

To use this technique, we should have pre-program data, and the data should show a reasonable degree of stability. The stability of the data is important to ensure reliable projection for the future. If the data have a high variance, then the accuracy of the trend line is in question. When the data are stable enough, then the trendline can be projected directly from historical data using a simple formula that is available in many calculators and software packages, such as Microsoft Excel. Figure 8.3 shows a trend line analysis of a marketing program intended to improve sales revenue.

FIGURE 8.3 Trend line analysis of sales revenue

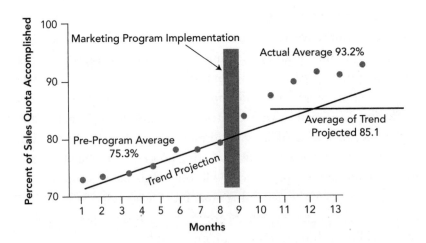

The vertical axis reflects the percentage of sales quota achievement, measured by the YTD sales revenue divided by the YTD quota. The horizontal axis represents time in months. Data reflect sales performance levels before and after a marketing program was implemented in August. As shown in the figure, an upward trend for the data existed prior to the marketing program implementation. The average pre-program quota achievement rate was 75.3 percent, and if the trend continued, it would have achieved 85.1 percent in the last quarter of the year. However, the program apparently had an effect on the sales revenue growth, as the actual average quota achievement was 93.2 percent, much greater than the projected average of 85.1 percent. The difference between the two numbers indicated the impact of the marketing program, which was 8.1 percent.

As another example, a company implemented a marketing program to reduce customer complaints. As Figure 8.4 shows, the percentage of customers who made complaints was 20 percent in January. Although the trend had been downward sloping, the rate was slow. It was estimated that the average percentage of customer complaints would be around 18.5 percent in the first six months of the year, and it would have reached

FIGURE 8.4 Trend line analysis of customer complaints

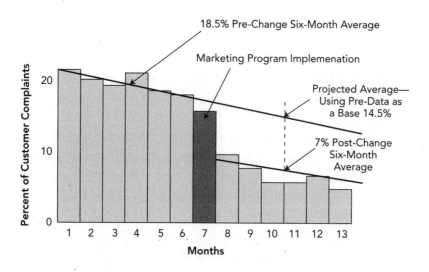

14.5 percent if the trend continued. The company implemented the marketing program in July and saw an immediate drop in the percentage of customer complaints. The actual six-month average of customer complaints was 7 percent, significantly lower than the projected percentage. The amount attributed to the marketing program is 7.5 percent, which equals the difference between 14.5 percent and 7 percent.

Mathematical Modeling

The trendline analysis assumes that there is no other significant variable influencing the outcome measures at the time of the marketing program implementation. However, what if a relevant variable indeed had a significant impact? As environments become increasingly less stable, we are more likely to face this type of challenge than in the past. Under this condition, we may use a statistical modeling method to isolate the effects of our marketing program.

When only one variable influences the outcome measures, we can write the relationship in the form of $y = ax + b$. Using this linear relationship, we can calculate a value of the anticipated performance improvement. In this equation, y represents the outcome, and x represents the variable that influenced the outcome. We assume that the relationship is established, and the mathematical model has been developed to link x to y. With this approach, we forecast the impact measure targeted by our marketing program based on the influence of the variable that has changed during the implementation or evaluation period of the program. We then compare the actual value of the impact with the forecast value, and the difference reflects the contribution of our marketing program.

If this discussion sounds too theoretical, let us use an example to demonstrate the application of the process.[2] A retail store of consumer electronic products is implementing an internal marketing program to enhance its sales associates' prospecting skills through training and role playing. The executives expect this program to help increase the sales volume for each sales associate. As an important measure of the program's success, the store uses the average sales per employee six months after the internal marketing program compared with the same measure prior to the program. We have the following information from the store's managers:

- The average daily sales were $1,100 per employee prior to the internal marketing program.
- Six months after the program, the average daily sales per employee were $1,500.

The difference between the pre-program and post-program daily sales per employee is $400. This means that six months after the internal marketing program was implemented, the daily sales per employee increased by $400. Can we claim the $400 as the impact of our internal marketing program? Before we do that, we need to ask ourselves one question: "Did other factors influence the actual sales level during this period?" Only when the answer is no, can we claim the $400 as program impact. However, after reviewing potential influencing factors, the store executives found that one factor, the level of advertising expenditure, appeared to have changed significantly during the period under consideration. In the month before the internal marketing program, the level of weekly advertising expenditure was $24,000. After the program, the level of weekly advertising expenditure was $30,000. When advertising expenditure goes up, the sales per employee will increase proportionately. Therefore, we cannot ignore the impact of the advertising expenditure changes when isolating the effects of our internal marketing program.

Using historical data stored in company records, marketers of the retail store develop a linear model yielding the following relationship: $y = 140 + 40x$. In this equation, y is the daily sales per employee, and x is the level of advertising expenditure per week (divided by 1,000), whereas the two numbers, 140 and 40, are two constants estimated from historical values. This equation is characterized by a straight line, corresponding to the relationship between the two variables, the level of advertising expenditure, and the daily sales per employee. As shown in Figure 8.5, we estimate the value of y by using the value of x. For example, when the level of weekly advertising expenditure was $24,000, the daily sales per employee were $1,100.

FIGURE 8.5 Forecasting daily sales based on weekly advertising (in $1,000 increments)

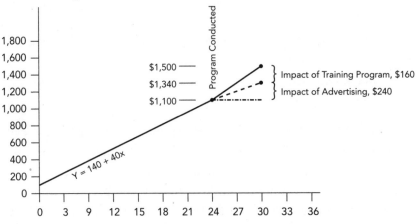

We can now use the relationship and the figure to forecast. For example, the figure shows that when weekly advertising expenditures increase, the daily sales per employee increase as well. Six months after the internal marketing program, the level of weekly advertising expenditures reached $30,000, and the daily sales per employee should be $1,340 as forecasted by the relationship. Since the new actual value is $1,500, the difference of $160 between the forecasted value and actual value ($1,500 – $1,340) must be attributed to the internal marketing program. That difference represents the impact of the training on sales associates' prospecting skills because the skills were not included in the forecasted value.

Qualitative Isolation Methods

Although the quantitative methods introduced above are generally credible and provide meaningful ways to isolate the effects of marketing programs, they may not always be available and will not always work in real-world applications. Sometimes, executives may not approve experiments such as the control group approach in their organizations. Sometimes, we may not have the resources, data, or expertise to run a trendline analysis or statistical models. Under these conditions, qualitative isolation methods serve as valid alternatives, if conducted properly. Although the qualitative approach is potentially weaker than the quantitative methods, it can be credible in many situations, and it can greatly enhance the credibility of the analysis if marketers take adequate precautions. Box 8.1 highlights the general steps to measure attribution using qualitative isolation methods.

Box 8.1   General Steps to Measure Attribution Using Qualitative Isolation Methods

If you find that a measure/indicator has improved, and you want to know how your marketing program influenced the improvement, use these steps:

- Identify the sources of data who know best about the improvement and what may have caused it (most credible sources).
- Decide on the most appropriate data collection method (self-administered questionnaire, action plan, interview, focus group, etc.).
- Ask:

  1. Given the amount of improvement in this measure, what are the factors that you believe have contributed to the improvement (you can leave this question open or provide a list of potential factors based on what you know, and then let the sources add to the list).
  2. Think through or discuss the linkage of each factor to the impact.
  3. As a percentage, how much of the improvement is due to your marketing program?

  _____

  4. On a scale of 0% to 100%, how confident are you that your estimate is accurate (100% = certainty; 0% = no confidence)?

  _____

(continued on next page)

5. Analyze your data using the formula:

A	B	C	D
Start with fact: measure improved	Estimate contribution of the program	Error adjustment (confidence estimate)	Adjusted contribution (A x B x C)
Improvement	%	%	Your program's value contribution

Adapted from Patricia Pulliam Phillips, Jack J. Phillips, Gina Paone, and Cyndi Huff Gaudet. *Value for Money: How to Show the Value for Money for All Types of Projects and Programs in Governments, Nongovernmental Organizations, Nonprofits, and Businesses.* Hoboken, NJ: John Wiley & Sons, 2019.

Essentially, we can divide the potential input for these estimates into four groups. The participants and customers directly involved in the programs are the first and second sources we should consider. If these sources are not available, we may use managers or significant others as other possible sources. Also, internal and external experts may provide insight into the causes of marketing performance improvement. We discuss the four categories of sources in the next sections.

Participants' Estimates of Impact

For many internal marketing programs, the most direct and easily implemented method of isolating the impact of a program is to obtain information from participants during program implementation. Since the participants are involved from beginning to end, experience the program firsthand, and take (or do not take) actions as a result of the program, they are capable of determining or estimating how much of the impact improvement is related to the internal marketing program implementation. Because of the same reasons, they may provide accurate and reliable data at different levels. Although still subjective estimates, the information they provide is likely to carry considerable weight because these participants are at the center of the change or improvement. We obtain the estimates by first defining the improvement and then asking participants to answer a series of questions, such as:

- What other factors have contributed to this improvement in marketing performance?
- What is the link between these factors and the marketing improvement?
- What percentage of this improvement can be attributed to the implementation of this marketing program?
- For each estimate, how much confidence do you have in this estimate, expressed as a percentage? (0 percent = no confidence; 100 percent = complete confidence)
- What other individuals or groups could provide a reliable estimate of this percentage to determine the amount of improvement contributed by this marketing program?

We illustrate this approach using an example of one participant's estimation. As highlighted in Table 8.1, the participant estimated the percentage of improvement caused by each potential factor identified. To ensure a conservative estimate, the participant was then asked to provide a confidence percentage for each value estimated. The confidence percentages reflect the extent to which participants are certain or uncertain about their estimates. For example, an 80 percent confidence suggests

TABLE 8.1 Example of a participant's estimate

FACTOR CAUSING IMPROVEMENT	PERCENTAGE OF IMPROVEMENT CAUSED	CONFIDENCE (%)	ADJUSTED PERCENTAGE OF IMPROVEMENT
Marketing program	40	80	32
Process changes	10	50	5
Environmental changes	40	60	24
Competition changes	10	80	8
Other	—	—	—
Total	100		

that the participant is only 80 percent certain that her answer is accurate, which suggests a potential error range around 20 percent. According to the fourth Guiding Principle, we should be conservative in the analysis and use the lowest estimated number. Therefore, we multiply the estimated value by 80 percent; this practice essentially reduces the number by 20 percent. With this approach, the estimate is multiplied by the confidence to yield the lower side of the range.

In the example highlighted in Table 8.1, the participant allocated 40 percent of the improvement to the marketing program and had a level of confidence in the estimate of 80 percent. The confidence percentage is multiplied by the estimate to produce a usable project value of 32 percent. This adjusted percentage is then multiplied by the actual amount of the improvement (post-program minus pre-program value) to isolate the portion attributed to the marketing program. If the actual amount of the improvement is $1 million, for instance, then the portion attributed to the marketing program is $320,000, using the participant's estimation approach.

Customers' Estimates of Impact

For both consumer marketing and business marketing programs, the target customers of the marketing programs serve as a credible data source for estimation. We may ask them why they chose a particular product or service, or we may ask them to explain how their reaction to the product or service has been influenced by individuals or systems involved in the marketing program. Customer input may constitute the most reliable, powerful, and convincing data if the input is complete, accurate, and valid. An excellent opportunity to collect input directly from customers regarding their reactions to new or improved products and service packages is through routine customer surveys. We can then combine this input with pre-program and post-program marketing and sales performance data to pinpoint the improvements spurred by our marketing program.

For example, a manufacturer recently launched a new high-efficiency furnace to the market.[3] Its marketing department supported the new product using both TV commercials and social media market-ing promotions. Six months after the consumer marketing program was implemented, the new product sales reached 420,000 units. At the same time, several other factors might have contributed to the sales results. One factor was the changing attitudes of the manufacturer's retail chan-nel partners, as they realized this new product offered a higher profit margin than existing products. Additionally, a major competitor suf-fered a product quality issue, and the negative publicity around it made many consumers reluctant to purchase that brand. Finally, the govern-ment was also providing tax incentives to households that purchased the high-efficiency furnace because of its environmental benefits. In essence, all four factors have led to the furnace's sales results of 420,000 units.

The marketing director of the manufacturer conducted a focus group analysis to isolate the impact of the promotional strategy (consisting of TV commercials and social media marketing) from other factors. Specifically, the company randomly selected and recruited 10 consumers who purchased the high-efficiency furnace. A neutral facilitator assisted in sorting out the cause and effect of each factor, following these steps:

- Describe the task to the 10 consumers so that they understand the expectations.
- Explain why the information was needed and how it would be used.
- Ask consumers to identify any other factors that may have con-tributed to their purchase decision.
- Have consumers discuss the link between each factor and their purchase decision.
- Provide consumers with any additional information needed to estimate the contribution of each factor.
- Obtain the actual estimate of the contribution of each factor. The total had to be 100 percent.
- Obtain the confidence level from each consumer for the estimate for each factor (100 percent = certainty; 0 percent = no confidence).

Based on the results of this focus group analysis, the marketing director and his team created a questionnaire to isolate the impact of their marketing program. Using a proper introduction and instruction, the consumers were able to complete the steps on their own without assistance. The questionnaire was sent to randomly selected consumers who purchased the furnace, and 1,000 questionnaires were collected.

The results from this survey were averaged as shown in Table 8.2. The amount attributed to the marketing program was determined by multiplying the percentage for the program factor times the confidence percentage. This, in effect, shows the impact of the marketing program. In this case, the numbers are $420,000 \times 39\% \times 81\% = 132,700$ and suggest that the marketing program has generated approximately 132,700 units of sale after controlling for the other factors.

TABLE 8.2 Consumer estimates for high-efficiency furnace purchase

HIGH-EFFICIENCY FURNACE MARKETING PROGRAM		
CONTRIBUTING FACTORS	AVERAGE IMPACT ON RESULTS	AVERAGE CONFIDENCE LEVEL
Marketing promotion program	39%	81%
Changing attitudes of retailers	11%	77%
Competitor's product quality issue	33%	60%
Incentives from government	12%	72%
Other	5%	85%
	100%	

Managers' Estimates of Impact

Although participants' estimates are preferred for internal marketing programs, this data source may not always be available. If this is the case, the participants' managers or supervisors may be asked to provide input regarding the program's role in improving marketing performance. Under certain conditions, the managers may be more familiar with the overall picture and less biased than the individual participants, and therefore the managers may be better equipped to provide estimates of impact. Both the questions asked and the analysis process for managers should be similar to those for participants. The managers' estimates should also be adjusted by the confidence percentages they reported.

In some settings, we may have collected estimates from both participants and their managers. You may ask which estimate we should use. According to Guiding Principle 3, we should choose the estimate that is more credible than the other, whether it's from participants or managers. If both estimates are equally credible, we should rely on Guiding Principle 4 and choose the most conservative approach by using the lowest value and including appropriate explanation.

Internal or External Experts' Estimates

Under certain conditions, we may choose internal or external experts to estimate the effects of our marketing programs.[4] For example, when the estimates from participants, managers, or customers are unavailable, less credible, or presumably biased, experts' estimates become our last resort of information. To use this technique, we must carefully select experts based on their knowledge of the marketing programs, the market segments, the products, and the situations. For example, an expert in customer service might be able to provide estimates of how much change in a customer satisfaction measure can be attributed to a service improvement program and how much can be attributed to other factors.

Select the Method

Isolating the effect of marketing programs is not an easy task, and selecting the most appropriate method for this task can be difficult. We are blessed with quantitative and qualitative, simple and complex, costly and inexpensive methods. But how do we make the choice? In general, no method is superior under all conditions, and some factors are more conducive for choosing one method over the other. The following factors should be considered when choosing among different methods:

- Credibility of the method with the target audience
- Feasibility of the method
- Accuracy associated with the method
- Cost to implement the method
- Amount of disruption in normal work activities associated with the method
- Time required for the method[5]

One way to ensure credibility and improve the accuracy of an isolating effects approach is to use multiple methods. Usually, two or more methods are better than one. Using multiple methods enables us to examine different aspects of the issue and allows an organization to experiment with different strategies and build confidence in the use of a particular technique. For example, if managers are concerned about the accuracy of participants' estimates, they may choose to combine the participants' estimates method with a control group arrangement and check the accuracy of the estimation process.

When we use multiple methods, we should choose the most credible method for ROI calculation. If they are all credible, then we should use the most conservative one, the one with the lowest value, in the calculation. We should always provide the target audience with adequate explanations of the process and the requirements. The audience, including management, should understand that even though the results might still be subject to error, we have made every effort to isolate our marketing program's impact. No matter which method or methods we choose, the result represents the best estimate of the impact given the constraints, conditions, and resources available.

Final Thoughts

Isolating the effects of a marketing program is an important step in answering the question of how much of the improvement in an impact measure was due to our program. Too often, however, marketers report and link results to their marketing programs with no attempt to isolate the real effects associated with the program. This practice leads to inaccurate evaluation and damages our credibility. As discussed in this chapter, we need to address the issue and isolate the effects early in the process for all major marketing programs. Without doing this, we lose respect, commitment, support, and funding. We presented multiple quantitative and qualitative approaches in this chapter to help marketers address this important issue. These methods are effective, are relatively easy to use, and have been implemented by some of the most progressive organizations. We also offered suggestions to marketers regarding how to select the most appropriate methods for their programs. After completing this important step, marketers must convert the data to monetary values, which we will discuss in the next chapter.

9

Make It Credible: Convert Data to Monetary Value and Identify Intangible Measures

Rod Tidwell: *Whatcha gonna do, Jerry?*
Jerry Maguire: *Show me the money!*
Rod Tidwell: *Unh! Congratulations, you're still my agent.*
JERRY MAGUIRE (1996) BY CAMERON CROWE

Global Engineering Company (GEC) is a major developer of low-power, high-definition (HD), and ultra-HD video compression and image processing solutions. The company produces system-on-chip (SoC) video chips and offers six different types of products to original design manufacturers and original equipment manufacturers nationwide through its direct sales force of 80 field salespeople. The company's products are used in a variety of professional and consumer applications, which include IP (internet protocol) security cameras, automotive cameras, flying cameras, sports cameras, wearable cameras, and broadcast infrastructure solutions. Some of GEC's target customers are GoPro, a leading maker of wearable sports cameras, and Ubiquiti Networks, a leading maker of IP security cameras. The field salespeople of GEC are responsible for both selling the products and providing professional services and technical support after customers' purchases.

In the past year or so, however, Michael, the vice president of sales at GEC, has noticed some changes. While the company is still growing, the rate of growth has started to slow down. Meanwhile, many of the company's competitors have grown at a much faster pace in this lucrative industry.

Another disturbing trend also draws his attention. GEC has been losing new business at an increasing rate. Finally, and this is the greatest concern for Michael, there are increasingly more complaints from customers about late orders, poor product quality, and lower levels of customer service quality than in the past. Michael is uncertain about how to improve the performance, so he decides to conduct some analyses.

Michael first reviews business records, and the data confirm his concerns. Specifically, the annual growth rate of GEC has dropped from 12 percent three years ago to 5 percent today, while the industry still grows at 10 percent annually. Similarly, both the number of contracts lost and the number of customer complaints doubled compared with the numbers three years ago. Additionally, the sales force turnover rate has increased from 10 percent per year to 30 percent per year.

His analyses also reveal the following:

1. Many GEC managers have strong science and engineering backgrounds, and they are comfortable hiring marketing specialists and salespeople with similar capabilities and experiences. Their training focuses more on the technical features of the products offered by GEC rather than a discussion with the customer.

2. Most customers are satisfied with GEC's established products, but unhappy with the company's new products because "they are too complex." Customers also complained that they are unable to get technical support from GEC salespeople, their phone calls were "never" returned, and their service requests were "never" answered. Some customers were asking why GEC did not hire more salespeople.

3. According to company sales reports, GEC salespeople have been working hard. Many salespeople complain that since the new products offered by GEC have become increasingly complex and there are strong demands from customers for technical support, they are struggling to balance providing personal selling and technical support services.

4. Industry data show that major competitors such as Ambarella, Maxim Integrated, Texas Instruments, and NXP Semiconductors N.V. have created in-house customer support centers to provide technical support and coordinate service efforts. Other companies such as Infineon Technologies AG and STMicroelectronics have established national key account teams to provide better service to important customers.

Michael understands that he is facing a tough situation and feels like his platform is on fire. Therefore, he hires a performance consulting firm for help. The consulting firm uses a systematic approach to assess the situation, analyze causes, and design solutions. It has also developed tools and techniques for all stages of the performance improvement process. Working as partners with consultants from the firm, Michael and members from different departments of GEC implement a marketing performance improvement project. This project involves multiple solutions, which include an internal marketing program to educate employees on the importance of customer focus. Michael also creates a national key account team and a customer service center, and he modifies the employees' performance evaluation criteria and reward scheme to reflect new priorities, as part of the efforts to address GEC's marketing performance issues systemically.

The marketing performance improvement project generates encouraging results and closes the performance discrepancies across the board. Six months after implementing the solutions, sales revenues of GEC's new products increase by 10 percent. Also, marketing data show that the number of contracts lost and the number of customer complaints are reduced by 30 percent and that the sales force turnover rate has been reduced by 20 percent. Michael is thrilled by the numbers and wants to place a monetary value on the outcomes before discussing the results with the CEO and other board members of GEC.

To ensure the credibility of the estimates, Michael understands that he needs to answer the question, "How much of this improvement is actually caused by the project?" Using suggestions from the consulting firm, Michael isolates the effects of the marketing performance project by utilizing estimations from participants, customers, and managers. This analysis follows the procedures introduced in Chapter 8 and increases the credibility of the estimations.

Michael is glad to see that the outcomes reflect improvements in multiple dimensions of marketing performance, including financial, activity, customer, and talent. All these dimensions are critical to GEC's strategies and organizational goals. Recall the marketing performance FACTs model discussed in Chapter 3. However, he still wants to place a specific monetary value on the total contribution of this important marketing performance improvement project. After all, both the CEO and CFO care about value and return on investment. Michael is wondering how he can convert improvements, such as the reduced number of complaints and lower employee turnover rates, to monetary value. Additionally, he is wondering how to estimate the total costs to calculate the ROI of the marketing performance improvement project.

• • •

The opening story illustrates an important trend, as executives and managers attempt to convert the hard-to-measure business outcomes of their programs to money. Across industries, executives, consciously and subconsciously, want marketers to show them the money.[1] To show the real money, marketers need to convert the improvement in impact measures that are attributable to the program (after isolating the effects of the program) to monetary values, which are then compared with program costs to calculate ROI. The monetary value is a way, if not the only way, for marketers to show executives the importance of business impact measures typically not converted to money. This represents the ultimate level in the five-level evaluation framework. In this chapter, we will demonstrate how marketers can develop monetary values, which can be used in the ROI calculation later.

Why Convert Data to Monetary Values?

It is not always clear to marketing managers why we need to convert business impact data to monetary values. After all, we can claim our marketing programs to be successful as long as we are able to demonstrate that the benefits created by our program exceed its costs, after isolating the effects properly. For example, an improvement in customer satisfaction, employee loyalty, product quality, or service quality could represent a significant benefit linked directly to a marketing program. However, this may not suffice for many executives, administrators, and sponsors, because they require actual monetary value corresponding to a marketing program. It is therefore in the interests of the marketing professionals to take the extra step of converting improvement to money.

Converting Improvement to Money Normalizes the Definition of Value

According to the FACTs framework described in Chapter 3, marketing performance has four important dimensions, reflecting the financial, activity, customer, and talent aspects of marketing outcomes. However, in the eyes of most executives, monetary value is still one of the primary criteria of success. Normalizing values from all dimensions into a common measure makes the process of resource allocation less difficult and defines value in a more impressive way.

Converting Improvement to Money Highlights the Contribution of Marketing

For some marketing programs, the business impact is more understandable and an easier way to highlight the contribution of marketing when it is stated in terms of monetary value. For example, consider the impact of a program aimed at improving an organization's customer relationship management (CRM) system.[2] Since a CRM system involves many departments and employees, the marketing program is likely to have an impact on most parts of the organization. The best and least confusing way to understand the value of this marketing program is to convert the outcomes and performance, at all dimensions, to monetary values.

Converting Improvement to Money Clarifies the Cost Issues

With the drive to gain sustainable competitiveness and to improve the efficiency of marketing management, awareness of the costs related to processes and activities is essential. Based on our experience, marketing programs may benefit an organization either through increasing revenue or through cost reductions or cost avoidance. Therefore, it is essential to understand the cost of a problem and the payoff of the corresponding solutions. Also, clarifying cost issues associated with marketing performance issues is important for budgeting and organizational operations.

Five Key Steps in Converting Data to Money

Converting data to monetary values involves the following five steps:

1. **Focus on a unit of measure.** First, we must define a unit of measure. The unit of measure can be a unit of product sold, one customer complaint resolved, one sales proposal submitted, or one error avoided. The unit of measure can also be time, such as the time to develop a new product, to deliver a product, or to process a customer request.

2. **Determine the value of each unit.** The second step involves placing a value (V) on the unit identified in the first step. We will describe multiple techniques in this chapter and provide an array of approaches for making this conversion.

3. **Calculate the change in performance data.** The third step of this approach involves calculating the change in marketing performance data. We label this incremental change as Δ, denoting that it is the performance improvement directly attributable to the marketing program, represented as the Level 4 business impact measure.

4. **Determine the annual amount of change.** We then annualize the Δ value and develop a value for the total change in the marketing performance data for one year (ΔP). For most short-term solutions, we only use the first-year benefits, even when the marketing program produces benefits beyond one year. This practice ensures our estimation to be conservative and credible.

5. **Calculate the annual value of the improvement.** As the fifth step, we calculate the total value of improvement by multiplying the annual performance change (ΔP) by the unit value (V) for the complete focal group. We then compare this value for annual program benefits with the costs of the marketing program to calculate the ROI.[3]

We use an example to demonstrate how we may use the five-step process to convert data to monetary values. In our example, a trucking company developed a marketing program to address a customer satisfaction crisis, as the company was experiencing an excessive number of complaints caused by inadequate or improper deliveries. Six months after program implementation, the total monthly number of customer complaints had declined by 25. After isolating the effects and following the five-step approach, we are able to calculate the total monetary value of the marketing program to be $228,000. We show details of the steps in Box 9.1.

Box 9.1 Converting Customer Complaint Data to Monetary Values

Setting. A business-to-business marketing program to address customer complaints for a trucking company.

Step 1: Define the unit of measure. The unit of measure is defined as one customer complaint based on delivery service.

Step 2: Determine the value (V) of each unit. According to internal experts (i.e., the customer care staff), the cost of an average customer complaint in this category was estimated at $1,500, when time and direct costs are considered ($V = \$1,500$).

Step 3: Calculate the change (Δ) in performance data. Six months after the project was completed, the average complaints per month had declined by 25. Sixty-five percent of the reductions were related to the project, as determined by the frontline customer service staff ("Isolating project impact"), with an average confidence of 78 percent. Use the six-month value of

$$25 \times 65\% \times 78\% = 12.7 \text{ per month}$$

Step 4: Determine an annual amount for the change (ΔP). The monetary amount is multiplied by 12 (months) to yield an annual improvement value of

$$12.7 \times 12 = 152$$
$$\Delta P = 152$$

Step 5: Calculate the annual value of the improvement.

Annual value = $\Delta P \times V$

= 152 x $1,500 = $228,000

Methods to Convert Impact Measures to Money

The five steps to convert a business impact measure to monetary value are straightforward and easy to understand, but the challenge is to follow them properly in complex situations. Out of the five steps, many marketers find Step 2, determining the value, to be particularly challenging. In the following sections, we discuss a variety of techniques that can be used to determine value. These techniques range from standard monetary values to the use of conservative estimates.

Standard Monetary Values

The first technique is using standard value, which is a monetary value assigned to a unit of measurement acceptable to executives and key stakeholders. Often, standard values are the measures that matter to marketing and the organization, that reflect problems or improvement opportunities, and that correspond to one or more dimensions of marketing performance we discussed in the FACTs framework. In Table 9.1, we show a list of sales and marketing measures that are often calculated and reported as standard values.[4] As you can see in the figure, some of these measures are related to financial performance (e.g., sales revenue and profit margin), customer performance (e.g., retention rate and churn rate), and activity performance (e.g., workload and inventories).

TABLE 9.1 Examples of standard values from sales and marketing

METRIC	DEFINITION	CONVERSION NOTES
Sales revenue	The sale of the product or service recorded in a variety of different ways: by product, by time period, by customer	The data must be converted to monetary value by applying the profit margin for a particular sales category
Profit margin (%)	The difference between sales revenue and cost for the product, customer, and time period as a percentage of sales revenue	Factored to convert sales to monetary value-add to the organization
Unit margin	Unit price less unit cost	Shows the value of incremental sales
Channel margin	Channel profits as a percentage of channel selling price	Used to show the value of sales through a particular marketing channel
Retention rate	Ratio of customers retained to the number of customers at risk of leaving	The value is the saving of the money necessary to acquire a replacement customer
Churn rate	Ratio of customers leaving to the number who are at risk of leaving	The value is the saving of the money necessary to acquire a new customer
Customer profit	The difference between the revenues earned from and the cost associated with the customer relationship during the specified period	The monetary value added is the profit obtained from customers, which all goes toward the bottom line
Customer lifetime value	The present value of the future cash flows attributed to the customer relationship	Bottom line; as customer value increases, it adds directly to the profits; as a customer is added, the incremental value is the customer lifetime average
Cannibalization rate	The percentage of new product sales taken from existing product lines	This is to be minimized, as it represents an adverse effect on existing product, with the value added being the loss of profits due to the sales loss

METRIC	DEFINITION	CONVERSION NOTES
Workload	Hours required to service clients and prospects	This includes the salaries, commissions, and benefits from the time the sales staff spends on the workloads
Inventories	The total amount of product or brand available for sale in a particular channel	Since inventories are valued at the cost of carrying the inventory, costs involve space, handling, and the time value of money; insufficient inventory is the cost of expediting the new inventory or the loss of sales because of the inventory outage
Market share	Sales revenue as a percentage of total market sales in an industry	Actual sales are converted to money through the profit margins, as a measure of competitiveness
Loyalty	The length of time the customer stays with the organization, the willingness to pay a premium, and the willingness to search	Calculated as the additional profit from the sale or the profit on the premium

Many internal marketing programs focus on improving talent performance, measures of employee-related improvement. Examples of talent performance measures include time saved, productivity improved, and employee turnover rate reduced. There are two ways we may utilize the standard value technique to determine the value creation. First, we can use employees' compensation, including salary and commission, to convert employee time to monetary value. For example, an internal marketing program implemented in a sales department saved an average of 74 minutes per day for a salesperson based on the estimates. Based on the average salary plus commission and bonus for a typical salesperson, the time of 74 minutes could be worth $31.25 per day, or $7,500 per year. The second way considers the fact that talent performance of employees may have profound effects on other dimensions of marketing performance such as financial or customer outcomes. For example, a marketing performance improvement project conducted by Sinotrac in China reduced the time an average salesperson spends in one retail store by 12 minutes. Because of this improvement, this salesperson is able to visit more stores and sell more merchandise, translating into $1,150 additional sales revenue for the client per year.

Using Historical Costs and Records

When standard values are not readily available, we have several alternative strategies for converting data to monetary values. One of them is using historical costs from records, which is a strategy that relies on identifying the appropriate records and tabulating the proper cost components for the item in question. Historical records can indicate the cost of a measure and the value of a unit of improvement. For example, historical data may show how much one customer complaint or 1 percent of employee turnover costs the organization. We can then use the historical costs to convert customer complaints and employee turnover reduction to monetary values.

Using Input from Internal and External Experts

When historical cost data are not available, we may consider inputs from experts on the marketing program to convert data items to monetary values. We can find internal experts in the departments in which the data originate. Internal experts are individuals who have knowledge of the situation and have the confidence of management. They must be willing to provide both the estimates and assumptions behind them. If we have reason to believe that the internal experts are biased regarding the measures or if the measures are not available, we can seek input from external experts. These external experts can be consultants, professionals, and suppliers in a particular area. For example, we may invite CRM experts to provide estimates on a marketing program addressing customer relationship issues.

Using Values from External Databases

For some measures, it may be appropriate to use the cost (or value) estimates based on the work and research of other individuals or institutions. This technique utilizes external databases that contain studies and research programs focusing on the cost of data items. The good news is that many databases include cost studies of data items related to marketing programs, and most are accessible on the internet. Data are available on the costs or value of customer complaints, customer lifetime value, brand equity, service quality, service failure, service recovery, new product failures, employee turnover, and even employee satisfaction. The challenge is to find a database with studies or research on a particular marketing program. Ideally, we will use data that originated from a similar setting in the same industry, but that is not always possible. Sometimes, data from other industries or organizations are appropriate and sufficient with potential adjustments to suit the focal marketing program.

Linking with Other Measures

If none of the standard values, records, experts, or external studies is available, we still have other feasible alternatives. One technique is known as linking with other measures. This method attempts to find a relationship between the focal measure and some other measures that can be easily converted to a monetary value. This technique involves first identifying existing relationships that show a strong correlation between one measure and another with a standard value and then estimating the monetary value of the focal measure indirectly but reliably. An example related to the talent performance of marketing outcomes is the negative correlation between job satisfaction and employee turnover. Suppose that after implementing an internal marketing program to enhance job satisfaction, we need to find a value to reflect changes in job satisfaction measures. Although a standard value for job satisfaction improvement is not available, we are aware of a predetermined relationship between increases in job satisfaction and reductions in turnover that directly link the two measures. Using standard data or external studies, we can determine the cost of turnover. Therefore, through the connection between turnover and job satisfaction, we can immediately convert a change in job satisfaction to a monetary value, or at least an approximate value.

Using Estimates from Customers, Participants, and Management

If none of the techniques we have introduced is available, as a last resort, we may rely on subjective estimates from customers and participants of internal marketing programs to convert the data to monetary value. This technique is appropriate when these individuals are capable of providing estimates of the cost (or value) of the unit of measure that has improved as a result of the marketing programs. To use this approach, it is important to provide customers and participants with clear instructions, along with examples of the type of information needed. The advantage of this approach is that the individuals, including both customers and participants, are most closely connected to the improvement and therefore may be able to provide the most reliable estimate of its value. Similar to isolating program effects, when we use subjective estimates to convert measures to monetary values, we need to make adjustments to reduce and control the error in those estimates.

In other situations, we may ask managers to review the estimates of customers, approve those of participants, and confirm, adjust, or reject those values. For example, a European pharmaceutical company designed a marketing program involving customer service representatives to reduce customer complaints. The program resulted in a reduction in complaints, but the company realized that it had to identify the value of a single customer complaint to determine the value of the improvement. Although customer service representatives knew certain issues surrounding customer complaints, their scope was limited, and their opinions might be biased. Therefore, the company asked its managers to provide the value. These managers had a broader perspective of the impact of a customer complaint, including the damage to the brand, and were able to provide estimates that were more accurate and reliable.

Guidelines for Selecting the Technique(s)

It is a blessing when we have so many techniques available, but it is a challenge to select one or more techniques appropriate for the situation and resources at hand. We have developed the following guidelines to help you with selecting a technique and finalizing the value. These guidelines come from our experiences with a variety of ROI evaluations. More detail on technique selection is available in the books and papers we've published.[5]

- Choose a technique appropriate for the type of data.
- Move from most accurate to least accurate.
- Consider data source availability and time.
- Use the source with the broadest perspective on the issue.
- Use multiple techniques when feasible.

To Convert or Not to Convert Data to Monetary Values

To convert or not to convert, this is a decision that deserves marketers' careful consideration at this step of the ROI Methodology. The assumption that each data item collected and linked to a marketing program can be and should be converted to monetary value is probably overly optimistic. It is especially dubious when highly subjective data, such as attitude change and perceived service quality improvement, are involved. This question posits potential risks for marketers. If the target audience and stakeholders sense that the estimates lack credibility, then they may find the whole process and the claimed contributions of our marketing programs questionable. To help marketers be better prepared to make this decision, we propose a four-stage test to deal with four important and sensitive issues. As illustrated in Figure 9.1, this test serves as a logical way to decide whether to convert data to monetary values or leave them as intangibles.

FIGURE 9.1 **A four-stage test: to convert or not to convert**

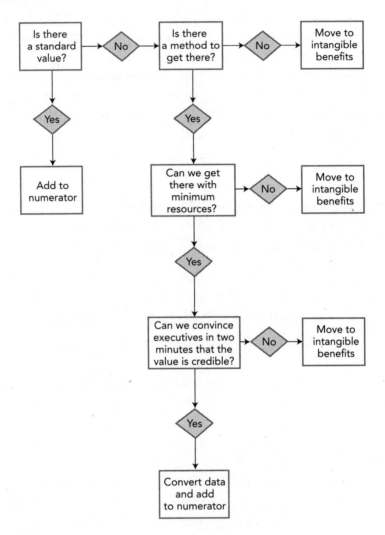

Identifying the Intangibles

In the ROI Methodology, we define intangibles as impact measures not converted to money because either the conversion would require too many resources, or the result would not be credible, or we choose not to convert the measures due to strategic reasons. Box 9.2 illustrates some typical examples from the vast number of possible intangibles in marketing.

Box 9.2   Typical Intangible Measures Linked with Marketing Programs

- Innovation
- Service quality
- Organizational climate
- Engagement
- Job satisfaction
- Organizational culture
- Brand awareness
- Brand image
- Brand personality
- Marketing effectiveness

- Creativity
- Attitude
- Customer satisfaction
- Customer loyalty
- Customer relationship
- Communication
- Cooperation
- Social responsibility
- Sustainability
- Marketing agility

The Importance of Intangibles

The way intangibles are defined may give people the impression that intangibles are not important. Unlike tangible assets, intangibles are invisible, difficult to quantify, and not tracked through traditional accounting practices. In contrast, tangible assets are required for business operations; they are readily visible, rigorously quantified, and routinely represented as line items on balance sheets. In reality, however, intangible assets are the key to competitive advantage and organizational success. As shown in Box 9.2, intangibles cover strategically important factors behind many well-known organizations' success. A highly innovative company continually develops new products and creative services. An organization with a strong culture and committed employees can develop marketing effectiveness and customer loyalty. A company that fulfills its social responsibilities enjoys a favorable brand image and sustainable competitive advantage. Intangibles are not only increasingly important but also critical to organizations.

Some items in Box 9.2, such as customer satisfaction, are classic intangibles. The good news is that more data once regarded as intangible are now being converted to monetary values. Customer satisfaction is an example of this. Over a decade ago, few organizations knew how to estimate the monetary value of customer satisfaction. Now more firms have taken the extra step to link customer satisfaction directly to financial outcomes such as revenue, profit, and other measures. For some marketing programs, customer satisfaction has moved into the tangible category. Meanwhile, more executives recognize the importance of intangibles and invest in projects like green marketing and cause marketing, primarily for the intangibles. They intentionally include a string of intangibles on their scorecards, operating reports, key performance indicators, and other reporting systems, and highlight these intangibles to customers and stakeholders. For many organizations, intangibles have become the dominant investment in the business.

Measuring Intangible Benefits

As we discussed, in some marketing programs, intangibles are more important than monetary measures. Therefore, we should monitor and report these measures as part of the evaluation process. In practice, all marketing programs will produce intangible measures. We should also monitor and report them as supplemental evidence of value creation. Several approaches are available for measuring intangibles. If the intangibles are customer complaints and conflicts, we can count the numbers. Most intangibles, however, are not things that can be counted, examined, and seen in quantities, but scholars have developed a variety of measurement scales so that we can assign a quantitative value to almost any intangible. For example, to connect the intangibles to a marketing program, we may ask a simple question: To what extent did this marketing program influence each of these measures? A 5-point or 7-point scale can be used for collecting responses from customers, participants, or managers. Other approaches include connecting soft measures to hard measures and developing indexes of different values. More details of these approaches can be found in the literature.[6]

Final Thoughts

In this chapter, we continued the discussion on key issues in making the evaluation of our marketing program credible. One issue discussed extensively involves converting business data to monetary values, after isolating the effects as discussed in the previous chapter. Regardless of the type of data, several techniques can help convert the data to monetary values to use in the ROI calculation. During this process, we need to follow several principles to ensure the results are both conservative and credible. If the benefits cannot or should not be converted to monetary value, we need to estimate the intangible benefits. Both converting business data to monetary value and estimating intangible benefits are important steps of the ROI Methodology. We will continue the discussion on key issues related to making results credible in the next chapter.

10

Make It Credible: Capture Costs of Program and Calculate ROI

The modern marketer is: an experimenter,
a lover of data, a content creator, and a justifier of ROI.

KIMBERLEY WALSH

Continuing the opening story in Chapter 9, Global Engineering Company (GEC) was facing serious challenges with issues related to financial, activity, customer, and talent performance. Michael, the VP of sales, and his team launched a marketing performance improvement project to address these issues. Using the ROI Methodology, the team started with the end in mind with the business measure of improved marketing performance along the four dimensions as the desired outcomes. The solutions included training the sales force, creating a key account team and a customer service center, and modifying the reward plan to focus on customer service. Six months later, there are signs of improvement across the board. Michael decides to estimate the monetary value of the improvement and calculate the ROI of this marketing project before discussing it with the GEC executive team.

Following the ROI Methodology, Michael and his team collect data at the four levels including reaction, learning, action, and business impact to measure and estimate the value created by this program. The data are collected from both GEC employees and customers to have a comprehensive assessment of the progress, whereas the business impact data are collected from sales records, reports, and customer surveys.

- **Reaction, Level 1.** At the reaction level, GEC conducts interviews and survey research to find how salespeople and customers react to the program. Specifically, salespeople are asked to what extent they find the program useful, easy to implement, and important to their work and performance. The team also asks the customers to assess the GEC employees' service and GEC products. Additionally, customers are asked to what extent they find the key account team and customer service center to be relevant, important, and helpful for improving their purchasing experience and adding value to their business.

- **Learning, Level 2.** The marketing performance improvement program involves a sales training component. After the training sessions, salespeople are tested on their knowledge of GEC products and service procedures. Role plays and observations are used to assess selling and customer service skills. The program also involves establishing a customer service center. To test customer learning, the GEC evaluation team conducts interviews and surveys to assess how many customers are aware of the assistance available at the service center and know how to utilize the customer service center to have their issues addressed and problem solved.

- **Action, Level 3.** The action-level data collected from the salespeople focus on the extent to which they apply the knowledge and skills they learned to provide professional services to customers. The data are collected through sales reports and managers' observations. The GEC team also assesses customers' actions by measuring the number of emails and phone inquiries received as well as the customers' interactions with salespeople through survey studies.
- **Business Impact, Level 4.** The data at the business impact level include sales revenue, number of customer complaints, number of lost orders, and employee turnover rate. The GEC team collects the data from company records.

Table 10.1 explains how the chain of impact works for this marketing performance improvement program with the results measured at different levels.[1]

To convert the improvements at the business impact level to monetary value, Michael and his team use the five-step approach by defining the unit of measure, determining the value of each unit, calculating the incremental changes, annualizing the changes, and calculating the total value. For financial performance, the team uses sales revenue in dollars as the unit of measure. The number of lost orders and the number of customer complaints are used as the units of measure for activity performance and customer performance, respectively. For talent performance, the number of voluntary turnovers of employees is used as the unit of measure. For each unit of measure, a standard value is used to determine the monetary value of the improvement. The improvements along the financial, activity, customer, and talent dimensions are isolated to reflect the true contribution of the marketing performance improvement program and annualized to determine the annual amount of change. This five-step approach shows that the total monetary value generated for the program over one year totals $3.58 million, an impressive number.

Had the evaluation stopped at that point, Michael and his team would be celebrating this impressive achievement and milestone. However, Michael wants to see the cost of the program before discussing it with

TABLE 10.1 Types and levels of data

		GEC MARKETING PERFORMANCE IMPROVEMENT PROJECT		
TYPE OF DATA	DATA COLLECTION METHOD	DATA SOURCES	TIMING	RESULTS
Reaction (Level 1)	Survey Interview	Employees	At the end of sales training	4.6 out of 5 rating on usefulness, ease of use, and importance
	Survey	Customers	One month after the program launch	4.4 out of 5 rating on salespeople's service and GEC products
Learning (Level 2)	Quiz Role play	Employees	At the end of sales training	88 out of 100 points on product knowledge 7 out of 10 on selling skills
	Survey	Customers	One month after the program launch	90% of customers are aware of the existence of the customer service center; 65% of customers know how to contact the center and get their problems solved
Action (Level 3)	Reports Records	Employees	Three months after the program launch	76% of salespeople are applying the new selling skills when interacting with customers
	Observation	Customers	Three months after the program launch	48% of customers contact the service center, and 39% of customers have their problems resolved

	GEC MARKETING PERFORMANCE IMPROVEMENT PROJECT			
TYPE OF DATA	DATA COLLECTION METHOD	DATA SOURCES	TIMING	RESULTS
Business impact (Level 4)	Monitor financial, activity, customer, and talent performance	Company records	Routinely	$3.58 million in one year
Cost	Monitor records	Cost statements	Routinely	$3.97 million cost in one year
ROI (Level 5)				–9.8%
Intangibles	Questionnaire	Employees	Quarterly	Increased commitment to the organization, engagement, employee satisfaction, and teamwork
		Customers	Quarterly	Increased customer satisfaction with GEC products and salespeople, loyalty, willingness to purchase, willingness to recommend GEC to others

the top management team. Following the Guiding Principles of the ROI Methodology, Michael and his team consider both direct and indirect costs during the process. The total cost includes the administrative cost, the salaries of the staff and their operating expenses, the bonus and commissions to employees, and any upfront development costs associated with the marketing program. When all costs are tallied, the total cost for the program comes to $3.97 million. Because the total costs exceed the monetary benefits of $3.58 million, there is a negative ROI:

$$\text{ROI (\%)} = \frac{\$3,580,000 - \$3,970,000}{\$3,970,000} \times 100 = -9.8\%$$

Michael and his team are very disappointed with the negative results and engage in a heated discussion. Many team members argue that although the ROI is negative, GEC should continue the program because of the intangible benefits it generated, such as employees' organizational commitment and customer loyalty. While this logic may be feasible for some marketing programs, Michael emphasizes that it does not work with this one. Because the nature of this program is based on enhancing profitability and growth through improving activity, customer, and talent performance, it will not be suitable to lose money on this program. Michael reminds the members of the team that they have an objective for a positive ROI, noting, "Although we didn't set a precise value for the ROI, we wanted it to create more value than it costs."

Two team members suggest a reassessment of the cost analysis. They distinguish the total cost into a direct cost component, which includes expenses directly related to the marketing program, and an indirect cost component, which includes the administrative cost of half a million dollars. They argue that the indirect cost has been allocated arbitrarily and is therefore misleading. Instead, they suggest that the team should focus on the difference between monetary value and the direct cost, which they label as the contribution margin of the marketing program.[2] They cite marketing and sales management books and literature to show the relevance and superiority of the contribution margin approach to the full cost approach. They show that if only direct costs are included, the cost of the program is $3.47 million, and the ROI will be positive:

$$\text{ROI (\%)} = \frac{\$3,580,000 - \$3,470,000}{\$3,470,000} \times 100 = 3.2\%$$

Michael acknowledges the importance of the contribution margin approach in marketing and sales management. However, he points out that the ROI Methodology follows conservative guidelines. Specifically, according to Guiding Principle 10, the costs of the solution should be fully loaded for ROI. Therefore, Michael insists to have both direct and indirect costs included for the ROI calculation and encourages the team to see where adjustments can be made to lower the program costs. The team conducts a systemic analysis and finds that there are too many staff members working at the customer service center. It appears, based on the data collected over two weeks, that the staff is only about 25 percent utilized in the newly established service center. Michael concludes that the service center can eliminate 50 percent of the positions without lowering service quality and job performance. He places the "eliminated" employees in open positions in the organization so that no one will lose his or her job. This reduces the costs by almost $1 million. With the new costs at $3.01 million, the ROI is positive:

$$\text{ROI (\%)} = \frac{\$3,580,000 - \$3,010,000}{\$3,010,000} \times 100 = 18.9\%$$

This story highlights three important issues in ROI analysis. First, unless we push the evaluation to the ROI level, we will not see the ultimate value and accountability of our marketing program. The monetary value may be impressive, but the value is discounted if the costs are very high. Second, if the ROI calculation generates a negative number, it does not mean the marketing program should be discontinued. Marketers should strive to adjust the program to deliver the desired value. Both the intangible benefits and strategic importance of the business impacts need to be considered to make the program adjustments in a comprehensive and strategic way. More importantly, a systemic analysis may be needed to identify the areas that can potentially be improved. Third, although the contribution margin approach is relevant and desirable,

225

and is often considered superior to the full cost approach in marketing and sales management, the ROI Methodology mandates we include both direct and indirect costs in the ROI calculation. This approach is consistent with the Guiding Principles and ensures that the ROI calculation is conservative and credible and that the results of our ROI analysis are comparable to those in other ROI studies and the literature.

In this chapter, we discuss the various techniques, processes, and issues involved in calculating and interpreting the ROI.

The Importance of Costs and ROI

One of the main reasons for monitoring costs is to create budgets for marketing programs. We usually estimate the initial costs of most marketing programs during the proposal process. These estimations are often based on the costs of previous programs. It is necessary to have a clear understanding of costs so that we can use that information to determine the costs of future marketing programs and future budgets. One way to make this task easier is to track costs using different categories, which we will explain later in this chapter.

Tabulating the Costs of the Program

Tabulating the costs of a marketing program is important for the following reasons. First, the cost of marketing programs has been skyrocketing. Today, corporate America spends hundreds of billions of dollars on various marketing activities each year. Second, many executives need to know the total cost of a marketing program, pushing the cost profile beyond direct costs to include indirect costs as well. Both trends increase the pressure for marketing managers and professionals to know how, where, and why money is spent. Third, we define value as the ratio of benefit and cost. Determining the monetary value of a marketing program's benefit is only part of the value story. The cost component represents the denominator of the ROI formula and serves an essential role in the value story. Finally, the ROI calculation must be consistent with accepted financial practices and based on credible and conservative assumptions. All the important issues related to the costs and ROI of marketing programs deserve exploration and discussion.

Fundamental Cost Issues

To address issues related to cost tabulation consistently, credibly, and conservatively, we need to apply several rules. A few guidelines for marketers are:

- Monitor all costs, even if they are not needed now.
- Costs must be realistic and reasonable.
- Some costs will not be precise; estimates are okay.
- Disclose all costs.

Additionally, according to Guiding Principle 10 of the ROI Methodology, we need to use fully loaded costs. Because we use a conservative approach to calculate the ROI, we should include a cost item even though we are not sure whether a cost should be included, even if the cost guidelines for the organization do not require it. The philosophy is "When in doubt, put it in." By doing so, we can ensure the credibility of the ROI calculation, and the calculation process should withstand even the closest scrutiny. Certainly, if the executives, including the CFO, insist on not using certain costs, then we should leave those costs out or report them in an alternative way. As suggested in the guidelines, we should disclose all costs, even if they are not included in the calculation.

Costs to Include

The specific policies and steps regarding cost tabulations may differ from one organization to another. In most cases, decisions made by the marketing team need to be approved by management. In some organizations, the finance and accounting staff may need to approve the list. For discussion, we list some common cost categories in Table 10.2 for a fully loaded, conservative approach to estimating costs related to a marketing program.[3]

TABLE 10.2 Marketing program cost categories

	COST ITEM	PRORATED	EXPENSED
1.	Initial analysis and needs assessment	✔	
2.	Design and development of solutions	✔	
3.	Acquisition of solutions	✔	
4.	Implementation costs:		
	Salaries/benefits for coordination time		✔
	Salaries/benefits for participant time		✔
	Materials and supplies		✔
	Travel/lodging/meals		✔
	Use of facilities		✔
5.	Maintenance and monitoring		✔
6.	Administrative support and overhead	✔	
7.	Evaluation and reporting		✔

As shown in the table, these cost categories cover major costs throughout the process of marketing program development, implementation, and evaluation. Some of the costs are prorated, which means these costs may be allocated over a longer period or across multiple programs. Therefore, only a portion of the costs should be allocated to the focal marketing program. Other costs are expensed, as they are more directly related to the program. Specifically, we have costs related to the following categories

Initial Analysis and Needs Assessment

In a marketing program, this cost involves marketing research, data collection, analysis, and assessments to better understand the situations and customer needs. The analysis can take place both online and offline. When a program is implemented without analysis, this cost is close to zero. However, when marketers invest in initial analysis and assessment, they have a better chance to develop a successful marketing program.

Design and Development of Solutions

These costs include the time and resources spent in both the design and development of the solutions for a marketing program. They may also include costs for purchasing supplies, technology, and other materials directly related to the solutions. For consumer and business marketing programs, these can be costs related to designing and developing solutions such as advertising, personal selling, public relations, and social media promotions.

Acquisition of Solutions

These costs are connected to the purchasing of solutions from agencies, consulting firms, and other sources, to use directly or in a modified format. They could be outsourcing to a full-service advertising agency or a group of manufacturers' representatives for consumer and business marketing programs. For internal marketing programs, they could be hiring a consulting firm to deliver training to the company sales force. The costs for these solutions include the purchase price, support materials, and licensing agreements.

Implementation Costs

These costs represent the largest cost segment in a marketing program, which includes the time (salaries and benefits), travel, and other expenses of all those involved in the program. These costs can be estimated using average or midpoint salary values for specific job groups. The costs can also be associated with program materials or hardware, software, and videos used for the marketing program. The use of facilities may include costs related to using media such as TV, radio, newspaper, and billboards for advertising if it is a consumer marketing program or those related to using conference rooms and hotel rooms if it is an internal marketing program.

Maintenance and Monitoring

These costs involve the routine expenses necessary to maintain and operate the marketing program. Typically, for marketing programs, these are ongoing expenses that allow the new solution to continue and may involve staff members, volunteers, and additional expenses.

Administrative Support and Overhead

This category includes the additional costs not directly charged to the marketing program. Typical items are the cost of administrative and clerical support, telecommunication expenses, office expenses, and other fixed costs. To allocate or not to allocate the administrative and overhead is debatable in the marketing context, as some researchers and managers believe allocating administrative costs arbitrarily may create misleading effects on the marketing contribution because none of the allocation schemes is perfect. As we discussed earlier, however, we intend to be conservative with the ROI Methodology, so we suggest including these costs.

Evaluation and Reporting

Costs in this category include developing the evaluation strategy, designing instruments, collecting data, analyzing data, preparing a report, and communicating the results of our marketing programs. Cost categories include time, materials, purchased instruments, surveys, any consulting fees, etc. This is an important cost category that completes the fully loaded costs.

Calculating the ROI

In this book, we define "return on investment" as an actual value determined by comparing the monetary value and the costs of a marketing program. The formula presented in this chapter uses annualized values so that the first year's impact of the investment can be calculated for short-term projects and programs. Many organizations use annualized values as an accepted practice for developing the ROI. This approach is considered a conservative and credible way to develop the ROI, because many short-term projects and programs have added value in the second or third year. By focusing on the first year of value only (and ignoring value added in the second year and beyond), we ensure our ROI is smaller and more conservative.

For long-term marketing programs, we should use a longer time frame. For example, many new product development projects take at least five years to complete. In an ROI analysis of such a project, we may choose a five-year time frame. However, for short-term marketing programs that take only a few weeks or several months to implement (such as a social media promotional program), we believe it is appropriate to use first-year values only.

In selecting the approach to measure ROI, we need to communicate to the target audience the formula used and the assumptions made in arriving at the decision. This way, we can prevent misunderstandings and confusion surrounding the process used to develop the ROI value. In this book, we use the following formula:

$$\text{ROI (\%)} = \frac{\text{program benefits} - \text{program costs}}{\text{program costs}} \times 100$$

With this formula, the numerator is the difference between the benefits and costs of the marketing program, which is also known as the net benefit, and the denominator is the program costs. We multiply the result by 100 to convert it to a percentage.

We use a marketing program to illustrate this calculation. Consider a business marketing program designed to reduce customer complaints. Imagine that the average monthly number of customer complaints dropped from 25 to 15 because of the program, after isolating effects. Further, assuming that the standard value for one customer complaint reduction is $5,000, the monthly benefit from this program is $50,000 (or $5,000 × 10). The annual savings are therefore $600,000 (or $50,000 × 12). If the program's total fully loaded costs are $400,000, then the ROI after the first year is

$$\text{ROI (\%)} = \frac{\$600,000 - \$400,000}{\$400,000} \times 100 = 50\%$$

This suggests that for every dollar invested in this marketing program, the dollar is recovered plus another 50 cents is returned.

Final Thoughts

This chapter focused on the key issues related to tabulating the costs and calculating the ROI of our marketing programs. Costs are important factors when determining value. Costs should be fully loaded in the ROI calculation, using direct and indirect costs because of the scrutiny ROI calculations of marketing programs typically receive. Including both direct and indirect costs makes the ROI number smaller, but this practice ensures the credibility of the process and comparability of the results. Therefore, we should include all costs even if the organization does not require it. Calculating the ROI is another critical issue discussed in this chapter. Calculating the ROI compares program costs with program monetary benefits and estimates the value of a marketing program. Now that we have fully explored the process of ROI calculation, our next chapter discusses how to report the results of the program evaluation by communicating a compelling story.

11

Tell the Story: Communicate Results to Key Stakeholders

Data is like garbage. You'd better know what
you are going to do with it before you collect it.

MARK TWAIN

Travis and Jenni are overjoyed to see the outcomes of their marketing program. After conducting a series of analyses, they are convinced that their program has indeed created significant values for their firm. The firm is Consumer Warehouse Co., known as CWC among many consumers, a national chain of 420 stores, located in most major US markets. CWC sells small household items, gifts of all types, electronics, and jewelry, as well as personal accessories.

Travis is the marketing director at CWC, and Jenni is a training special-ist there. They have been working on an internal marketing program for nearly three months.

The program started with a concern Travis shared with other exec-utives at CWC regarding the slow sales growth in many of their stores. Additional concerns focused on the sales team's interaction with custom-ers. It appeared the CWC sales associates were not actively involved in the sales process, usually waiting for a customer to make a purchasing decision and then proceed with processing the sale. Most sales associates are not college graduates and have just a few months of retail store experi-ence. Travis thought that more communication with the customers would boost sales but was not sure how to accomplish that. He contacted the CWC training department for help, as he thought that the major cause of these issues could be the sales team's lack of interactive selling skills.

Jenni, the training specialist for the sales team, suggested starting the project with some analyses. After observing how salespeople interacted with customers at different stores, Jenni and Travis conducted interviews and survey studies to understand the needs of the sales team and the customers. They found that most sales associates did not have adequate techniques to probe and guide the customer to a purchase decision in the store. Further analysis revealed that many customers would appreciate the sales associates using these techniques when assisting them. Based on these analyses, Travis and Jenni designed an internal marketing pro-gram for CWC sales associates to improve five interactive selling skills critical for sales success.

The process for obtaining funding for the program, however, was not easy. The retailing industry notoriously suffers low profit margins, and executives are understandably careful with extra spending. To save costs, Travis decided to use learning materials, including videos from an exter-nal supplier, to train salespeople, and use mobile apps for reminders on the job. To test the value of this internal marketing program, Travis and Jenni implemented the program in three stores with 16 salespeople from each store. Travis and Jenni also selected three other, similar stores as the control group. In order to ensure credibility, the program was facilitated by a consulting firm for a predetermined facilitation fee. Travis's plan was to implement the program and monitor the results before launching it to the whole organization.

Three months after the pilot marketing program launch, evaluations show that the results are positive. Travis is confident that CWC should implement the program in all 420 stores immediately. He is wondering what will be the best way to communicate the program results with the top management team, including the CEO and CFO, for the needed financial resources and support. Based on Jenni's suggestions, he uses a seven-step communication approach to accomplish his goal.

First, Travis analyzes and lists the reasons why he needs to communicate the results. Specifically, he wants to demonstrate the results of the internal marketing program and discuss the importance and implications of these results. He will also explain the techniques used in order to establish the credibility of the marketing and training departments. Ultimately, Travis would like to earn support from the CWC top management team and secure funding for the organization-wide implementation of the program.

Second, understanding the importance and costs of the communication tasks, Travis and Jenni spend time planning their efforts. They identify executives, store managers, sales associates, and training directors and trainers, as well as customers, as potential audiences. They also go through the results of the marketing program and summarize the data at different levels.

Next, Travis selects the target audiences. Although there are many potential stakeholders who may be interested in the program as identified in the previous step, Travis understands that the executives should be his primary target based on the goals he wants to achieve. Because an organization-wide implementation will need support from the training department, Jenni and Travis also select the training director and her team as the secondary target audience.

As the fourth step, Travis and Jenni develop communication reports for the two selected audiences. For the primary target group of executives, they focus on data at Level 4, Impact, and Level 0, Input (including costs). After isolating the effects of the program, Travis can calculate the ROI. For the secondary target of training director and trainers, Jenni understands that they are more interested in more tactical issues, such as training design and results at Level 1, Reaction, and Level 2, Learning, and how learning leads to Level 3, Action.

In the fifth step, Travis and Jenni choose appropriate media for their target audience. Treating the current program as a pilot study, Travis writes an interim and progress report for the executives to inform them about the status of the marketing program, and he asks for additional funding and continuous support. Additionally, Travis requests commitment from the top management group to launch the program in all 420 stores. To satisfy the needs of the training director and her team, Jenni writes the marketing program into a case study, not only highlighting the results of the program but also making the point that training adds value in a systematic way. Travis and Jenni also plan to use meetings as additional media for communication.

The sixth step involves presenting and delivering the message and information. Following the communication principles, Travis makes a personal presentation in front of the executives. He not only demonstrates the business impact and performance improvements but also makes sure that the top managers understand the process used to achieve and evaluate these results. He focuses on the benefits the program brings to the organization and makes specific requests for executive support of an organization-wide implementation. As a member of the training department, Jenni makes a personal presentation to the training director and her colleagues. She presents the process, the outcomes, and the challenges she faces when working on the program. At the end of the presentation, Jenni discusses the benefits for trainers and marketers working as business partners and invites the leaders and staff of the training department to support the organization-wide implementation of the program, if approved by the top executives.

The seventh and last step of the communication process involves analyzing the audience members' reactions and addressing their concerns. A more important measure of the effectiveness of the communication effort is the extent of the commitment and support attained from the managers, executives, and sponsors. The allocation of more resources and voiced commitment from top management are strong evidence of management's positive perception of the communicated results. Because the CEO is interested in the value created by the marketing program, in addition to the business impact and ROI, Travis also discusses the intangible benefits of the CWC marketing program. These intangibles include customer satisfaction, customer loyalty, improved brand and store image, employee job satisfaction, employee loyalty, and organizational commitment. Additionally, Jenni invites Travis to meet her director at the training department to discuss how the two functions can collaborate more effectively.

These communication efforts have positive impacts on both the executives and trainers. The senior executives approve Travis's request for additional funding and voice their support of this program to all employees. They also allocate resources to provide financial incentives for the salespeople to participate in the program. The training director is also supportive and asks her team to work closely with the marketers as partners on the important marketing program.

* * *

In essence, the process of marketing is just like the process of storytelling. Marketing, first and foremost, is about the customers we serve. Similarly, a story is like a product we develop. But storytelling is not only about our story; it is about the people, the audience, and the customers we are trying to connect with. For both marketing and storytelling, we need to understand the needs and preferences of our target customers and audience, to carefully design and develop our product or story, to select the media or channel that people prefer, and to deliver the product or story effectively and professionally. Further, similar to marketing, storytelling is not only about serving the needs of the audience or customers. It is also about prompting desirable actions and behavior of the audience and customers to accomplish the organizational goals.

A good marketing program starts with a good understanding of customer needs. Additionally, marketers need resources and expertise to develop products and services to satisfy customer needs. Similarly, a good understanding of the audience's needs is critical for good storytelling, and we need to deliver information and data systematically to satisfy our audience. In previous chapters, we discussed collecting data at the reaction, learning, action, and impact levels, isolating the effects, calculating ROI, and estimating intangibles. The data may show that our marketing program is a success, or they may reveal certain aspects that need to be improved. Either way, marketing programs do not end when we have data in hand. Instead, we should use the data to tell the story of our marketing program. "Tell the Story" is the eleventh step of the ROI Methodology and the focus of this chapter. The performance improvement standard in this step is "Work in Partnership." Once a marketing program is complete, marketers must communicate to all stakeholders and let them know the success of the program. In this chapter, we provide guidance for presenting evaluation data to various audiences in the form of both oral and written reports.

The Importance of Communicating Results

Communicating the results of a program is critical. Achieving results without communicating them is like planting seeds but failing to fertilize and cultivate the seedlings. That will not yield optimal outcomes. We need to communicate the results to stakeholders upon completion of the program so that they can see the value the marketing program has created. We also need to communicate throughout the duration of the program to maintain a continuous flow of information. Communication is necessary because we can never take it for granted that all stakeholders will see our contribution. Communication is also the key to making important adjustments and meaningful improvements at all phases of the program. In addition, communication is one of those issues that can be sensitive. If we are not careful, our communications may cause major problems. We must recognize the varied audience needs and tailor the communications individually to accommodate each audience, before constructing and delivering the communications effectively and fairly to all key stakeholders.

Principles of Communicating Results

Effectively communicating results requires skills that are almost as sensitive and sophisticated as those needed for obtaining the results. Both the style and the substance of the communication are equally important. We recommend the following general principles for communicating the results of marketing programs:

- Communication must be timely.
- Communications should be targeted to specific audiences.
- Media should be carefully selected.
- Communication should be unbiased and modest in tone.
- Communication must be clear and consistent.
- Testimonials must come from respected individuals.
- Presenters must have credibility.

The Seven-Step Process for Communicating the Results of a Marketing Program

In this chapter, we introduce a seven-step approach for marketers to manage their communication process effectively.[1] This approach fulfills the purposes of communicating the results of a marketing program, consistent with the 12 Guiding Principles of the ROI Methodology and guidelines, and is both systematic and systemic. The process includes seven components in the sequence highlighted in Figure 11.1.

Step 1. Analyze Reason for Communication

As shown in Figure 11.1, the first step involves analyzing the need to communicate the results from a marketing program. Just as it is necessary to explore customer needs before any marketing program, it is important to outline the specific reasons why we need the communication. Do we need more support for our marketing programs? Do we

239

FIGURE 11.1   A communications model for results

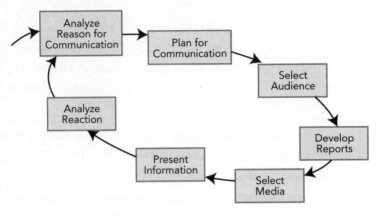

need to maintain or adjust the funding for our programs? Alternatively, do we need to instill confidence among stakeholders or build credibility for our marketing programs? The specific reasons for communicating results will depend on the nature of the marketing program, the setting, and the unique needs of each party.

Step 2. Plan for Communication

To achieve maximum results, we need to carefully plan for communication, which is the focus of the second step. Communication consumes resources, time, and energy. The planning of the communication is important to ensure that each audience receives the proper information at the right time and that necessary actions are taken as expected. Planning should focus on when and to which audience the communication should be presented, the specific types of data to be communicated, and the action items to be addressed. We list several crucial issues in this critical step of planning the communication of results:

- Who is the target audience?
- What will be communicated?
- When will the data be communicated?
- How will the information be communicated?

- Where will the information be communicated?
- Who will communicate the information?
- What are the specific actions required or desired?

Because communication is such an important component of marketing program development and management, we should start to consider the communication plan even before implementing the program.

Step 3. Select Audience

Similar to selecting target segments of customers, the third step involves selecting the target audiences for communication. The reason we should recognize different audiences is that each audience typically has its own needs. We should consider an overall communication strategy for all groups and carefully design and artfully craft delivery of the message for each specific group to fit the needs. We identify several common target audiences and list them in Table 11.1. The figure also briefly discusses the basis for each audience selection.

TABLE 11.1 Common target audiences

PRIMARY TARGET AUDIENCE	REASON FOR COMMUNICATION
Customer and client	▪ To gain support and help secure approval for the program
Regulators and policy makers	▪ To gain support for this program and future programs
Users and participants	▪ To secure agreement with the issues
Top executives	▪ To enhance the credibility of the marketing program ▪ To improve the results and quality of future feedback
Managers	▪ To reinforce the processes used in the program ▪ To prepare participants for the program
Program team	▪ To drive action for improvement ▪ To identify the best way to engage the customer ▪ To create the desire for a participant to be involved

(continued on next page)

PRIMARY TARGET AUDIENCE	REASON FOR COMMUNICATION
Other key stakeholders	▪ To show the complete results of the program
Support staff or agency	▪ To explain the techniques used to measure results
All employees	▪ To demonstrate accountability for expenditures
Prospective customers and participants	▪ To market future programs

Step 4. Develop Reports

Developing reports is the fourth step of the communication process. This step involves written materials to explain the results of a marketing program to a particular audience group in a format desired and appreciated by that group. It is similar to the product development process of marketing. Depending on the needs of the audience, the written materials can be a brief summary of the results, or they can be detailed research documents on the evaluation process and outcomes. Typically, marketers develop a complete report, select parts or summaries from the report, and use them for different media to serve different communication goals and purposes. We present a possible outline for an impact study report of a marketing program in Box 11.1.

Box 11.1   Outline for an Impact Study Report

1. General information
   - Background
   - Objectives of study
2. Methodology for impact study
   - Levels of evaluation
   - ROI process
   - Collecting data

- Isolating the effects of the program
- Converting data to monetary values

3. Data collection analysis issues
4. Results: General information
   - Response profile
   - Success with objectives
5. Results: Reaction
   - Data sources
   - Key issues
6. Results: Learning
   - Data sources
   - Key issues
7. Results: Action
   - Data sources
   - Key issues
8. Results: Impact
   - Data sources
   - Isolating the effects of the program
   - Key issues
9. Results: ROI
   - Converting data to money
   - Project costs
   - ROI and its meaning
10. Results: Intangible measures
11. Barriers and enablers
    - Barriers
    - Enablers
12. Conclusions
13. Recommendations
14. Exhibits

It is important not to boast about the results of a marketing program. Grand claims of overwhelming success can quickly turn off the audience and can be counterproductive for the delivery of the desired message. Further, credit for the success must go to the parties that deserve it, which may be team members, participants, and their managers. For audiences who are not familiar with either the ROI marketing methodology or the marketing program, we should clearly explain the methodology and the program. In contrast, if the audience understands the basic concepts of the ROI marketing methodology or is familiar with the marketing program, then a brief one-page summary may be appropriate. We provide an example of such a one-page summary for a marketing program in Figure 11.2.

Step 5. Select Media

The fifth step of the communication process is media selection. Choosing certain methods of communication that a target group will respond to favorably is similar to selecting a distribution channel for a target customer segment. Although many options are available for the dissemination of program results, none of them is perfect. These options all have their pros and cons, which make some options more appropriate for certain audience groups than others. We list some common options in Table 11.2.

TABLE 11.2 Communication options

MEETINGS	DETAILED REPORTS	BRIEF REPORTS	ELECTRONIC MEDIA	MASS PUBLICATIONS
Executives	Impact study	Executive summary	Websites	Announcements
Management	Case study (internal)	Slide overview	Emails	Bulletins
Stakeholders	Case study (external)	One-page summary	Social media/ blogs	Newsletters/ white papers
Staff	Major articles	Brochure	Videos	Brief articles

Figure 11.2 One-page summary

An Internal Marketing Program to Improve Sales Effectiveness

The Business Challenges and Action Plans
- Two-day training with action plans and support tools
- Each participant develops an action plan to apply the skills in the field.

Target:
Field Sales Team 970
Sample 72
(18 managers, 4 regions)

Reaction—Objectives Met

Relevance	✓
Important	✓
Intent to use	✓

Action Objectives on a 5-Point Scale

Extent of use	4.3
Frequency of use	4.5
Success with use	3.9

Barriers

Not enough time	23%
Lack of support	18%
Doesn't fit	14%
Other	10%

Learning Objectives Met Pre-Post-Improvements	
1. Prospecting skills	48%
2. Sales planning skills	57%
3. Presentation and listening skills	42%
4. Objection handling skills	69%
5. Closing skills	53%
6. Follow-up skills	67%

Methods of Isolation: Participant Allocation, Adjusted for Error

Impact Objectives
Two Objectives Each Participant

- Costs 23%
- Satisfaction 17%
- Sales 21%
- Quality 29%
- Other 10%

Method of Converting Data to Money

- Estimate 13%
- Expert Input 63%
- Standard Value 24%

Costs—Direct $355,370
Indirect—Prorated $9,890
Total $365,260

Total Monetary Benefits = $538,640

Intangibles
- Engagement
- Satisfaction
- Stress

BCR = 1.47   **ROI = 47%**

Step 6. Present Information

The sixth step is presenting and delivering the message about the program results in the form of appropriate information. Just as with a successful sales presentation, the key to delivering the message is to understand the audience members and their perspectives and then show what benefits there are for them. Darlene Price, a communications expert, makes the following suggestions for delivering the message:

- Do not try to perfect your communication but try to connect with your audience.
- Organize your presentation with persuasive logic and use an effective structure.
- Ensure the delivery to be dynamic and confident every time with live presentations.
- Engage your audience whenever possible to make the message meaningful and memorable.
- Use PowerPoint more effectively to reinforce your message and to optimize impact.
- Manage nervousness and create a great first impression.
- Cultivate a variety of image enhancers that will subtly lend power to your presentation.[2]

There are different types of situations, under which we choose appropriate communication forms to present the program results. We discuss three types of communication situations in the following sections.

Presentation of Results by Providing Feedback

For most marketing programs, marketers routinely collect and analyze data at multiple levels. A primary reason for doing so is to provide feedback to various audiences in order to make adjustments and improvements throughout the program. We recommend the following steps for providing feedback and managing the overall process based on the concepts and recommendations of Peter Block in his successful book *Flawless Consulting*.[3]

- Communicate quickly.
- Use negative data in a constructive way.
- Use positive data in a cautious way.
- Simplify the data.
- Carefully choose the language of the communication.
- Ask the audience for reactions to the data.
- Ask the audience for recommendations.
- Use support and confrontation carefully.
- Secure agreement from all key stakeholders.
- Keep the feedback process short.

Following these steps does not guarantee success, but it will help move the program forward and generate useful feedback, which will lead to necessary adjustments that are supported and executed.

Presentation of Results by Storytelling

We cannot rely on only numbers and data to tell the whole story. Other means of communication, such as storytelling, are required to define and articulate the results. Storytelling is a uniquely useful technique in its ability to bring people together and to organize and present information in an efficient and accessible manner. Storytelling creates a richer experience and fosters greater insight into the nature of the program, therefore enabling key stakeholders to understand how the marketing program contributes to organizational success.[4]

There are empirical evidence and compelling reasons why storytelling works, as discussed by Paul Smith. We summarize them into the following:

1. Storytelling is simple.
2. Storytelling is timeless.
3. Stories are contagious.
4. Stories are easier to remember.
5. Stories inspire.
6. Stories appeal to all types of audiences.
7. Stories fit in the workplace where most of the work happens.
8. Telling stories shows respect for the audience.[5]

It is helpful to have a logical structure when developing a story. Box 11.2 presents a checklist for developing stories effectively and efficiently. The checklist includes the major components of a story structure, although the structure may vary depending on the audience and situation.

Box 11.2　Story Structure Checklist

Hook
- Why should I listen to this story?

Content
- Where and when did it happen?
- Who is the hero? (Is the hero relatable?)
- What does the hero want? (Is that worthy?)

Challenge
- What is the problem/opportunity? (Relevant?)

Conflict
- What did the hero do about it? (Honest struggle?)

Resolution
- How did it turn out in the end?

Lesson
- What did you learn?

Recommended Action
- What do you want me to do?

Presentation of Results to Senior Management

The third type, and probably the most challenging and stressful type of communication, is presenting the results of a marketing program to senior management. For many marketing programs, senior managers are the sponsors, supporters, and, sometimes, the clients. The challenge is convincing this highly skeptical and critical group that we have achieved outstanding results in a very reasonable time frame. We need to not only address the performance issues but also make sure that the top managers understand the process. We have several guidelines to help ensure that we plan and execute this process properly, which are shown in Box 11.3.

Box 11.3   Guidelines for the Executive Meeting

Purpose of the meeting:

- Create awareness and understanding of ROI.
- Build support for the ROI Methodology.
- Communicate the results of the study.
- Drive improvement from the results.
- Cultivate the effective use of the ROI Methodology.

Use these ground rules:

- Do not distribute the impact study until the end of the meeting.
- Be precise and to the point.
- Avoid jargon and unfamiliar terms.
- Spend less time on the lower levels of evaluation data.
- Present the data with a strategy in mind.

Follow this presentation sequence:

1. Describe the program and explain why it is being evaluated.
2. Present the methodology process.
3. Present the reaction and learning data.
4. Present the action data.
5. List the barriers to and enablers of success.
6. Address the business impact.
7. Show the costs.
8. Present the ROI.
9. Show the intangibles.
10. Review the credibility of the data.
12. Summarize the conclusions.
13. Present the recommendations.

Step 7. Analyze Reaction

The seventh step is analyzing the audience's reactions to the communication efforts. When we communicate the results of our marketing programs, we should monitor the reactions of the target audience. These reactions include verbal remarks, written comments, nonverbal gestures, and other actions that may reveal how the audience received and perceived the messages. We may collect the reaction data in various ways. For example, when we present the results face-to-face in a meeting, we may have some indication about how the group reacts to our presentations by observing people's facial expressions, by listening to their comments, and by answering their questions. When we communicate major program results, we may use a feedback questionnaire to determine the extent to which the audience understood and believed the information presented. The survey can be administered to the entire audience or a sample of the audience. We can also evaluate the interest and attitudes of the audience members online by reading the comments they make to social media posts or replies to our emails. Comments about the results, both online and offline, should be noted and tabulated.

For many situations, the analysis can be informal. For communication efforts that are extensive and more involved, we may need a formal and structured feedback process. However, monitoring reactions is not where the effort ends. Depending on the nature of these reactions, we can adjust our subsequent strategies for better communication of the program results. The reaction data can also be used for adapting future program communications. A more important measure of the effectiveness of our communication effort is the extent of commitment and support attained from the managers, executives, and sponsors. The allocation of more resources and voiced commitment from top management are strong evidence of management's positive perception of our communication of the results.

Final Thoughts

Communicating results is a crucial step for the success of a marketing program. We need to execute our communications properly and adequately in order to demonstrate the value of the marketing program, establish credibility, and win more support, resources, and funding. We started the chapter with a discussion about the importance of communication, guidelines, and general principles. These general principles are vital to the overall success of the communication effort. We then introduced a seven-step approach for communicating program results and showed the importance of inducing desirable behaviors in the target audience to accomplish our communication goals.

This chapter highlighted the importance of communicating all results, whether they are positive or negative. If the results are not satisfactory as expected, the communication will lead to the necessary adjustments for performance improvement. In the next chapter, we will discuss the topic of optimizing the results, the last step of the 12-step ROI Methodology.

12

Optimize Results: Use Performance Improvement to Increase Funding

What the great learning teaches, is to illustrate illustrious virtue;
to renovate the people; and to rest in the highest excellence.

CONFUCIUS

onvey Air Taxi Services (CATS) is a privately held company that offers personal and on-demand flight services. A group of friends who all had experience in the airline industry founded this company using their own savings and investments from venture capitalists. A former commercial pilot, Robert is a cofounder and the CEO of CATS. He and his friends recognize an increasing demand from time-conscious travelers who prefer quick, luxurious, and cost-effective jet transportation to avoid the hassle of commercial airline travel.

As a newcomer to the air taxi industry, CATS has little brand recognition. To better understand customer needs, Robert and his team conduct market research. They first gather secondary data on air traffic patterns, popular destinations for private jet travelers, and travel frequency for business and leisure customers. They then use focus groups, interviews, and survey studies to collect primary data on potential customers regarding where they would like to see CATS operate and what features they would like the service to offer. The market research efforts reveal the following findings:

- Business travelers value the air taxi service more than those who travel for leisure.
- Leisure travelers plan ahead and need less on-demand service.
- Business travelers prefer one-way flights, whereas leisure travelers need round-trip flights.
- Business travelers value time, and leisure travelers value comfort.
- Among the business travelers, consultants and sales professionals have greater need for on-demand air taxi services than the other business travelers.

Based on these results, CATS develops a marketing plan to guide its marketing efforts. In terms of target marketing, the company identifies consultants from mid- to large-size consulting firms as its primary target market and salespeople as its secondary target segment. To address the challenges of low customer awareness and a constrained marketing budget, Robert and the executive team use promotions to reach potential customers and build interest in the benefits of the company's service. In order to create demand and build brand equity, the CATS marketing department launches a comprehensive promotional campaign by combining advertising, direct marketing, personal selling, and content marketing. The company positions itself as a provider of speedy air services that are more convenient and comfortable than traditional airline flights but cost far less than private jet ownership.

CATS sets the marketing objectives at different levels. Objectives are set for reaction, learning, and action levels to monitor the progress of this marketing program. Since it is a new business, the ROI objective is set at zero. The Level 4 (Impact) objectives for the first year include (1) selling 5,500 flight itineraries, (2) attaining 90 percent "highly satisfied" customers, and (3) achieving repeat purchases from 50 percent of customers.[1] The CATS marketing department uses print ads and sends out direct marketing materials to the identified target customers. Additionally, the company utilizes salespeople to communicate important product and service messages to key clients. Public relations and social media coverage are also used to promote the first CATS flight and create online and offline buzz.

CATS officially launches the air taxi service in May, and the marketing department has been carefully monitoring the market responses at multiple levels. Six months later, however, it becomes clear that not everything has been on the right track. Specifically, the CATS marketing managers find the following information on their dashboard:

- In total, CATS has sold only 1,856 flight itineraries in the first six months after the initial launch, significantly below the YTD goal of 2,500 itineraries.
- In total, only 67 percent of customers report to be "highly satisfied" with the service CATS provides, below the goal of 90 percent "highly satisfied" customers.
- In total, only 38 percent of customers who used the service are making repeat purchases or express that they are willing to repurchase, far below the goal of a 50 percent repeat purchase rate.

These numbers disappoint almost everybody. Two salespeople working on key accounts in the consulting industry left the company, and more employees begin to complain about lack of support, inadequate resources, and fierce competition. Robert and the CATS marketing managers decide to use the ROI Methodology to monitor the effectiveness of their promotional efforts to identify the cause of the situation. Their investigations paint a slightly rosy picture. Specifically, the survey data show that 90 percent of the target audience have heard of CATS, and most of these people view the service as innovative, interesting, and potentially beneficial, with an overall rating of 4.3 out of 5. Quarterly surveys conducted by the CATS marketing department show that 80 percent of target customers who received the CATS marketing messages understand the major benefits of the company's services. Since the promotion began, phone call and email inquiries about its services have increased by 15 percent on a monthly basis, and the CATS website traffic (including the number of visitors and number of web pages they visit) has increased by 30 percent on a monthly basis.

The CATS marketing managers are perplexed about the situation. They simply do not understand why a seemingly effective marketing program fails to generate satisfactory financial results. Understandably, Robert and other CATS executives are very concerned as well. They are wondering what has gone wrong, and more importantly, what is needed in order to improve the situation. To fully understand the situation and answer these questions, Robert and the marketing managers take the following actions.

First, they assess the marketing performance and conclude that the major performance issues are related to unsatisfactory sales results and inadequate repeat purchases. Both are financial performance issues at Level 4. Second, considering external and internal factors, they determine that the original goals are still achievable, but significant improvement is needed within three months. Therefore, as the third step, they collect more data from sales transactions, survey results, and other internal records. These data show that in the past six months:

- The primary target market of business consulting travelers bought less than 30 percent of the 1,856 flight itineraries, were less likely to be satisfied with the air taxi service (only 45 percent of consultants who bought the services were highly satisfied), and were less likely to repurchase (only 25 percent repurchased or were willing to repurchase).
- In contrast, the secondary target market of sales professionals was more interested in the service than were business

consultants. Sales professionals not only bought more than half the flights; they were also more likely to be highly satisfied (85 percent) and more willing to repurchase (65 percent) than their consultant counterparts.

- In total, less than 100 flight itineraries were purchased by leisure travelers, confirming a previous conjecture that leisure travelers may not be a good target audience for the service.
- Surprisingly, there was a very strong demand from customer service representatives in the technology and engineering industries. Although there was no direct promotion toward them, this group purchased nearly 25 percent of total flights, with 90 percent of these customers highly satisfied with the service and 88 percent willing to repurchase.

The marketing managers then conducted more analyses on the activity reports, which revealed the following:

- Although 60 percent of CATS' marketing efforts have been targeted toward business consultants, only 17 percent of the phone and email inquiries were from this group.
- Approximately 52 percent of the phone and email inquiries were from sales professionals.
- Only 6 percent of the phone and email inquiries were from leisure travelers.
- Although not a target segment, customer service representatives constituted 25 percent of the phone and email inquiries.

Meanwhile, the CATS marketing managers conducted several focus groups and interviewed selected customers from each segment. Then they conducted survey research based on the focus group studies. The results showed:

- The demand from business consultants is not as strong as expected. Many consultants enjoy their frequent-flyer benefits with major airlines. More importantly, the flight expenses are typically billed to the clients, rather than being covered by the consulting firm's budget.

- There are stronger demands from sales professionals and customer service representatives than initially estimated, especially
in the technology sector. With intense competition in the tech
industry, both sales and customer service representatives strive to
respond to customer requests in a timely manner. The CATS air
taxi service meets this need at a reasonable price.

These analyses prompted Robert and the marketing managers to
conclude that the current marketing strategy is ineffective and is the
main cause of the subpar financial performance. To address the issue,
they propose to modify the company's marketing strategy by shifting
attention from business consultants to sales professionals. In addition,
they will explore the segment of customer service representatives from
the technology industries as another target segment. Robert and his
team understand that modifying the targeting strategy means they need
to reconsider almost every element of their marketing program. They
need to incorporate the unique needs of the new segments (sales professionals and customer service reps from the high-tech industry) into the
process of redesigning the service features and pricing. They also need
to find appropriate media and best positioning statements to effectively
communicate with the new segments. However, Robert and his team
are hopeful that these modifications will lead to improved financial performance, better customer satisfaction, and employee loyalty so CATS
can establish itself in the highly competitive and rapidly growing air taxi
service industry.

The Importance of
Continuous Improvement

No marketing program is perfect. If a marketing program is not as successful as expected, marketers can analyze the data collected and use the
analysis outcomes to make changes for improvement. If the marketing
program is indeed successful, the data may be used to find ways to make
the program even more successful. Marketers need to have the mindset of

continuous improvement in order to reach excellence in terms of maximum value. In this chapter, we discuss the final step in the ROI Methodology process, "Optimize Results: Use Performance Improvement to Increase Funding." Essentially, this also involves using design thinking and performance improvement processes to increase funding.

As discussed in Chapter 2, the design thinking principle in this step is "a new competitive logic of business strategy," and the performance improvement standard is "Add Value." Our ultimate goals in this step are to improve value, optimize the ROI, and secure allocation of more funds. We need to build the case for more investment in our marketing programs. To accomplish this, it is beneficial to integrate design thinking and performance improvement with the ROI Methodology. We design for the desired results, collect and use data to improve the program and optimize ROI, and then make the case for more funding. With intense competition for resources, showing key funders and supporters the value of our marketing programs is not optional. It is a mandate. With the right mindset and right methodology, marketers can keep and even improve the budget. Figure 12.1 shows the connection between evaluation and the allocation of funds.

FIGURE 12.1 Optimize results

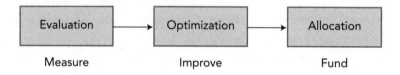

Retail Merchandise: A Case Study in Marketing Performance Improvement

Retail Merchandise is an American chain of retailing stores that sell women's apparel, handbags, shoes, and beauty products, as well as electronic products and other household merchandise.[2] It has nearly 20,000 employees working in over 400 stores nationwide. Last year, the firm implemented a marketing program to accelerate sales growth, address problems with customer experience, and explore better business models. Samantha, the chief marketing officer, was newly recruited from a major competitor. Samantha and her marketing team designed the internal program by introducing an interactive selling skill as an effort to enhance the quality of interactions between store salespeople and customers. The selling skill program was a result of marketing research, indicating that both customer satisfaction and store sales revenue would benefit from enhanced dialogue between salespeople and their customers.

The internal program started with a pilot study conducted with 48 sales team members in three stores, with 16 participants from each. Three other stores of similar size and with comparable locations and past performance were selected as control groups to evaluate the effectiveness of the internal marketing program. Three weeks after the pilot program implementation, the experimental control group analysis showed impressive results. Specifically, the sales team in the experimental group achieved a 16 percent increase in sales revenue, whereas its counterparts in the control group achieved only 1 percent during the same period. The increased financial performance generated enough profit that the program yielded an ROI of 118%.

The impressive results from the pilot study were presented to the members of the management team, and this earned their support to implement the marketing program throughout the 420 stores. Four weeks into the program, however, the organization-wide implementation was not generating results as expected. Although some stores did see improvement similar to that of the pilot study, two-thirds of the stores did not see any significant improvement. The disappointing outcomes put Samantha and her team in an awkward position because the marketing program was costly, consuming both financial and human resources. Some executives, including the CFO, were weighing the option to either cut the budget of the program or discontinue the program and move organizational resources elsewhere.

Samantha refused to give up. She and her team began conducting analyses and specifically taking the following steps to improve the outcomes as a way to earn support:

1. They assess the marketing performance of the stores and find that although 20 percent of the stores are able to achieve or exceed the expected 16 percent revenue growth, other stores on average can only achieve 3 percent revenue growth, compared with what they achieved prior to the program.

2. Based on this assessment, Samantha and her team set a marketing performance improvement (MPI) objective of increasing the sales revenue by 16 percent nationwide in six months.

3. The team conducts more analyses and identifies a performance discrepancy. Most of the sales teams in the underperforming stores are not using the interactive selling skills, whereas the sales teams in the top stores use the skills frequently. In all stores, salespeople react positively to the program and are able learn the interactive skills.

4. Samantha and her team then analyze potential causes of the issue. They identify the following two major causes:
   - Unlike their counterparts in the top stores, the sales teams in the underperforming stores indicate their managers do not expect them to use the interactive skills.
   - There are no tools or job aids to support the use of the skills.
   As a result of these findings, Samantha believes that the MPI objective (set in Step 2) is reasonable, and there is no need for adjustment. The MPI objective is used to guide all subsequent activities.

5. Working with store managers, Samantha designs three solutions to deal with the pain point of lack of action:
   - She asks all store managers to articulate their strong expectation of and support for salespeople using the interactive skills with all customers.
   - Working with store managers, she and her team create an activity quota and design a sales contest around using the selling skills.
   - The marketing team develops job aids and tools to support the sales teams' use of the skills.

6. The solutions are implemented in all stores, and objectives are set at multiple levels. Samantha and her team pay particular attention to the objective at Level 3, the action level, because the key to this marketing performance improvement project is to address the pain point of lack of action and induce desirable selling behaviors.

7. Evaluation is conducted at all levels. One encouraging finding is that, at Level 3, the frequency and extent to which store salespeople use the interactive selling skills with customers have been significantly increased. Consequently, after isolating the effects of the program, the total sales revenue has increased by nearly 20 percent.

8. To sustain the positive changes and performance improvement, Samantha works with store managers to take several measures. A training course is designed to focus on the interactive selling skills and becomes part of the sales team's onboarding process. Tools and job aids are also developed and made available. In addition, sales managers receive training on how to motivate the teams to use effective selling skills and improve job performance.

Samantha summarizes the marketing performance improvement data in a report and shares it with the top management team. She highlights the value created by the systematic efforts and establishes a convincing connection between the steps taken and the improvement achieved. She also discusses the measures taken to sustain the improvement. Her communications and success of the marketing program have created a positive impact and earned the support of the top executives, including the CFO. Consequently, she secures more funding for the marketing function and the marketing program.

• • •

This case study shows how marketing performance improvement can lead to optimization, and optimization can lead to allocation of funds. The process not only ensures the success of a marketing program but also reveals the areas that can be adjusted to increase the success in the future. As a result, marketers are in a position to deliver even more results through their marketing programs. In a convincing way, marketers can use the results to earn endorsements from top management, ensure funds are allocated for their programs, and implement programs with support throughout the organization.

The case also shows that it is beneficial to have a systematic approach as a way to better manage and coordinate performance improvement efforts. A systematic approach increases effectiveness because it considers factors at multiple levels, thus providing better opportunities to identify real causes and optimal solutions. A systematic approach also ensures efficiency, because it enables organizations to better allocate resources and spend time and energy wisely. Although it is possible to cycle through the 12 steps in the ROI Methodology, a more concise set of steps can be helpful. The marketing performance improvement methodology is recommended as a systematic process.

Marketing Performance Improvement Is the Key

The marketing performance improvement methodology highlighted in the case study is an eight-step methodology that originated in the performance improvement literature and is consistent with marketing theories and practice. Over the years, it has been taught in academic settings and applied in real-world projects.[3] The methodology can be used to improve marketing performance when a program is not delivering results as expected. It can also be used as a tool for marketers to regularly examine their daily practices and conduct continuous performance improvement. Figure 12.2 shows the steps of the MPI model.

FIGURE 12.2   The eight steps of marketing performance improvement

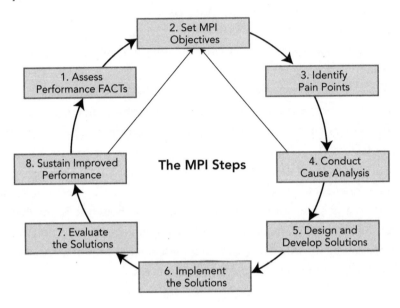

Step 1. Assess Performance FACTs

As shown in the figure, the first step of the marketing performance improvement process is to assess the current marketing performance situations. The FACTs framework denotes the four dimensions of marketing performance, namely, financial, activity, customer, and talent; and we should compare the current levels of the four performance dimensions with strategies and goals of the marketing program. From the perspective of the ROI Methodology, most if not all measures related to the four dimensions of marketing performance are at Level 4 (Impact). Because executives care about the business impact the most, it makes sense to start the process with a marketing performance assessment.

Step 2. Set MPI Objectives

Comparing the current performance levels with the strategic expectation, the first step, is likely to identify performance gaps. The gap could be sales revenue or lack of profit to reach the financial performance goals, or it could be customer satisfaction or customer complaints to reach the customer performance goals. The gap could also be related to talent performance, such as employee turnover rates that exceed expectation, or activity performance that is substandard at product delivery time, or customer requests responses that are not satisfactory. Marketers need to set SMART objectives—objectives that are specific, measurable, attainable, relevant, and time bound—to close the gaps as described in Chapter 3.[4]

Step 3. Identify Pain Points

Pain points need to be identified before conducting a cause analysis (Step 4). Pain points refer to discrepancies or ignored opportunities that are directly causing or related to the performance gaps identified in Step 2. These discrepancies and opportunities are likely to be at one or more levels, from Level 0 (Input), to Level 1 (Reaction), Level 2 (Learning), and Level 3 (Action). These lower-level measures may have influenced the performance gaps at Level 4 (Impact), that were identified in Step 2 through the chain of value effects. This step attempts to explore whether and where discrepancies, barriers, and opportunities exist. If a significant barrier exists, we can then conduct a cause analysis to gain a better understanding before taking measures to address the barrier by trying to minimize, remove, or go around it. We must examine each of the levels.

Step 4. Conduct Cause Analysis

After identifying the pain points, the next step is to conduct a cause analysis. There are meaningful differences between the cause analysis in this step and the cause analysis during program design. As discussed previously, during the process of designing a marketing program, our goal is selecting or developing the right solutions for the marketing program. Therefore, we need to analyze factors both external and internal to the organization including market conditions and organizational strategies. In contrast, the task of cause analysis here is focusing on fine-tuning certain aspects of the marketing program for better results, which is more concentrated and directed. Therefore, we conduct cause analysis in this step primarily on the factors related to the pain points at one or more levels of input, reaction, learning, and action.

Some of these factors, especially those related to one level and one level only, are obvious. For example, we find that the pain point is related to using the wrong communication channel. Others are more complex when they are related to more than one level. As shown in the opening story, when a program targets the wrong customer segment, there will be discrepancies at the input, reaction, learning, and action levels. Under these conditions, it is critical to identify the root pain points, such as the wrong targeting strategies. As shown in Figure 12.2, we have the option to revise the MPI objective if cause analysis reveals additional information that may influence the extent to which we accomplish the original objective.

Step 5. Design and Develop Solutions

The solutions designed and developed at this step are remedies directly related to the pain points identified and cause analysis conducted. The remedies should be specifically designed to address the barriers at one or more levels from input to action. The solutions may also take advantage of the neglected opportunities. Some solutions could be quick fixes, such as increasing the number of times target customers see our advertisement. Other solutions may require more changes. For example, targeting a new customer segment typically involves modifying the product package, promotional messages, pricing, and distribution channels.

Step 6. Implement the Solutions

Although the causes identified and solution designed in previous steps tend to be specific and focused, solution implementation involves systemic changes and should be treated as a change management process. The business alignment model we discussed in previous chapters provides such a systematic framework because the changes will occur from

Level 0 to Level 4 through the chain of impact. Before implementing the solution, objectives should be set at different levels to guide the process and make the necessary changes when one or more measures are not as desired. If the solution is implemented at lower levels such as input and reaction, higher-level objectives need to be set in order to monitor the learning and action induced by the solution. When we implement a solution to address issues at higher levels, changes need to be made at the input and reaction levels to start the change management process.

Step 7. Evaluate the Solutions

The business alignment model also guides the evaluation process. The evaluative component of the alignment model, as we discussed in previous chapters, provides procedures and tools to conduct an evaluation of the outcomes of the solution at different levels. The ultimate goal of any marketing performance improvement solution is to enhance the business impact and add value. To achieve that ultimate goal, we need to examine and monitor the chain of impact starting at Level 0 (Input), and moving through to Level 3 (Action). The chain of impact enables us to make necessary adjustments to achieve the marketing performance improvement objective. In Step 7, the evaluative outcome is compared with the MPI objective to determine to what extent this has been accomplished.

Step 8. Sustain Improved Performance

Marketing performance improvement is a continuous process, not a one-time event. If the performance improvement efforts generate positive outcomes, we need to manage factors at the individual and environmental levels to sustain the improved performance. At the individual level, we recognize that the improved business outcomes are likely caused by the changed and enhanced actions of customers and employees. We should take measures to reward these actions as a means to sustain the improved performance. Many organizations develop a loyal customer program to induce and maintain desirable customer behaviors. In addition, organizations can use advertisements and social media marketing to remind customers of the great benefits they are receiving as a way to sustain desirable purchasing behaviors. For internal marketing programs, organizations may use bonuses, commissions, or recognition programs to induce and maintain the desirable behavior of employees. Desirable actions can also be encouraged by sharing successful stories. Organizational-level factors will likely have greater impact on employees' behavior. It is critically beneficial to modify policies, procedures, and processes to create a climate that is conducive to the desirable actions that will sustain the improved marketing performance.

Influencing Budget Allocation

One goal of this book is to help marketers influence the funding allocations for marketing programs. This influence may have one or more of the following desirable outcomes: minimizing the reductions in the budget, maintaining the current budget, or increasing the budget. In terms of budget allocation, marketers need to move beyond avoiding budget cuts and maintaining existing budgets to increasing budgets. This is possible in the face of reductions in other areas, as long as marketers are able to demonstrate enough value created by the marketing programs. Some organizations may actually increase marketing program budgets during a recession, when budgets are being cut in other places. This influence can be powerful, if we are able to demonstrate value throughout the process.

> *Costs are like fingernails, you have to cut them constantly.*
> CARLOS ALBERTO SICUPIRA

Investment Versus Cost

Facing fierce competition and demanding customers, executives always look for budgets that can be easily cut. For many executives, cutting the budget is not an enjoyable task. However, it must be done for the benefit of the whole organization. With or without an economic downturn, the uncertainty and volatility embedded in the marketplace often create anxiety among executives, who have the tendency to embrace a leaner budget as a way to alleviate stress and prepare for the unknown. After all, economic recessions have a lasting effect on many organizations. Consequently, executives feel the pressure not only to keep their budgets in check but to ensure up-front accountability before implementing any new programs.

As discussed in previous chapters, the concepts of cost and investments have meaningful differences. Although both refer to expenditures, costs represent expenditures incurred but are not expected to generate future cash flows, whereas investments represent expenditures expected to generate future cash flows as well as other benefits. In other words, the fundamental difference between a cost and an investment is the extent to which the expenditure can lead to improved business outcomes and intangible benefits. Therefore, to influence executive decisions on budget allocation, it is critical to influence the perceptions of marketing programs. When an executive perceives a marketing program as a cost or an investment, the subsequent implications can be dramatically different.

As shown in Figure 12.3, if executives perceive a marketing program as a cost or an expense, they are more likely to control it, to reduce it, or even to eliminate it. In contrast, if executives perceive the marketing program as an investment, they are more likely to maintain it, to enhance it, and to protect it. The higher the expected ROI of the marketing program, the more likely it is to secure and increase the marketing budget. With the managerial and financial support from executives, we are able to improve customer relationships and business partnerships. As we gain more influence on the organizational decision-making process, we earn a seat at the table, and competing for funding becomes a little bit easier. If executives see marketing programs as valuable investments, they can resist the temptation to cut our budgets even when facing tough economic and financial conditions. The key is to convince them that the marketing programs have a direct and positive impact on business results. We need to constantly convince and remind the executives that investing in marketing programs produces a positive ROI. Without that perception, support for marketing programs will not continue.

FIGURE 12.3 Costs versus investment perception

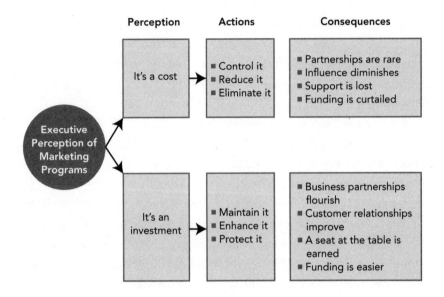

Competition for Funding

The competition for funds is fierce, especially during economic uncertainty, as anxiety and downturns often translate into cost reduction. Under the pressure to deliver and as managers become more demanding, no function in an organization feels that its budget is adequate. Indeed, functions within an organization have many activities that represent costs. As we discussed in previous sections, the perception of executives about these costs becomes critical in the budget approval process. If executives see the activity as an investment with a positive ROI, then they are willing to support it, or at least they are reluctant to minimize or reduce it. When a department fails to show its activity has an impact, or there are no credible data to show its effects, then executives often have a desire to reduce, minimize, control, or even eliminate the activity.

In the budget approval process, you get what you can sell.
These days, it's easier to sell impact and ROI.
JAC FITZ-ENZ

As stated by Jac Fitz-enz, the key to winning support is to show the impact and ROI of the marketing program, and the goal is to convince top executives to see our programs as an investment, instead of a cost. To achieve this goal, marketers must make sure there is a systematic analytical approach, equipped with solid data collected from creditable sources. We must have convincing data and analysis to build the case that marketing programs are making a difference and that the proposed budget contributes to that. The contributions highlighted should be measures of business impact, with supporting data collected at the reaction, learning, and action levels. We will compare the monetary benefit with the cost and demonstrate the value created with an ROI calculated in a systematic and credible way. The more credible and specific the data, in terms of impact and ROI, the more convincing the story, and the more likely the budget will be approved and even increased.

Final Thoughts

This chapter wraps up the 12-step ROI Methodology and serves as the capstone of the results-based philosophy of the book.[5] It shows why we need a serious approach for evaluation. We face serious challenges to protect the marketing budget. If we fail to do so, there are serious consequences. If we cannot convince executives and decision makers that marketing programs are sound investments that add value, we may not only lose funding, but also lose influence and opportunities to establish partnerships. We must show the value and, more importantly, how this value is created by the marketing program. In this chapter, we introduced marketing performance improvement, a systematic approach that guides and enables marketers to continuously improve the business impact and optimize the ROI of their marketing programs. With this increased ROI, marketers can influence the allocation of funds. The key is to convince executives that the marketing program is an investment instead of a cost. The approach is not to measure our way to a positive ROI but to design the entire process to deliver ROI. That is what is needed, and that is what this book focuses on.

13

Forecast the ROI

The most reliable way to forecast the future
is to try to understand the present.

JOHN NAISBITT

Six students in a row hurried into Konstantin Gonyshev's small tattoo parlor one day this month with identical requests to ink a domino, and quick. Days earlier, Domino's Pizza in Russia had announced a promotion that was supposed to run for two months offering lifelong free pizza to anyone who showed up with the company's logo in a tattoo. But that morning, Domino's posted on social media that it was ending the promotion—although those who were being inked right then could still make the midday cutoff.[1]

"More than a million people would have come to demand pizzas" if the promotion had lasted the full two months, guessed 24-year-old Natalia Koshkina, who got a small Domino's logo tattooed above her left kneecap, just below a skull embellished with roses and butterflies. "After all, this is Russia," she said.

Bargains and freebies are powerful draws here. The Soviet period—where foodstuffs were often cheap but in short supply—and the economic hardships of the 1990s have conditioned many Russians to pounce on a good deal. A stagnant economy has left average disposable incomes stuck around $500 a month, and Ms. Koshkina said the free pizza would help her put aside a bit of money from her salary working at a piercing and tattoo parlor. "Who doesn't want free food?" she said.

Russia is also a country of citizens with multiple tattoos. They love tattoos, and an iconic American brand is a desirable option. Some individuals, when informed that it was too late to meet the deadline, even got the tattoo anyway. Tattoos in Russia have long been associated with criminals who have used them to depict status in the underworld. But in recent years, they have become part of a broad assimilation of American hipster culture that includes craft beer, skateboards, and boutique barbershops.

A spokesman for Domino's Pizza Inc., the US-based owner of the Domino's Pizza brand, said the Russian franchisee had been overwhelmed by the response, receiving more applicants in days than it had expected in months.

Social media campaigns have become a staple of marketers looking to generate online buzz—and, in this case, turn people into lifelong walking advertisements. But the efforts can go awry. McDonald's, for example, pulled a Twitter campaign with the hashtag #McDStories in 2012 after consumers used it to complain about the company.

US fast-food brands poured into Russia after the Soviet Union collapsed, and they quickly gained popularity in a country where people had grown used to standing in line for basic foodstuffs. Domino's first opened a store in Russia in 1998, and master franchisee DP Eurasia NV now has more than 100 restaurants, predominately in Moscow.

Now, brands such as Yum Brands, Inc.'s KFC and Restaurant Brands International Inc. unit Burger King are common and are facing a crowd of competition from local fast-food companies and firms that deliver orders from restaurants placed via apps on smartphones.

Domino's announced the launch of its tattoo promotion named "Domino's Forever" on VKontakte, the Russian equivalent of Facebook, on August 31. The conditions were minimal: Applicants should post a photo on social media of a real tattoo in a visible place with the hashtag

#domino'sforever. They would receive a certificate allowing them to receive 100 free pizzas a year of any size for 100 years, the company said.

When the campaign was halted, 381 people had qualified for free pizza. The lifelong pizza was defined as 100 pizzas a year of any size for 100 years. Just for the four days of the campaign, it could cost the franchise as much as $15 million over that period.

• • •

This marketing campaign went astray and turned into a near disaster. Understanding what went wrong is a good exercise. We will explore this following the process that is presented in this book.

1. What was the reason for doing the marketing campaign? This is not so clear. It could be that it was to drive business, create loyal customers, build the brand, or some other reason. The key to any project is to have a clear understanding of the business measures desired.

2. Given that the correct business measures are identified, the next question is whether this is the right marketing campaign to deliver the objectives. In this case, it is not clear that this project was the correct solution.

3. Expect success by ensuring that the objectives are set for the project along the way and that everyone understands the desired impact. There are no indications that this was achieved.

4. It is not clear that a forecast was made for this marketing program.

5. When forecasting, it is important to have experts estimate the amount of improvement in the impact measure that will be connected to the solution. For example, how much of the additional sales would be generated from this solution? In this situation, a good forecast would have made a difference in this program.

Someone has suggested that maybe Domino's implemented this campaign as a marketing gimmick to bring attention to the brand, realizing it would stop the campaign early. Even if that was the goal of the program, it is not clear that was accomplished.

The Importance of Forecasting ROI

Confusion sometimes exists about when to develop the ROI. The traditional approach, which we described in previous chapters, is to base ROI calculations on the business impact obtained after the marketing project is implemented. This chapter focuses on ROI calculated at earlier stages—even before the project is initiated. Forecasting may be appropriate when projects are expensive or when they demand costly changes. Forecasting may also be appropriate when dealing with high risks and uncertainty. Forecasting may provide additional benefits. For example, comparing actual results with a forecast helps evaluate the success of a marketing program. If the forecast becomes a reliable predictor of the post-project analysis, then the forecast ROI might substitute for the actual ROI and save money. In certain industries, various regulatory, legal, and managerial forces require organizations to forecast ROI before undertaking major programs. In other situations, forecasting ROI can be a powerful marketing tool.

The Trade-Offs of Forecasting

Forecasting is never perfect and always involves trade-offs. In the case of ROI forecasting, the ease, convenience, and costs involved in capturing an ROI forecast often create trade-offs in accuracy and credibility. As shown in Table 13.1, the ROI can be developed at different times and with different levels of data. The figure also shows the relationship between the timing of the ROI and the factors of credibility, accuracy, cost, and difficulty. Five approaches to developing ROI include:

- **Pre-project ROI forecasting approach.** The least expensive and least difficult approach to forecast ROI is the pre-project approach. Although sometimes lacking credibility and accuracy, the pre-project forecast can be an easy-to-use and cost-efficient tool for marketers to forecast the ROI of their marketing programs. We discuss this approach in detail in the next section of this chapter.

- **ROI forecasting approach using reaction data.** Marketers can use reaction data collected at Level 1 to forecast ROI. To use this approach, marketers ask customers and participants to anticipate the chain of impact as a marketing program is implemented. While accuracy and credibility increase from the pre-program basis, this approach still lacks the credibility and accuracy desired in many situations. However, the data can be easily collected, and the goal can be readily accomplished. It is a low-cost option to forecast ROI. We will discuss it in detail in the next section together with the pre-program approach.

- **ROI forecasting approach using learning data.** In marketing programs that involve a significant learning component—for example, a complex marketing message—learning data can be used to forecast the ROI. This approach is applicable only when there is a relationship between knowledge learned and subsequent impacts. When this correlation is available (it is usually developed to validate the test of knowledge), knowledge data can be used to forecast subsequent purchases, and the ROI can be calculated. This approach has less potential as a forecasting tool and will not be discussed in subsequent sections.

- **ROI forecasting approach using action data.** When the actions of customers and participants are linked to business impact, the actions can predict the impact. For example, a desired action of a marketing program is to have potential customers view a product website through a specific link. If the analysis shows that 10 percent of potential customers who remain on the site for over five minutes will actually purchase the product, then this action becomes a predictor of sales. While this is particularly helpful in situations where appropriate analyses have been developed, it may have limited applications in other programs.

- **ROI estimating approach using impact data.** Finally, the ROI can be developed from business impact data converted directly to monetary values and compared with the cost of the project. This is not a forecast. It is a post-program evaluation and the basis for the ROI calculations in this book. It is the preferred approach.

However, considering the pressures presented earlier, marketers may find examining ROI calculations at other times and with other levels of data is sometimes necessary.

TABLE 13.1 Time intervals when ROI can be developed

ROI WITH	DATA COLLECTION TIMING (RELATIVE TO PROJECT)	CREDIBILITY	ACCURACY	COST TO DEVELOP	DIFFICULTY
1. Pre-project data	Before project	Can have low credibility	Can be inaccurate	Inexpensive	Not difficult
2. Reaction data	During project				
3. Learning data	During project	↓	↓	↓	↓
4. Action data	After project				
5. Business impact data	After project	Very credible	Very accurate	Expensive	Very difficult

In the following sections, we will review in detail the pre-project ROI forecasting approach and the ROI forecasting approach based on reaction.

Pre-Project ROI Forecasting

Forecasting the ROI of a marketing project is probably one of the most useful ways to convince an executive or a sponsor that a project is beneficial and deserves resources and support. The forecasting process is similar to the post-project analysis except that the extent of the impact must be estimated along with the project costs.

Basic Model

In Figure 13.1, we demonstrate the basic model for capturing the data necessary for a pre-project forecast. This basic model is a modified version of the post-program ROI process model presented in Chapter 4. When forecasting ROI using the pre-project approach, we estimate the project outcomes, rather than collect actual data after project implementation. Data collection with the pre-project approach is simple and relies on subjective approaches such as interviews, focus groups, or surveys of experts. It may also be helpful to tap into benchmarking studies or locate previous relevant studies.[2]

FIGURE 13.1   Pre-project forecasting model

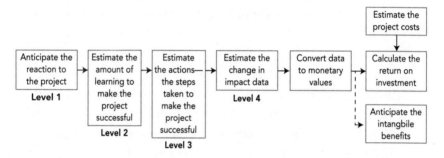

Beginning at the reaction level, we capture anticipated or estimated reaction data. Next, we develop the anticipated learning and anticipated actions that must occur. Here, the estimates focus on what must be accomplished for the project to be successful and may be based on the objectives set at each of these levels. Finally, the impact data are estimated by experts, which may include specialists, managers, or potential participants in the project. In this basic model, the levels build on each other. Having data estimated at Levels 1, 2, and 3 enhances the quality of the estimated data at Level 4, Impact, which is needed for the ROI forecasting analysis.

Notably, in the basic model, there is no need to isolate the effects of a project as in the post-project model. Instead, we ask the individual experts providing the impact data the following question: "How much will the impact measure change as a result of the project?" Because this question ties the anticipated change in the business impact measure directly to the marketing project, isolation is not needed here.

Consequently, this approach makes the forecasting process easier than the postevaluation model, where isolating project impact is always required. It is a straightforward process to convert data to monetary value using the techniques described in Chapter 9. The specific steps to develop the forecast are detailed next.

Basic Steps to Forecast ROI

We highlight 18 detailed steps in this section, which are necessary to develop a credible pre-project ROI forecast using expert input:

1. **Understand the situation.** Both the individuals providing input to the forecast and those conducting the forecast must have a good understanding of the situation and task. This is a typical requirement for selecting the experts.

2. **Predict the present.** Many measures in marketing projects often lag the present situation and may be based on data taken several months ago. Due to the dynamic influences in the marketplace, it may be beneficial to estimate where the measure is now. For example, market share data are often several months old. Looking at trending market share data and examining other influences driving market share can help marketers understand the current situation.

3. **Observe warnings.** We need to observe warning signs and red flags, which are signals that something is going against the measure in question, causing it to go in an undesired direction or otherwise not move as it should. We must factor these warning signals into the situation as the forecasts are made.

4. **Describe the new process, project, program, or solution.** We must describe the project completely and clearly to the experts so they fully understand the mechanics of what will be implemented. Typically, we need to include the project scope, the individuals involved, time factors, and whatever else is necessary

to express the magnitude of the program and the profile of the solution.

5. **Develop specific objectives.** Objectives provide clear direction toward the project's end. These objectives should mirror the levels of evaluation and should include reaction objectives, learning objectives, action objectives, and impact objectives. The cascading levels represent the anticipated chain of impact that will occur as we implement the project.

6. **Estimate how customers or participants will perceive the project.** In this step, the experts are trying to determine how customers or participants will react to the offering of the project. Will they find the offering to be valuable? Important to them? Will they support the project? Answers to these questions help determine reaction.

7. **Estimate what the customers or participants will learn.** Every marketing project involves learning, and the experts will estimate what and how learning occurs, identifying specific knowledge, skills, and information. Using the learning objectives, the experts will determine what marketing message the customers will acquire and how participants will learn as they become involved in the project.

8. **Anticipate what customers or participants should do because of the project.** In this step, the experts will identify what actions the customers or participants will take as the project is implemented successfully. This step details specific actions taken, tasks followed, processes implemented, and technology used.

9. **Estimate the improvement in business impact data.** This is a critical step, because the impact data generated are needed for the purpose of the financial forecast. The experts will provide the estimate, in either absolute numbers or percentages, about the change in the business impact measure (ΔP) as a result of the marketing project.

10. **Apply the confidence estimate.** To ensure the accuracy of the estimate attained in the previous step, we need an error adjustment. We develop it by deriving a confidence estimate on the

value identified in the last step. Specifically, the experts are asked to indicate the confidence they have in the previous data. The confidence level is expressed as a percentage, with 0 percent indicating "no confidence" and 100 percent indicating "certainty." This becomes a discount factor in the analysis, denoted by c.

11. **Convert the business impact data to monetary values.** Using one or more methods described in Chapter 9, we can convert the data to money. If the impact measure is sales, the value represents the gain obtained by having one more unit of the measure. If the impact measure is what the organization is trying to reduce, such as product returns, errors, or customer complaints, then the value is the cost that the organization incurs as a result of one incident. For example, the cost of product returns may be 5 percent of sales. This value is noted by V.

12. **Develop the estimated annual impact of each measure.** The estimated annual impact is the first-year improvement directly related to the marketing program. In formula form, this is expressed as $\Delta I = \Delta Pc \times V \times 12$ (where ΔI = annual change in monetary value, ΔP = monthly change in performance of the measure, c is the confidence factor − error adjustment, and V = the value of that measure). If the measure is daily, weekly, or monthly, we must convert it to an annual amount. For example, if three product returns will be prevented each month, the number avoided represents a total of 36.

13. **Factor additional years into the analysis for programs that will have a significant useful life beyond the first year.** For projects with a significant useful life beyond the first year, the factor should reflect the diminished benefit of subsequent years. Marketers should use the best data and information sources available to determine the amount of the reduction and the values developed for the second, third, and successive years. Consistent with the ROI Methodology principles, it is important to be conservative by using the smallest numbers possible.

14. **Estimate the fully loaded project costs.** In this step, use all the cost categories described in Chapter 10 to estimate the fully

loaded costs, and denote the value as *C* when including it in the ROI equation. Include all direct and indirect costs in the calculation, as guided by the ROI principles.

15. **Calculate the forecast ROI.** Use the total projected benefits and the estimated costs in the standard ROI formula to calculate the forecast ROI as follows:

$$\text{ROI (\%)} = \frac{\Delta I - C}{C} \times 100$$

16. **Show variation.** It is beneficial to use sensitivity analysis to develop several potential ROI values with different levels of improvement (ΔP). When more than one measure is changing, the analysis may take the form of a spreadsheet showing various output scenarios and the subsequent ROI forecasts. The break-even point will be identified from this analysis.

17. **Identify potential intangible benefits.** Anticipate intangible benefits using input from the individuals who are most knowledgeable about the situation, based on assumptions from their experience with similar projects. As discussed previously, the intangible benefits are those benefits not converted to monetary value but are connected to the project and possess value.

18. **Communicate the ROI forecast and anticipated intangibles with caution.** The target audience must clearly understand that the forecast is based on assumptions. Although the assumptions are clearly defined and the values represent the best possible estimates, they may include a degree of error. Use with caution.

Following these 18 steps will enable an individual to forecast the ROI with confidence in a systematic way.

Forecasting Can Prevent Problems

A good forecast can avoid the problem of missing the mark, which can be expensive and devastating. The opening story in this chapter explored a very expensive snafu made by Domino's with its franchise in Russia. This, perhaps, could have been easily avoided if a serious approach had been taken to forecasting the ROI before the project was implemented. Using the process outlined in this chapter could have produced a credible forecast that might have prevented or radically altered the promotional offer that was communicated to the Russian public.

Sometimes a marketing campaign involving TV advertisements can miss the mark on the positive side and be very successful. Consider this example of a series of television ads for the state of Utah to increase visitors to the national parks in that state.

Six years ago, Utah tourism officials launched a "Mighty 5" marketing campaign to entice more visitors to the state's spectacular national parks. State officials got more than they bargained for.[3]

Frustrated locals are now dealing with the consequences of the explosive growth that followed. The number of visitors to the five parks—Zion, Bryce Canyon, Capital Reef, Canyonlands, and Arches—has soared to 10.6 million visitors in 2018 from 6.3 million in 2013, a 68 percent increase that state officials say was due in large part to the advertising. Other factors, they say, included the national economic recovery and social media.

Few places have seen the impact more than Moab, Utah, a city of 5,300 that sits beneath towering red rock cliffs near the entrances to two of the parks, Arches and Canyonlands. Once known as a relaxed getaway for mountain biking and four-wheeling, Moab is being swarmed by 3 million visitors annually. On peak days, visitors create hour-long waits at restaurants, are responsible for empty store shelves, and turn the city's quaint Main Street into a parking lot. With infrastructure and facilities strained, officials in the parks and their gateway communities have pushed back on both state and local promotion efforts. Grand County, which includes Moab, in June opted not to pursue a $250,000 state grant to aim more marketing at prospective visitors in Texas and Illinois. After hearing the complaints, the Utah Office of Tourism, which ran the Mighty 5 campaign, put on the brakes.

This ad campaign was too successful, generating more tourists than the cities could handle. This success turned out to be a disaster for some of the local areas. The key question is, could this success have been predicted? If so, the campaign could have run for a shorter period, or the cities could have been given more notice to prepare for the increase in visitors. The key issue is that you can control the outcomes of projects if there is an understanding and a forecast of those outcomes. The challenge is to determine if the process outlined in this chapter can be used to forecast the success.

Some experts understand this type of tourism ad and also the environment in which such ads are being offered. This campaign was launched in the face of a great economic boom, and social media often attracts people to tourism as well. So perhaps some indication of these other factors could have been helpful. Certainly, there must have been some experts who could have examined history to offer some estimates of the program outcomes. If so, the planning could have been much better.

For some organizations, having too many results from an ad campaign is a good thing. But for others, when it causes bottlenecks and other problems, advertising can do more harm than good. The critical point is that a good, credible forecast can make a difference.

Forecasting with a Pilot Project

To deal with the inaccuracies inherent in a pre-project forecast, marketers may choose a better approach by developing a small-scale pilot project with the ROI based on post-project data. This approach involves the following steps:

1. As introduced previously, develop Level 1, 2, 3, and 4 objectives.
2. Select a small-scale sample to implement the pilot project. Exclude all the bells and whistles to keep the project costs low without sacrificing integrity.
3. Fully implement the project with one or more target segments or groups.
4. Develop the ROI using the ROI process model for post-project analysis as outlined in previous chapters.
5. Use the results of the pilot project to decide whether to implement the project throughout the organization or in the national market.

Estimating ROI with a pilot project provides less risk than developing an ROI forecast. For example, large organizations such as Walmart can use this method to evaluate a pilot project to reduce the risk of implementing a project throughout its chain of stores.

ROI Forecasting with Reaction Data

Another possibility is to develop a forecast based on reaction data. The reaction data are collected after the customers or participants are involved in the project. To forecast ROI at this level, marketers need to ask customers specifically what actions they will take and what results they anticipate. The actions could include signing up to be a new customer, purchasing the product, or agreeing to an upgrade. We can easily convert these actions to monetary values. Customers can provide a confidence factor with their responses, which is used for the next step when adjusting estimates for the confidence level. When tabulating data, the confidence levels are multiplied by annual monetary values to produce a conservative estimate for use in data analysis.

Forecasting ROI Using Reaction Data

Transoft is one of the largest software companies for the trucking industry. With more than 12,000 users, Transoft dominates the trucking landscape. Transoft provides software solutions for carriers, brokers, logistics companies, and shippers. A variety of software solutions are available, including products for financial operations, fleet management, document systems, dispatch operations, freight management, and broker management. Its most popular software, ProfitPro, integrates a variety of software solutions, all aimed at improving the efficiency and profitability of the trucking company. The trucking industry is highly competitive, often producing low margins. Having an efficient operation is usually the difference in profit or loss. ProfitPro has a reputation for helping trucking companies meet profit goals.[4]

Transoft has just completed an upgrade on ProfitPro and has released it to the sales team to begin selling the upgrade. An upgrade costs the client from $1,000 to $3,000, depending on the scope of operations. For the client, the upgrade provides some new features and streamlines some of the previous processes. It should help make clients more profitable by reducing the time to complete certain documents, ensuring on-time filing, reducing invoicing errors, and improving other operating efficiencies.

To support the campaign, the marketing department created an email message with a link to a four-minute video that will be sent to all the ProfitPro users. The email encourages the users to take just four minutes and view the details of the new upgrade of this important software. The thinking was that the users of the system would be curious about the upgrade and that some users would welcome an upgrade. A high percentage of customers were expected to click on the video and watch it. Then, the users were sent another email containing two questions with a reward of a $25 Starbucks gift certificate for answering the questions. The two questions are:

1. "As a result of what you saw in the video about this upgrade, on a scale of 1 to 10, what is the likelihood of you purchasing the upgrade?"
2. "On a scale of 1 to 10, where 10 is complete confidence (meaning your previous estimate is 100 percent accurate), and 1 indicates no confidence, please provide an assessment of your confidence in your answer to question 1."

This was all the data the customers had to supply in return for the $25 gift certificate, and the rate of questionnaires returned was high.

The analysis was conducted as follows: For the first survey question, an answer such as 8 on the likely-to-purchase scale translated into 80 percent of the sale. However, the confidence adjustment was the way to adjust the estimate for error, as described in Chapter 9. For example, if someone answered 8 for the likely-to-purchase question and also answered 8 on the scale of confidence, those two numbers would be multiplied together to equal 64. This meant that the person was 64 percent likely to purchase this upgrade. This was then multiplied by the purchase price to obtain the actual monetary amount.

Those who did not respond to the email asking for these two data items were considered to be zero, meaning that they will not purchase the product. This approach was very conservative and followed Guiding Principle 6 of the ROI Methodology.

When the numbers were multiplied and the total monetary value was developed, the monetary value was multiplied by the profit margin, which was 20 percent. These values were totaled and compared with the cost of the four-minute video, including design, development, production, and implementation costs as well as the cost of the gift certificates for those who responded. When the total costs were compared with the monetary benefits, the ROI was calculated. In this case, the ROI turned out to be over 200 percent. Essentially, this was the ROI on the marketing video about the upgrade based on reaction data from the customers.

This forecast was completed before the sales team took the mobile learning course and helped increase sales. This example shows how forecasting is a great way to get an early indicator of the marketing campaign.

Forecasting Guidelines

Compared with today's enterprise, the enterprise of the future will be more likely to implement and utilize continuous analysis of past business performance and events to gain forward-looking insight to drive business decisions and actions.[5] With the different forecasting time frames outlined in this chapter, we propose the following guidelines known to drive the forecasting possibilities within an organization. These guidelines come from our experiences in forecasting in a variety of projects and programs.[6] More discussions are available in the books and papers we published.[7]

1. If you must forecast, forecast frequently.
2. Make forecasting an essential part of the evaluation mix.
3. Forecast different types of data to develop an overall assessment.

4. Secure input from those who know the process best.
5. Forecasting works best when it covers a short time frame.
6. Expect forecasts to be biased, and understand their limitations.
7. Manage the effort of serious forecasting.
8. Review the success of forecasting routinely.
9. Communicate the assumptions clearly.
10. Use the forecasting to achieve important organizational goals.

Final Thoughts

Most marketers focus only on impact data for ROI calculations. In this chapter, we illustrated that ROI calculations can be developed at different times and at different evaluation levels. There is a growing need to forecast impact and ROI earlier in the process. It is possible to satisfy this need by forecasting ROI using reaction, learning, and action data, as well as using a pre-project approach. Although pre-project ROI forecasts have an image of low credibility and accuracy, they also have the undeniable advantage of being inexpensive and relatively easy to develop. ROI forecasts developed before a marketing project begins and during implementation can be useful to executives, sponsors, customers, and participants. The reality is that forecasting is an important part of the measurement mix and should be pursued routinely and used regularly in decision-making. Using the guidelines introduced in this chapter, marketers can make their ROI forecasts based on estimates of impact data more credible and accurate.

14

Make It Work: Sustain the Change to a Value-Driven Marketing Program

Change is inevitable. Progress is optional.

GARY MARX

"Natural Beauty is dedicated to enhancing consumers' wellness and beauty naturally through superior products and extraordinary service," claims Laurie, the chief marketing officer of Natural Beauty Laboratories, Inc. Since she joined the company last year, this mission has inspired Laurie to work tirelessly in the rapidly growing organic cosmetics industry. As more consumers are becoming open to green and natural products, Natural Beauty quickly establishes itself as a leading provider of a variety of natural cosmetics including skin care, moisturizers, perfumes, lipsticks, nail polishes, and facial makeup products. The company's products are available both online and at retail stores all around the nation.

Marketing is one of the most important functions within Natural Beauty. Laurie's team consists of brand managers, social media managers, advertising managers, and public relations managers, as well as specialists in search engine optimization, marketing analysts, and web content writers. She also manages the company sales force through a sales director and store managers. To better manage her team and optimize the budget, Laurie has been constantly seeking best practices in the marketing management field. Several months ago, she attended a conference and heard about the ROI Methodology. She feels that this process is exactly what she has been looking for.

Laurie understands that to implement the ROI Methodology in her organization, she needs support from both the marketing team and the executives. Therefore, she asks Sophia, a recent MBA graduate on her marketing team, to work on the initiative. After collecting books and case studies on the ROI Methodology, Sophia develops two PowerPoint presentations, one for the executive team and another for the marketing department. At the monthly meeting of the Natural Beauty executive committee, Laurie and Sophia present the ROI Methodology to the executives. Using charts, graphs, and flowcharts, they highlight clearly and convincingly the logic of implementing the methodology in Natural Beauty.

Some questions are asked at the meeting, such as, "How long has the methodology been around?" "Who else has been using the methodology?" and "How well has the methodology worked for others?" However, there is little controversy. The initiative receives approval from the executives without much discussion. The presentation, the discussion at the meeting, and the CMO's backing seem to produce an agreement.

Laurie is happy with the meeting and moves forward to implement the ROI Methodology in Natural Beauty. She asks Sophia to distribute ROI articles to department heads and develops a one-day session to train the marketing teams. Laurie asks all marketing teams, including advertising, sales, social media, and content marketing, to implement at least one ROI project, and she demands to see results within three months. To her surprise, most members of the marketing teams are not excited about the initiative. They complain about the disruption this new initiative will create for their job and protest that it will be difficult to take time to attend the training session from their busy schedules. "How will this approach help my writing?" asked the web content writer. Even partners at the advertising agency complain that they do not have time to collect the learning and action data needed for evaluation and assessment of Natural Beauty's advertisements.

Laurie tries to explain the rationale for introducing the methodology but finds that she will have to spend days on the phone listening to the complaints and answering questions. Each team has many members who want to continue running their business the way they are used to. They have come up with a wide variety of excuses to avoid using the new approach. The social media team states there is no reliable way for it to measure consumers' actions when the interactions with consumers are primarily virtual. The sales director protests that isolating the effects of his coaching on sales performance is not doable because there are so many factors beyond his control. The public relations manager also challenges Laurie. She states that all her PR campaigns benefit the brands of Natural Beauty, but there is just no credible way to convert the benefit to monetary value.

It goes on and on and on. Laurie's attention is being diverted to dealing with the avalanche of calls, complaints, concerns, and issues. Laurie feels that she has hit a wall. Introducing the ROI Methodology to Natural Beauty turns out to be a much tougher task than she thought.

• • •

Transforming the marketing function of an organization and pursuing value-driven marketing programs represent significant changes. It must be a high priority for the executives and marketers of the organization to develop capability in the ROI Methodology and implement results-based, value-driven marketing programs throughout the organization. However, as we have learned from the opening story, the change will be resisted. Although some of the resistance to change is based upon actual barriers and real obstacles, most concerns originate from fear and misunderstanding. If not properly integrated, fully accepted, and adequately supported by those who must make it work within the organization, even a step-by-step, logical, and simple process like the ROI Methodology may fail. In this final chapter, we focus on some of the most effective means of overcoming resistance so that we can effectively implement the ROI Methodology and successfully transform our organization.

Overcoming Resistance and Facilitating Change

An organization is an entity that consists of people, and it is part of human nature to resist something new. When we are trying to introduce a new model, new concept, and new idea, such as the ROI Methodology, to our organization, resistance is almost inevitable. New models and processes create uncertainty, challenge the status quo, and cause doubts or even fear. Understandably, some people will intuitively say no to the new model to stay within their comfort zone.

John P. Kotter, a professor at Harvard Business School and author of multiple bestsellers, is an expert on the topics of change and leadership. He and his colleagues interviewed approximately 400 individuals from 130 organizations and found the following:[1]

- Highly successful organizations know how to overcome resistance that rejects anything new.
- Successful organizational changes occur in eight stages, as shown in Box 14.1.

- The central challenge of organizational change is changing people's behavior.
- People's behavior can be changed by either giving them an analysis to influence their thoughts or helping them to see a truth to influence their feelings. The latter is more convincing and effective than the former for behavioral change.

Box 14.1 The Eight Steps for Successful Organizational Change

Step 1. Increase urgency.

Step 2. Build the guiding team.

Step 3. Get the vision right.

Step 4. Communicate for buy-in.

Step 5. Empower action.

Step 6. Create short-term wins.

Step 7. Don't let up.

Step 8. Make change stick.

The fourth finding of Kotter's study is important because it echoes what psychologists have been telling us for a long time, that our brain has an emotional side and a rational side.[2] Jonathan Haidt, an NYU professor and psychologist, uses an analogy to explain the two sides of our brain when he labels the emotional side as the elephant and the rational side as the rider.[3] The rider of the elephant appears to be in control but can be easily overwhelmed and overpowered by the elephant when there is a disagreement between them, as the elephant usually wins.

Chip Heath and Dan Heath build on this analogy and propose three categories of approach to change people's behavior.[4] The first option is to direct the rider, that is, to influence people's rational brain by providing data, analysis, and logic. The rational brain is responsible for reasoning, directing, and planning but can be paralyzed by overanalyzing and overthinking. The second option is to motivate the elephant, that is, the emotional brain. The emotional brain can be influenced by people's feelings and appreciates quick and instant gratification. The third option is to shape the path for the elephant and rider, where the path can be the surrounding environment that makes change easier.

Academic research provides meaningful implications for marketers and managers. In order to induce people to adopt the ROI Methodology in our organizations, we have three strategic choices. We may choose (1) to show data to change an individual's thinking, (2) to reveal the truth to influence the individual's feelings, and (3) to modify policies and processes to facilitate changes. Similarly, drawing on decades of research and practice, ROI Institute has identified a series of steps critical for influencing behavior and overcoming resistance at the organizational level.[5] As shown in Figure 14.1, these actions are treated as building blocks for this purpose. In the remainder of this chapter, we will present several strategies and techniques based on the building blocks in Figure 14.1 and the steps highlighted in Box 14.1.

FIGURE 14.1 Building blocks for overcoming resistance

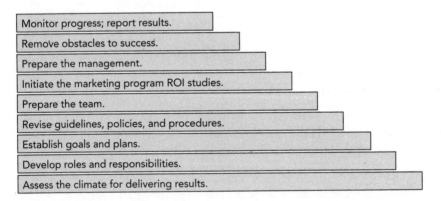

Monitor progress; report results.
Remove obstacles to success.
Prepare the management.
Initiate the marketing program ROI studies.
Prepare the team.
Revise guidelines, policies, and procedures.
Establish goals and plans.
Develop roles and responsibilities.
Assess the climate for delivering results.

Assess the Climate and Increase Urgency

Some organizations assess the current organizational climate as a first step toward adopting new approaches. The assessment is in the form of a survey to the marketing team. An example of the survey is in Appendix C. The focus of this assessment is the extent to which an organization is ready to make necessary changes and adopt the new model. With an awareness of their organization's current status, marketers can plan for significant changes.

One way to induce change is by directing "the rider," or the rational side of the brain, using the approach of analyze-think-change. This approach focuses on presenting data and analysis to make people think and change. As discussed in the opening story, this approach may not always be adequate. Alternatively, we may choose to motivate "the elephant," or the emotional side of the brain, using the approach of see-feel-change. This approach dramatically presents evidence and creates an urgency that touches an individual's feelings, which, in turn, motivates the individual to change. As observed by Kotter and his colleagues, the second approach has contributed to the success of many organizational change efforts. The following examples illustrate this see-feel-change approach.[6,7]

- **The videotape of the angry customer.** A marketing executive was disappointed that his customer service representatives were too slow to respond to customers' requests. After discussing this with one of the unhappy customers, he sent a team to interview the customer and made a 15-minute video. In the video, the customer candidly shared his experience and the issues he had been having with the company's customer service. When the video was played to the customer service representatives, most of them were genuinely surprised, and some were even offended by the angry customer and his story. Their eyes were glued to the TV screen, and a few mouths dropped open. Although a few representatives thought the customer was wrong and felt defensive, the majority of the team felt the urgency to fix the problems, and keep them fixed, to retain satisfied customers.
- **Gloves on the boardroom table.** An executive believed that his company's purchasing process had been wasting money. To improve efficiency, he was determined to redesign the process to drive down purchasing costs by $1 billion. The plan was resisted across the board since a change of this scale meant a big shift in the established process. To obtain a sense of the magnitude of

the problem, the executive studied the gloves used in the company's factories and found that 424 different kinds of gloves were purchased at various prices because each factory had its own supplier and negotiated the prices. He and his team then collected a sample of every one of the 424 gloves, tagged each one with the price on it and the factory it was used in, and put them in the boardroom. The executive then invited all the division presidents to visit the room and showed them the gloves stacked high on the boardroom table. The division presidents were shocked to see the total number of gloves used and the different prices paid by the factories. The demonstration of gloves was so impressive that it became part of a traveling roadshow so that more people in different divisions and plants had the opportunity to look at the stacks of gloves. As a result, the urgency created by the demonstration and roadshow quickly led to a mandate for change, as executives were convinced to take action.

- **A sledgehammer in the showroom of Haier.** Haier is a multinational company headquartered in Qingdao, China. It designs, manufactures, and markets household appliances and consumer electronic products. In the showroom of Haier Group's headquarters, one can find a simple sledgehammer. This blunt instrument represents the great transition of Haier from a dysfunctional, near-bankrupt refrigerator manufacturer into one of China's most successful companies. In the 1980s, when China opened up to world markets, foreign corporations began investing in China, and one of them, a German refrigerator company, Liebherr, built a joint venture with China's Qingdao Refrigerator Co. Although the installation of Liebherr's equipment quickly updated the technology, most local workers from the planned economy era were still sluggish, careless, and so undisciplined that the CEO had to stop them from urinating on the factory floor. One day in 1985, when a dissatisfied customer returned a faulty fridge to the plant, Zhang Ruimin, the legendary CEO of Haier, inspected the factory's inventory and found many appliances were broken too. The frustrated CEO lined up 76 flawed refrigerators on the shop floor and handed out sledgehammers. "Destroy them!" he commanded the workers. The workers hesitated because, in 1985, each fridge was worth two years of a worker's pay. Zhang grabbed a sledgehammer and smashed it into a fridge himself. Soon the factory floor was littered with fragments of plastic and metal, and all the workers got the CEO's message: workers must shatter the old ways and put product quality first. Since then, Zhang has transformed Haier into a leading manufacturer with 24 plants, 70,000 employees, and a commanding share of the global market for household appliances.

In all three examples, the executives used the see-feel-change approach. It takes both courage and creativity to do so. However, if done properly, the approach creates a sense of urgency and helps overcome employee resistance and complacency.

Build the Guiding Team and Develop Responsibilities

A sense of urgency motivates more people to support the initiative and take action. However, it is necessary to get the right people in place with both the emotional commitment and the technical expertise to guide the process and lead the way. A powerful guiding team must have both the right people and the right team dynamic. To ensure the effectiveness of the team, we also need to define specific roles and responsibilities for each team member in order to address many of the resistance factors and help pave a smooth path for adoption and implementation.

Establish Vision, Goals, and Objectives

The ROI Methodology is not just another technique to conduct marketing programs. It provides an excellent opportunity for organizations to revisit their visions. When a new or revised vision on value is established, marketers should work with stakeholders to create goals, targets, and objectives for the adoption of the ROI Methodology and the implementation of results-based and value-driven marketing programs. This includes the detailed planning documents for the overall process of adoption and the individual marketing programs to be implemented. One key issue related to goals and plans is setting specific targets at different levels, which are important for the organization to monitor progress with measurement and evaluation.

Communicate for Buy-In and Support

Establishing vision, goals, and strategies is the starting point of organizational change. To make the vision a reality, we need to engage in effective and continuous communication to ensure understanding, buy-in, and support among all stakeholders. Ideally, our communication alone can lead to senior management buy-in. With top management's support and endorsement, we can design and implement the initial marketing program. This top-down approach enables us to have an organization-wide impact quickly. Alternatively, we may focus on getting employee buy-in and make incremental changes at departmental and functional levels. This bottom-up approach may take longer and require more effort. However, once top management understands the value created and shows support, the organizational change will be more sustainable because employees are the ultimate users of the marketing programs.

Initiate ROI Studies

The best demonstration of the value of using the ROI Methodology can be seen at the initiation of the first marketing program for which an ROI calculation is planned and conducted. It is therefore critically important to identify appropriate marketing programs and keep them on track. As discussed before, only certain types of marketing programs are appropriate for this comprehensive and detailed analysis. For example, ROI Institute recommends that at least 5 to 10 percent of marketing programs should be evaluated at the ROI level. Characteristics of initial marketing programs suitable for analysis include programs that are:

- Consistent with the vision and mission of the organization
- Important to strategic objectives
- Linked to major marketing performance problems and opportunities
- Targeted to large groups of external and internal customers
- Expensive
- Time consuming
- Highly visible[8]

This is by no means a comprehensive list. However, it covers major aspects of a marketer's consideration when choosing appropriate marketing programs.

Empower Actions and Remove Obstacles

Earlier in the chapter, we discussed an analogy of the elephant-rider-path used by psychologists for overcoming resistance and facilitating change. When both the elephant and rider are prepared and ready to go, it is time to clean the path for a smooth and successful journey. In the psychological analogy, the path here refers to the surrounding environment that people work in, which includes both the actual job procedures and people's psychological climate. A highly successful change will not occur unless people are empowered to take action, and empowering action is all about removing barriers. Therefore, to ensure the successful adoption of ROI and the implementation of value-driven marketing programs, it is important to remove the obstacles that will inevitably crop up during the process. Many of the obstacles are based on the concerns discussed in this chapter. Although some of the concerns may be valid, many others are based on unrealistic fear, misunderstanding, or even myths.

Dispel Myths

As part of the efforts to remove obstacles, we should strive to dispel the myths and remove or minimize the barriers. Much of the controversy regarding ROI, value, and accountability comes from misunderstandings about the process. To help marketers recognize and dispel myths, we present a brief quiz on many of the myths in Appendix B. The answers to this ROI quiz are also located in Appendix B.

Using the Data

Another tremendous obstacle is the failure to use data. It is a waste of resources and opportunity if no action is taken after evaluation and data collection. After all, the data are essentially the justification for undertaking the evaluation in the first place. If used properly, the data can provide useful information for improvement. They will become action items for the team to make changes and adjustments. Table 14.1 shows how the different levels of data can be used to improve different aspects of the programs.

TABLE 14.1 Use of evaluation data

USE OF EVALUATION DATA	APPROPRIATE LEVEL OF DATA				
	1	2	3	4	5
Adjust program design	✔	✔	✔		
Improve implementation	✔	✔	✔	✔	
Influence action and program impact			✔	✔	
Improve management support for the program			✔	✔	
Improve stakeholder satisfaction			✔	✔	✔
Recognize and reward participants		✔	✔	✔	
Justify or enhance budget				✔	✔
Reduce costs		✔	✔	✔	✔
Market programs in the future	✔		✔	✔	✔
Optimize ROI				✔	✔

Monitor Progress and Make Change Stick

Monitoring the overall progress made and communicating that progress to all stakeholders is the final element of the adoption and implementation process. Although often overlooked, effective communication plans and progress reports help keep the implementation process on target and let team members and stakeholders know what the process is accomplishing. There are two target audiences, the marketing team and the senior managers, and both are critical for progress reporting. The marketing team members should be informed of progress, and senior managers should know the extent to which the value-driven, results-based process is being implemented. They also need to know how it is working and creating value within the organization. Adopting and implementing the ROI Methodology into an organization's marketing function represents a great change, and change can be fragile. It takes continuous effort and frequent feedback to make change stick.

Final Thoughts

The ROI Methodology empowers marketers to create, demonstrate, and improve value. It, therefore, should be an essential component of any marketing function. However, introducing something new into an organization is never easy, as it is part of human nature to resist change. In this chapter, the final chapter of this book, we discussed the theory and practice behind overcoming resistance to change and facilitating the adoption of an innovative model like the ROI Methodology. Change and adoption can be achieved by presenting facts and data to influence thoughts, by demonstrating truth in a dramatic way to influence feelings, and by modifying the surrounding environments to make adoption easier.

Additionally, the chapter presented the different building blocks that must be considered and issues that must be addressed to ensure that implementation of the results-based, value-driven marketing program is smooth, uneventful, and sustained. Following these instructions, marketers can integrate the ROI Methodology into their value creation process and endeavor to contribute to organizational success in a systematic, logical, and sustainable way.

This book outlined the relevant steps necessary to analyze performance, deliver results, optimize the ROI, and use the outcomes to gain support and secure the budget for the marketing function. If done properly, the ROI Methodology will provide great opportunities for marketers to transform their marketing department and even the whole organization into a value-driven and results-based entity. It is possible and worth the effort! Good luck.

APPENDIX A

Answers to Exercise 5.1

OBJECTIVE	EVALUATION LEVEL
After completing the marketing program, customers (participants) should:	
Improve sales revenue by 20 percent in six months.	4
Initiate at least three new product development ideas in 15 days.	3
Achieve an average cost reduction of $20,000 per project.	4
Increase the use of interactive selling skills in 90 percent of business-to-business sales calls.	3
Achieve a 2:1 benefit-to-cost ratio one year after the new product quality program is implemented.	5
Be able to identify the five features of the recently launched new product.	2
Increase the external customer satisfaction index by 25 percent in three months.	4
Address customer complaints with the five-step process in 95 percent of complaint situations.	3
Perceive the new social media marketing message to be interesting.	1
Achieve a product knowledge test score average of 75 out of a possible 100.	2
Conduct a performance review meeting with key account sales professionals to establish performance improvement goals.	3
Provide a 4 out of 5 rating on the appropriateness of the new ethics policy.	1

(continued on next page)

OBJECTIVE	EVALUATION LEVEL
Decrease the time to recruit new account managers from 35 to 20 days.	4
Complete marketing action plans in three months.	3
Perceive the new compensation and incentive plan as influencing their intent to remain with the organization.	1
Be involved in the career enhancement program at a rate of 15 percent of all employees.	3
Decrease the amount of time required for product managers to complete a new product development project.	4
Achieve a post-test customer service knowledge score increase of 30 percent.	2
Use the new digital marketing app daily, as reflected by an 80 percent score on an unscheduled audit of use.	3
Submit ideas or suggestions for improvement in the first year (10 percent objective).	3

If you have questions about the answers, we would be delighted to discuss them with you. Please contact us at info@roiinstitute.net.

APPENDIX B

ROI Quiz

For each of the following statements, please choose whether it is true or false:

	TRUE	FALSE
The ROI Methodology collects or generates just one data item, expressed as a percentage.	☐	☐
A program with monetary benefits of $200,000 and costs of $100,000 translates into a 200% ROI.	☐	☐
The ROI Methodology is a tool to strengthen and improve marketing programs, projects, and processes.	☐	☐
After reviewing a detailed ROI impact study, senior executives will usually require ROI studies on all marketing programs.	☐	☐
ROI studies should be conducted very selectively, usually involving 5–10 percent of marketing programs.	☐	☐
While it may be a rough estimate, it is always possible to isolate the effects of a marketing program on impact data.	☐	☐
A marketing program costing $100 per customer, designed to support 100 customers, is an ideal program for an ROI study.	☐	☐
Data can always be credibly converted to monetary value.	☐	☐
The ROI Methodology contains too many complicated formulas.	☐	☐
The ROI Methodology can be implemented for about 3–5% of my budget.	☐	☐

(continued on next page)

	TRUE	FALSE
ROI is not future oriented; it only reflects past performance.	☐	☐
ROI is not possible for green marketing programs.	☐	☐
A negative ROI will kill my marketing program.	☐	☐
The best time to consider an ROI evaluation is three months after the marketing program is completed.	☐	☐
In the early stages of implementation, the ROI Methodology is a process improvement tool and not a performance evaluation tool for the program team.	☐	☐
If senior executives and managers are not asking for ROI, there is no need to pursue the ROI Methodology.	☐	☐

Answers to the Quiz

1. F	**9.** F
2. F	**10.** T
3. T	**11.** F
4. F	**12.** F
5. T	**13.** F
6. T	**14.** F
7. F	**15.** T
8. F	**16.** F

If you have questions about the answers, we would be delighted to discuss them with you. Please contact us at info@roiinstitute.net.

APPENDIX C

How Results-Based Are
Your Marketing Programs?

Instructions: For each of the following statements, please circle the response that best matches the extent to which marketing programs at your organization deliver business results. Select only one choice. Please be candid with your responses. All marketing organizations deliver business results. These are impact measures of output (sales, new accounts), quality (customer complaints, product returns), time (call time, response time), and costs (shipping costs, rebates).

1. The direction of our marketing programs:
   a. Shifts with requests, problems, and changes as they occur.
   b. Is determined by top executives and leaders and adjusted as needed.
   c. Is based on a mission and a strategic plan for the organization or the community.

2. The primary rationale for our marketing programs is:
   a. To respond to requests by managers and leaders to deliver programs and services.
   b. To help management and leaders react to crisis situations and reach solutions through programs and services.
   c. To implement many programs in collaboration with clients and leaders to prevent problems and capitalize on opportunities.

3. The goals of our marketing programs are:
   a. Set by the program teams based on perceived demand for programs.
   b. Developed consistent with the organization's plans and goals.
   c. Developed to integrate with operating goals and strategic plans of the organization or the community.

4. Most new marketing programs are initiated:
   a. By request of top leaders and administrators.
   b. When a program appears to be successful in another organization.
   c. After a needs assessment has indicated that the program is needed.

5. The proper solution, driven by our marketing programs, is:
   a. Obvious.
   b. Part of the request for the programs.
   c. Derived from a performance analysis.

6. To define plans to support marketing programs:
   a. Program teams choose from a list of existing actions.
   b. Participants are asked about their support needs.
   c. Needs are systematically derived from a thorough analysis of performance problems.

7. The responsibility for results from marketing programs:
   a. Rests primarily with the program team.
   b. Is the responsibility of the marketing support team that ensures that results are obtained.
   c. Is a shared responsibility of the program team, participants, designers, facilitators, managers, and others with all working together to ensure business success.

8. Objectives for each marketing program are set at:
   a. The reaction and learning levels, to create expected reactions and learning to make the program successful.
   b. The action level to define what participants and clients must do to make the program successful.
   c. The reaction, learning, action, and impact levels.

9. Systematic, objective evaluation, designed to ensure that a marketing program is successful:
   a. Is never accomplished; the only evaluations are during the program launch, and they focus on how clients and participants reacted to the program.
   b. Is occasionally accomplished; clients are asked if the message was received.
   c. Is frequently and systematically pursued; action and impact are evaluated frequently.

10. New marketing programs are designed and developed:
    a. Internally; a team of designers and specialists is used.
    b. By suppliers; we usually outsource marketing programs modified to meet our needs.
    c. By using internal staff and suppliers; this is accomplished in the most economical and practical way to meet deadlines and cost objectives.

11. Costs for our marketing programs are accumulated:
    a. On a total aggregate basis only.
    b. On a program-by-program basis.
    c. By specific process components such as design, development, launch, and evaluation, in addition to a specific program.

12. Steps are taken to improve marketing programs:
    a. Occasionally.
    b. When a problem is identified.
    c. Routinely at each step in the process.

13. To ensure that a marketing program is properly implemented, we:
    a. Encourage clients and participants to apply what they have learned and report results.
    b. Ask managers and influencers to support and reinforce and report results.
    c. Utilize a variety of strategies appropriate for each situation.

14. The marketing program team's interaction with operating and field management is:
    a. Rare; issues are almost never discussed with them.
    b. Occasional; issues are discussed during activities such as needs analysis or program coordination.
    c. Regular; communication is used to build relationships as well as to develop and deliver programs.

15. A method to show the attribution of major marketing programs on impact measures:
    a. Is never pursued.
    b. Is sometimes discussed and implemented.
    c. Is always implemented.

16. Most clients or funders view our marketing programs as:
    a. Questionable—they waste too much time.
    b. Necessary activities that probably cannot be eliminated.
    c. Important resources that can improve organizations, clients, and individuals.

17. Marketing programs are:
    a. Activity oriented (all customers receive rebates).
    b. Individual results based (the customer will purchase the product).
    c. Organizational results based (sales growth will be 25 percent).

18. The return on investment in our marketing programs is measured primarily by:
    a. Subjective opinions.
    b. Observations by management and reactions from customers.
    c. Tracking sales, new accounts, customer loyalty, customer satisfaction, customer complaints, etc.

19. New marketing programs are implemented at my organization without some formal method of evaluation:
    a. Regularly.
    b. Seldom.
    c. Never.

20. Marketing programs are initiated when a very specific:
    a. Awareness need is identified.
    b. Behavioral need is identified.
    c. Business need is identified.

21. The results of marketing programs are communicated:
    a. When requested; to those who have a need to know.
    b. Occasionally; to members of management only.
    c. Routinely; to a variety of selected target audiences.

22. Management (or influencer) involvement in marketing program evaluation:
    a. Is minor; no specific responsibilities and few requests.
    b. Is moderate; consists of informal responsibilities for evaluation, with some nonroutine requests.
    c. Is very specific; all managers and significant others have some responsibilities in evaluation.

23. The results of our marketing programs are used to:
    a. Validate the need for the program.
    b. Reward those who made it successful.
    c. Secure more funds for programs in the future.

24. During a business decline at my organization, our marketing programs will:
    a. Be the first to have their budget reduced.
    b. Be retained at the same budget level.
    c. Go untouched in budget reductions, and possibly be increased.

25. We provide funders (or donors) with:
    a. Participation data to show who is involved.
    b. Data about success with program launch.
    c. Impact data defining the specific contribution of the marketing program.

26. Budgeting for our marketing programs is based on:
    a. Last year's budget.
    b. Whatever the marketing director can "sell."
    c. A zero-based system built around need and feasibility of proposed programs.

27. The principal person or group that ultimately approves marketing program expenditures is:
    a. The program leader.
    b. A top executive.
    c. The funders or sponsors.

28. Over the last two years, the budget for our marketing programs has:
    a. Decreased.
    b. Remained stable.
    c. Increased.

29. Top leaders' involvement in the implementation of marketing programs:
    a. Is limited to sending invitations, extending congratulations, recognizing success, etc.
    b. Includes monitoring progress, making presentations to the team, providing statements on the importance of the program, etc.
    c. Includes participation to see what's involved, conducting segments of the program, requiring key managers to be involved, etc.

30. When a participant is involved in an internal marketing program, his or her manager (or significant other) is likely to:
   a. Make no reference to the program.
   b. Ask questions about the program and encourage the use of the program content or material.
   c. Require use of the program material and provide rewards when the program is successful.

Score the assessment instrument as follows. Allow:

- 1 point for each (a) response.
- 3 points for each (b) response.
- 5 points for each (c) response.

The total will be between 30 and 150 points.

The interpretation of scoring is provided below. The explanation is based on the input from hundreds of organizations and program evaluators.

SCORE RANGE	ANALYSIS OF SCORE
120–150	**Outstanding Environment** for achieving results with your marketing programs. Great management support. A truly successful example of results-based marketing.
90–119	**Above Average** in achieving results with your marketing programs. Good management support. A solid and methodical approach to results-based marketing.
60–89	**Needs Improvement** to achieve desired results in your marketing programs. Management support is ineffective. Programs do not usually focus on results.
30–59	**Serious Problems** with the success and status of your marketing programs. Management support is nonexistent. Programs are not producing or showing the value of the program to funders, sponsors, and donors.

The survey should be adjusted to fit your terminology. These results provide a gap analysis for improvements. When the survey is repeated each year, the results provide a measure of progress.

NOTES

CHAPTER 1

1. "The Coca-Cola Company Announces Senior Leadership Appointments." Coca-Cola Company. Accessed March 5, 2020. https://www.coca-colacompany.com/press-releases/coca-cola-announces-senior-leadership-appointments.
2. Handley, Lucy. "Chief Marketing Officers Will Have to 'Grow or Go' as Fortune 100 Companies Switch to 'Chief Growth Officer' Roles." November 7, 2017. http://www.cnbc.com/2017/11/07/chief-marketing-officers-might-become-chief-growth-officers.html.
3. Pemberton, Chris. "2017–2018 CMO Spend Survey Highlights Demand for Results." November 20, 2017. http://www.gartner.com/smarterwithgartner/2017-2018-cmo-spend-survey-highlights-demand-for-results/.
4. "2 in 3 CMOs Feeling Pressure from the Board to Prove Marketing's Value." Marketing Charts, August 29, 2013. https://www.marketingcharts.com/brand-related/brand-metrics-36293.
5. "Media Advertising Spending in the United States from 2015 to 2022." Statista. Accessed March 5, 2020. https://www.statista.com/statistics/272314/advertising-spending-in-the-us/.
6. "Marketing Budgets Vary by Industry." CMO Insights and Analysis from Deloitte. *Wall Street Journal*. Accessed March 5, 2020. https://deloitte.wsj.com/cmo/2017/01/24/who-has-the-biggest-marketing-budgets/.
7. "7 in 10 Enterprise CEOs Believe They Are Wasting Money on Marketing Initiatives." Marketing Charts, November 25, 2014. https://www.marketingcharts.com/business-of-marketing-48692.
8. Kerin, Roger A., and Steven W. Harley. *Marketing*, 14th ed. Dubuque, IA: McGraw-Hill, 2019.
9. Marshall, Greg W., and Mark W. Johnston. *Marketing Management*, 3rd ed. New York: McGraw-Hill, 2018.
10. "CMO vs. CGO: The Renewed Importance of the Chief Growth Officer." Mondo. Accessed March 5, 2020. https://www.mondo.com/cmo-vs-chief-growth-officer.
11. Handley, Lucy. "Procter & Gamble Saves $750 Million on Advertising and Cuts Agencies by 50 Percent." January 24, 2018. https://www.cnbc.com/2018/01/24/pg-slashes-ad-budget-by-750-million-and-agencies-by-50-percent.html.
12. "Definitions of Marketing." American Association of Marketing. Accessed March 5, 2020. https://www.ama.org/the-definition-of-marketing-what-is-marketing/.

13. Kotler, Philip, and Kevin Lane Keller. *Marketing Management*, 15th ed. London: Pearson Education, 2015.

14. Porter, Michael E. *Competitive Strategy: Techniques for Analyzing Industries and Competitors*, 1st ed. New York: Free Press, June 1, 1998.

15. MASTERCODEAV. "Steve Jobs' Marketing Strategy." April 17, 2016. YouTube Video, 6:53. https://www.youtube.com/watch?v=H5zToMreEoU.

16. Kerin, Roger A., and Steven W. Harley. *Marketing*, 14th ed. Dubuque, IA: McGraw-Hill, 2019.

17. Ibid.

18. Value. Dictionary. Accessed March 5, 2020. https://www.dictionary.com/browse/value?s=t.

19. Kaplan, Robert S., and David P. Norton. *Translating Strategy into Action: The Balanced Scorecard*. Boston: Harvard Business School Press, 1996.

20. Zoltners, Andris A., Prabhakant Sinha, and Sally E. Lorimer. *Building a Winning Sales Force: Powerful Strategies for Driving High Performance*. New York: AMACOM, 2009.

CHAPTER 2

1. Brown, Tim. *Change by Design: How Design Thinking Transforms Organizations and Inspires Innovation*. New York: Harper Business, 2009.

2. Mootee, Idris. *Design Thinking for Strategic Innovation: What They Can't Teach You at Business or Design School*. Hoboken, NJ: Wiley, 2013.

3. Phillips, Patricia Pulliam, and Jack J. Phillips. *The Business Case for Learning: Using Design Thinking to Deliver Business Results and Increase the Investment in Talent Development*. West Chester, PA: HRDQ and Alexandria, VA: ATD Press, 2017.

4. "ISPI's 10 Standards." *ISPI Online*. Accessed February 24, 2020. https://ispi.org/page/10Standards.

5. Phillips, Jack J., and Patricia Pulliam Phillips. *Show Me the Money: How to Determine ROI in People, Projects, and Programs*. San Francisco: Berrett-Koehler, 2007.

CHAPTER 3

1. Moeller, Leslie H., and Edward C. Landry. *The Four Pillars of Profit-Driven Marketing, How to Maximize Creativity, Accountability, and ROI*. New York: McGraw-Hill, 2009.

2. Kerin, Roger A., and Steven W. Harley. *Marketing*, 14th ed. Dubuque, IA: McGraw-Hill, 2019.

3. Ibid.

4. Johnston, Mark W., and Greg W. Marshall. *Sales Force Management Leadership, Innovation, Technology*, 11th ed. New York: Routledge, 2013.

5. Van Tiem, Darlene, James L. Moseley, and Joan C. Designer. *Fundamentals of Performance Improvement: Optimizing Results Through People, Process, and Organizations*. San Francisco: Pfeiffer, 2012.

6. Chevalier, Roger. *A Manager's Guide to Improving Workplace Performance*, 1st ed. New York: AMACOM, 2007.

7. Fu, Frank Q. "Marketing Performance Improvement." Working Paper, University of Missouri–St. Louis, 2019.

8. Kaplan, Robert S., and David P. Norton. *Balanced Scorecard: Translating Strategy into Action*. Boston: Harvard Business School Press, 1996.

9. Zoltners, Andris A., Prabhakant Sinha, and Sally E. Lorimer. *Building a Winning Sales Force: Powerful Strategies for Driving High Performance*. New York: AMACOM, 2009.

10. Rothwell, William J., Carolyn K. Hohne, and Stephen B. King. *Human Performance Improvement: Building Practitioner Performance*, 3rd ed. New York and London: Routledge, 2018.

CHAPTER 4

1. Rothwell, William, Caroline K. Hohne, and Steven B. King. *Performance Improvement: Building Practitioner Performance*, 3rd ed. New York and London: Routledge, 2018.
2. Ibid.
3. Gilbert, Thomas F. *Human Competence: Engineering Worthy Performance*. Silver Spring, MD: International Society for Performance Improvement, 1978.
4. Chevalier, Roger. *A Manager's Guide to Improving Workplace Performance*, 1st ed. New York: AMACOM, 2007.
5. Six Boxes: The Performance Thinking Network. Accessed March 3, 2020. https://www.sixboxes.com/.
6. Kerin, Roger A., and Steven W. Harley. *Marketing*, 14th ed. Dubuque, IA: McGraw-Hill, 2019.
7. Ripley, David, and Peter Dean. *Performance Improvement Pathfinders: Models for Organizational Learning*. Silver Spring, MD: International Society for Performance Improvement, 1997.
8. Robinson, Dana, and Jim Robinson. *Zap the GAPS! Target Higher Performance and Achieve It!* New York: HarperCollins, 2002.

CHAPTER 5

1. Kerin, Roger A., and Steven W. Hartley. *Marketing*, 14th ed. New York: McGraw-Hill, 2019.
2. "General Mills Using 'Greener' Bowls for Warm Delights." *Packaging Strategies*. Accesssed March 4, 2020. https://www.packagingstrategies.com/articles/85585-general-mills-using-greener-bowls-for-warm-delights.
3. Phillips, Patricia Pulliam, and Jack J. Phillips, *The Business Case for Learning, Using Design Thinking to Deliver Business Results and Increase the Investment in Talent Development*. West Chester, PA: HRDQ and Alexandria, VA: ATD Press, 2017.
4. Wendel, Stephen. *Designing for Behavior Change: Applying Psychology and Behavioral Economics*. Sebastopol, CA: O'Reilly Media, 2014.

CHAPTER 6

1. Crawford, Merle, and Anthony Di Benedetto. *New Products Management*, 11th ed. New York: McGraw-Hill, 2015.
2. Kotler, Philip, and Kevin Lane Keller. *Marketing Management*, 15th ed. London: Pearson, 2015.
3. Yoon, Clara. "Assumptions That Led to the Failure of Google Glass." NYC Design, August 2, 2018. https://medium.com/nyc-design/the-assumptions-that-led-to-failures-of-google-glass-8b40a07cfa1e.
4. Kottasová, Ivana. "McDonald's Pulls Ad About a Boy Whose Father Died." CNN Money, May 17, 2017. https://money.cnn.com/2017/05/17/news/mcdonalds-advertisement-dead-father/.
5. Kerin, Roger, and Steven Hartley. *Marketing*, 13th ed. New York: McGraw-Hill, 2016.
6. Ibid.

7. Fishbein, M., and I. Ajzen. *Belief, Attitude, Intention and Behavior: An Introduction to Theory and Research*. Reading, MA: Addison-Wesley, 1975.
8. Lutz, Richard J. "Changing Brand Attitudes Through Modification of Cognitive Structure," *Journal of Consumer Research*, March 1975, pp. 49–59.
9. Phillips, Patricia Pulliam, Jack J. Phillips, Gina Paone, and Cyndi Huff Gaudet. *Value for Money: How to Show the Value for Money for All Types of Projects and Programs in Governments, Nongovernmental Organizations, Nonprofits, and Businesses*. Hoboken, NJ: John Wiley & Sons, 2019.
10. Kerin and Hartley. *Marketing,* 13th ed.
11. Marshall, Greg W., and Mark W. Johnston. *Marketing Management*, 3rd ed. New York: McGraw-Hill, 2018.

CHAPTER 7

1. Fishbein, M., and I. Ajzen. *Belief, Attitude, Intention, and Behavior: An Introduction to Theory and Research*. Reading, MA: Addison-Wesley, 1975.
2. Ajzen, Icek. "From Intentions to Actions: A Theory of Planned Behavior." In Julius Kuhl and Jürgen Beckmann (eds.), *Action Control: From Cognition to Behavior*. Berlin: Springer. 1985, pp. 11–39. ISBN 978-3-642-69748-7.
3. Davis, F. D., "Perceived Usefulness, Perceived Ease of Use, and User Acceptance of Information Technology." *MIS Quarterly*, 13(3): 319–340 (1989).
4. Bagozzi, R. P., F. D. Davis, and P. R. Warshaw. "Development and Test of a Theory of Technological Learning and Usage." *Human Relations*, 45(7): 660–686 (1992).
5. Phillips, Patricia Pulliam, and Jack J. Phillips. *The Business Case for Learning: Using Design Thinking to Deliver Business Results and Increase the Investment in Talent Development*. Alexandria, VA: HRDQ and Alexandria, VA: ATD Press, 2017.
6. Phillips, Jack J., and Patricia Pulliam Phillips. *Show Me the Money: How to Determine ROI in People, Projects, and Programs*. San Francisco: Berrett-Koehler, 2007.
7. Phillips, Patti P., and Jack J. Phillips. *ROI Basics*, 2nd ed. Alexandria, VA: ATD Press, 2019.
8. Kerin, Roger A., and Steven W. Harley. *Marketing*, 14th ed. Dubuque, IA: McGraw-Hill. 2019.

CHAPTER 8

1. Phillips, Patricia Pulliam, Jack J. Phillips, Gina Paone, and Cyndi Huff Gaudet. *Value for Money: How to Show the Value for Money for All Types of Projects and Programs in Governments, Nongovernmental Organizations, Nonprofits, and Businesses*. Hoboken, NJ: John Wiley & Sons, 2019.
2. Phillips, Patricia Pulliam, and Jack J. Phillips. *Handbook of Training Evaluation and Measurement Methods*. New York: Routledge, 2016.
3. Phillips, Phillips, Paone, and Gaudet. *Value for Money*.
4. Phillips, Patricia Pulliam, and Jack J. Phillips. *Making Human Capital Analytics Work: Measuring the ROI of Human Capital Processes and Outcomes*. New York: McGraw-Hill, 2015.
5. Phillips, Patricia Pulliam, and Jack J. Phillips. *The Green Scorecard: Measuring the Return on Investment in Sustainability Initiatives*. Boston: Nicholas Publishing, 2011.

CHAPTER 9

1. Phillips, Jack J., and Patricia Pulliam Phillips. *Show Me the Money: How to Determine ROI in People, Projects, and Programs.* San Francisco: Berrett-Koehler, 2007.
2. Kerin, Roger A., and Steven W. Harley. *Marketing,* 14th ed. Dubuque, IA: McGraw-Hill, 2019.
3. Phillips, Patricia Pulliam, Jack J. Phillips, Gina Paone, and Cyndi Huff Gaudet. *Value for Money: How to Show the Value for Money for All Types of Projects and Programs in Governments, Nongovernmental Organizations, Nonprofits, and Businesses.* Hoboken, NJ: John Wiley & Sons, 2019.
4. Farris, Paul W., Neil T. Bendle, Phillip E. Pfeifer, and David J. Reibstein. *Marketing Metrics: 50+ Metrics Every Executive Should Master.* Upper Saddle River, NJ: Pearson Prentice Hall, 2006.
5. Phillips, Phillips, Paone, and Gaudet. *Value for Money.*
6. Phillips, Patricia Pulliam, Jack J. Phillips, Gina Paone, and Cyndi Huff Gaudet. *Value for Money: How to Show the Value for Money for All Types of Projects and Programs in Governments, Nongovernmental Organizations, Nonprofits, and Businesses.* Hoboken, NJ: John Wiley & Sons, 2019.

CHAPTER 10

1. Phillips, Patricia Pulliam, Jack J. Phillips, Gina Paone, and Cyndi Huff Gaudet. *Value for Money: How to Show the Value for Money for All Types of Projects and Programs in Governments, Nongovernmental Organizations, Nonprofits, and Businesses.* Hoboken, NJ: John Wiley & Sons, 2019.
2. Johnston, Mark W., and Greg W. Marshall. *Sales Force Management Leadership, Innovation, Technology,* 11th ed. New York: Routledge, 2013.
3. Phillips, Patricia Pulliam, and Jack J. Phillips. *The Business Case for Learning: Using Design Thinking to Deliver Business Results and Increase the Investment in Talent Development.* West Chester, PA: HRDQ and Alexandria, VA: ATD Press, 2017.

CHAPTER 11

1. Phillips, Patricia Pulliam, Jack J. Phillips, Gina Paone, and Cyndi Huff Gaudet. *Value for Money: How to Show the Value for Money for All Types of Projects and Programs in Governments, Nongovernmental Organizations, Nonprofits, and Businesses.* Hoboken, NJ: John Wiley & Sons, 2019.
2. Price, Darlene. *Well Said! Presentations and Conversations That Get Results.* New York: AMACOM, 2012.
3. Block, Peter. *Flawless Consulting,* 3rd ed. San Diego, CA: Pfeiffer, 2011.
4. Mootee, Idris. *Design Thinking for Strategic Innovation: What They Can't Teach You at Business or Design School.* Hoboken, NJ: Wiley, 2013.
5. Smith, Paul. *Lead with a Story: A Guide to Crafting Business Narratives That Captivate, Convince, and Inspire.* New York: AMACOM, 2012. Used with permission.

CHAPTER 12

1. Marshall, Greg W., and Mark W. Johnston. *Marketing Management,* 3rd ed. New York: McGraw-Hill, 2018.

2. Phillips, Patricia Pulliam, and Jack J. Phillips. *The Business Case for Learning: Using Design Thinking to Deliver Business Results and Increase the Investment in Talent Development.* West Chester, PA: HRDQ and Alexandria, VA: ATD Press, 2017.

3. Fu, Frank Q. "Marketing Performance Improvement." Working Paper, University of Missouri–St. Louis, 2019.

4. Doran, George T. "There's a S.M.A.R.T. Way to Write Management's Goals and Objectives." *Management Review*, 70(11): 35–36 (1981).

5. Phillips, Patricia Pulliam, Jack J. Phillips, Gina Paone, and Cyndi Huff Gaudet. *Value for Money: How to Show the Value for Money for All Types of Projects and Programs in Governments, Nongovernmental Organizations, Nonprofits, and Businesses.* Hoboken, NJ: John Wiley & Sons, 2019.

CHAPTER 13

1. Marson, James, and Thomas Grove. "Domino's Free Pizza Offer Backfires in Age of Ink." *Wall Street Journal*, September 18, 2018.

2. Phillips, Jack J., and Patricia Pulliam Phillips. *The Consultant's Guide to Results-Driven Business Proposals.* New York: McGraw Hill, 2010.

3. McKinnon, John D., and Brent Kendall. "Utah's Ads Lure Swarms to Its Parks." *Wall Street Journal*, September 17, 2019.

4. Phillips, Patricia Pulliam, and Jack J. Phillips. "Measuring ROI in a Mobile Learning Solution for Sales." *Value for Money: Measuring the Return on Non-Capital Investments.* Birmingham, AL: ROI Institute, Chap. 17, 2018.

5. Maisel, Lawrence S., and Gary Cokins. *Predictive Business Analytics: Forward-Looking Capabilities to Improve Business Performance.* Hoboken, NJ: Wiley, 2014.

6. Bowers, David A. *Forecasting for Control and Profit.* Menlo Park, CA: Crisp Publications, 1997.

7. Phillips, Patricia Pulliam, Jack J. Phillips, Gina Paone, and Cyndi Huff Gaudet. *Value for Money: How to Show the Value for Money for All Types of Projects and Programs in Governments, Nongovernmental Organizations, Nonprofits, and Businesses.* Hoboken, NJ: Johns Wiley & Sons, 2019.

CHAPTER 14

1. Kotter, John P., and Dan S. Cohen. *The Heart of Change: Real-Life Stories of How People Change Their Organizations.* Boston: Harvard Business Publishing. 2012.

2. Verghis, Phillip. "Direct the Rider, Motivate the Elephant, and Shape the Path." *HDI*, July 29, 2016. https://www.thinkhdi.com/library/supportworld/2016/direct-the-rider-motivate -the-elephant-shape-the-path.aspx.

3. Haidt, Jonathan. *The Happiness Hypothesis: Finding Modern Truth in Ancient Wisdom.* New York: Basic Books, 2006.

4. Heath, Chip, and Dan Heath. *Switch: How to Change Things When Change Is Hard.* New York: Crown Publishing, 2010.

5. Kotter and Cohen. *The Heart of Change.*

6. http://www.haier.net/en/about_haier/news/201404/t20140426_218091.shtml.

7. Schuman, Michael. "Zhang Ruimin's Haier Power: The World's Largest Appliance Maker Wants to Transform the Meaning of Made in China." *Haier*, April 22, 2014.

8. Phillips, Patricia Pulliam, and Jack J. Phillips. *ROI Basics*, 2nd ed. Alexandria, VA: ATD Press, 2019.

INDEX

Page numbers followed by *f*, *t*, and *b* refer to figures, tables, and boxes respectively.

ABOUT THE AUTHORS

Jack J. Phillips, PhD, chairman of ROI Institute, is a world-renowned expert on accountability, measurement, and evaluation. Former bank president, Phillips provides consulting services for Fortune 500 companies and major global organizations. The author or editor of more than 75 books, he conducts workshops and presents at conferences throughout the world.

Phillips has received several awards for his books and work. On three occasions, Meeting News named him one of the 25 Most Powerful People in the Meetings and Events Industry based on his work on ROI. In 2017, Jack received the Brand Personality Award from Asia Pacific Brand Foundation for his work as an international consultant, author, teacher, and speaker. The Society for Human Resource Management presented him an award for one of his books and honored a Phillips ROI study with its highest award for creativity. The American Society for Training and Development gave him its highest award, Distinguished Contribution to Workplace Learning and Development for his work on ROI. Jack and his wife, Patti Phillips, were the first recipients of the Center for Talent Reporting's Distinguished Contributor Award. This award recognized their outstanding and significant contributions in the measurement and management of human capital. In November 2019, Jack and Patti were named two of the top 50 coaches in the world, by the Thinkers 50 organization. In addition, they were named finalists for the Marshall Goldsmith Distinguished Achievement Award for Coaching. Jack's work has been featured in the *Wall Street Journal, BusinessWeek*, and *Fortune* magazine. He has been interviewed by several television programs, including CNN.

Dr. Phillips' expertise in measurement and evaluation is based on more than 27 years of corporate experience in the aerospace, textile, metals, construction materials, and banking industries. Dr. Phillips has served as training and development manager at two Fortune 500 firms, as senior human resource officer at two firms, as president of a regional bank, and as management professor at a major state university.

Dr. Phillips regularly consults with clients in manufacturing, service, and government organizations in over 70 countries in North and South America, Europe, Middle East, Africa, Australia, and Asia.

Dr. Phillips has undergraduate degrees in electrical engineering, physics, and mathematics; a master's degree in Decision Sciences from Georgia State University; and a PhD in Human Resource Management from the University of Alabama. He has served on the boards of several private businesses and nonprofits and associations, including the American Society for Training and Development, the National Management Association, and the International Society for Performance Improvement, where he served as president (2012–2013).

Dr. Jack Phillips can be reached at jack@roiinstitute.net.

Frank Q. Fu, PhD, CPT, is an Associate Professor of Marketing at the University of Missouri–St. Louis. He obtained his PhD in marketing from the University of Houston. He also holds an MBA in marketing from the University of Rochester. He brings a diversity of methodological approaches, including quantitative modeling and behaviorally oriented survey research, to questions regarding the sales-marketing interface for new product success. His current research interests focus on marketing performance improvement and sales performance improvement. He won the 2006 AMA Sales SIG Award for best doctoral dissertation in professional selling and sales management. In 2005, he was selected as one of the four winners to receive an AMA Sales SIG/DSEF Sales Dissertation Research Grant.

Dr. Fu has published articles in the *Journal of Marketing, Marketing Letters, Journal of Marketing Theory and Practice, Journal of Personal Selling and Sales Management, Journal of Strategic Marketing, Human*

Performance, and *Performance Improvement,* among others. He has also presented research papers at various national and international conferences. Currently, he serves as an associate editor of *Performance Improvement Quarterly* and as an editorial review board member for the *Journal of Marketing Theory and Practice.*

Prior to joining academia, he gained valuable sales, marketing, and management experience in the pharmaceutical and medical equipment industries. For five years, he worked as sales representative, commercial supervisor, and district sales manager for a Johnson & Johnson Company in China. As sales manager, he worked on several new product launches and was responsible for a $12 million sales budget. In 2006, he was inducted into the Beta Gamma Sigma Honor Society for collegiate schools of business. He joined the Alpha Mu Alpha National Marketing Honorary Society as a faculty member in 2012.

In addition to doing academic research and teaching, Dr. Fu helps American and Chinese companies improve their marketing performance through consulting and advising efforts.

He can be reached at fuf@umsl.edu.

Patti P. Phillips, PhD, CPT, is CEO of ROI Institute and a leader in measurement and evaluation. Since 1997, Patti has been a driving force in the global adoption of the ROI Methodology. Her work as an educator, researcher, consultant, and coach spans private sector, public sector, nonprofit, and nongovernmental organizations in over 70 countries.

Patti serves as a member of the Board of Trustees of the United Nations Institute for Training and Research (UNITAR). She serves as chair of the Institute for Corporate Productivity (i4cp) People Analytics Board; Principal Research Fellow for The Conference Board; a board member of the International Federation for Training and Development Organizations (IFTDO); board chair for the Center for Talent Reporting (CTR); and is an Association for Talent Development (ATD) Certification Institute CPTD Fellow. Patti also serves on the faculty of the UN System Staff College in Turin, Italy. She is a Certified Performance Technologist (CPT) with the International Society of

Performance Improvement (ISPI). Her work has been featured on CNBC, Euronews, and in more than a dozen business journals.

Patti, along with her husband Jack J. Phillips, contributes to a variety of journals and has authored a number of books on the subject of measurement, evaluation, analytics, and ROI.

Patti Phillips can be reached at patti@roiinstitute.net.

Hong Yi, CPT, serves as the President of Beijing Sinotrac Consulting Co. Ltd. She is a leading performance improvement consultant in China, a Certified Performance Technologist, and the President of the ISPI China Chapter. Ms. Yi is also a certified action learning facilitator, an adjunct professor at the University of International Business and Economics in Beijing, and a certified instructor registered at the PRC Ministry of Personnel.

With 25 years of experience in training and consulting, Ms. Yi has served clients including Chinese and multinational companies, such as IBM, Samsung, Johnson & Johnson, Novo Nordisk, Sinopec, China Unicom, China Telecom, and China Merchants Bank, among others.

Ms. Yi has published two books and multiple journal articles on performance improvement in China and completed more than 200 marketing performance improvement cases in a variety of industries.

She may be reached at yihong@sinotrac.com.